MORE PORTS MORE STORMS

THE SECOND VOLUME IN THE ZANDER TRILOGY

Johnny Jones

ILLUSTRATIONS BY J PAUL JONES

ISBN 978-1-9162125-1-0

Illustrator: J. Paul Jones
Cover design & Typesetting: Raspberry Creative Design
Edinburgh

First Published as an E book in 2012
Rewritten and Improved 2020

Printed by Martins the Printers, Berwick-upon-Tweed

CONTENTS

LIST OF ILLUSTRATIONS

A number of scene-setting photographs associated with the first two volumes of the Zander Trilogy, can be viewed on the website, **https://johnnyjones.co.uk**

PREFACE

At the end of the first book in this trilogy, A Storm in Any Port, Zander is closing in on middle age. More Storms More Ports, as well as giving an account of some of the things he got up to in his earlier, formative years, also reveals that while his life has moved on, Zander has not.

Be aware that while you are reading the following stories, some of the locations and details benefit from a bit of literary license. Nevertheless, all of the events contain a core of reality. Anyone who recognises themselves or an incident portrayed therein, should ignore any inaccuracies that may have crept into the narrative and just enjoy the story in the spirit of fun intended.

Although these tales have a sailing theme, the boats are simply the links tying them together. As you will soon realise, I have only a rudimentary knowledge of the sea and boats. Whatever sailing I have done has been as a passenger and observer, so it follows that the few nautical terms I have used, are the ones most landlubbers will likely recognize.

I did take 'expert' advice on the ways and means of sailing, but my haphazard use of nautical terms was ever prone to missing the mark – by a nautical mile, so I resisted the temptation.

Off To A Running Start

PROLOGUE

No No No – Yes

Are you sitting comfortably? Good. I am about to tell you a series of stories about the adventures of one extraordinary man, and believe me – you do want to be sitting down for this.

Yes, I know you have heard many stories before, exciting stories, thrilling stories, stories that set your heart pounding and your blood racing. However, these particular stories are different. They are funny ones that make your heart sing, your body convulse with laughter and leave you to enjoy a warm contented glow. You may think yourself a veteran of the works of tellers of tales and can no longer be surprised, but these stories have something that those others do not; they have Zander. So relax while I reveal just how interestingly unlucky, irresponsibly thoughtless and innocently insensitive this one man and his pals can be.

This taster story begins in a railway station, one of the big ones crammed full of people, some travelling out and others returning; the building part has been modernised in a desperate attempt to conceal the sad fact that the overworked station is a dying relic of bygone days.

*

An ever-moving mass of people are bustling about the station concourse, filtering past each other, going to and arriving on trains. A red-faced man carrying a holdall is making a fair fist of sprinting along the broad platform between two trains. The guard's whistle had already blown and the train is relentlessly gathering speed. On the train, another bigger, powerful looking man is holding open a carriage door, anxiously encouraging the man to run faster.

Though everyone around him is getting on with their own travel arrangements, those who do notice the runner take a second look – something about him tells them that they have not often seen his likes before.

The man is dressed in a Harris Tweed jacket, border check shirt, striped club tie and grey flannel trousers – an outfit, that like the rest of him is ordinary enough looking, but in spite of his look of desperation, it is his face that catches your attention.

A tousled mess of black hair hangs down over a broad browed forehead and in the midst of a strong, slightly weather-beaten complexion is an upside down, but not unattractive, smile while in his unforgettable grey blue eyes, lurks mischief. The whole face looks lived in, likeable and promises a world of fun.

With a last desperate lunge he throws his holdall into the carriage and helped by a strong pull from the door holder, he jumps into the compartment, flops on to a seat and out of breath but triumphant, smiles up at his friend and says jubilantly,

"I told you I'd make it."

An elderly, white whiskered minister sitting in a corner of the carriage watching the escapade over the top of his 'Scotsman', nodded approvingly to the late arrival and his helper and said, "Well done lads, you're lucky you managed to get on board; its four hours 'till the next train to Carlisle!"

"Carlisle!" the flabbergasted pair gasped,

"But our boat's in Oban."

*

The Station is Edinburgh Waverley in the days when it was open plan. The platform is one of the West bound double ones and in their haste, the pair chose to take the train on their left instead of the one on the right.

What follows, are tales about Zander, the runner and his pal Grunt, who held the carriage door open for him which tells us how – fortunately for the writer – without really thinking about it they regularly make the wrong choice.

GROWING PAINS

Wee Johnny

1

The Boy   Portobello

Imagine sitting in a darkened cinema watching the flickering start of a black and white movie. White letters appear on the screen's black backdrop, spelling out,

PORTOBELLO SUMMER 1939

The lettering fades out and a jerky moving picture emerges. Four athletic young men in knee–length shorts and long sleeved vests are carrying a bulky rowing boat over a broad stretch of sandy beach towards the sea.

The image now switches to a close up, highlighting the contented face of a toddler sitting at the back of the boat. The scene fades and fresh lettering appears,

ALEXANDER M^CLEAN DUFF
AN EARLY VOYAGE

The close-up of the child returns to the screen to let us see the chubby cheeks, fair curly hair and innocent expression of the youngster. This is Zander, who will grow up to become the principal character of these stories.

One of the stalwarts carrying the boat is Zander's teenage brother, George, who every weekday has to look after his younger brother. When baby Alexander first came into the world, George – for some undefined reason – possibly some difficulty with the pronunciation, abbreviated his young brother's name to Zander. His constant usage influenced the Duff family into calling their younger son by that name.

Due to the nature and demands of their work Mr and Mrs Duff, were unable to spend as much time with their young sons as they would have liked, but it took their combined salaries to provide them with the decent standard of living they enjoyed.

Mr Duff was a history teacher and local councillor, his wife a leading light in the local repertory company. Mornings in the family home began with a rushed breakfast, followed by a few fleeting words from their parents, before George took his little brother off to school. Later in the day, George would collect him and look after him until his parents came home from work.

The family spent their evenings sitting in the parlour, the parents either catching up with, or preparing for the next day's work; Mother reading the script of some play or other, while father made inroads into the copious amounts of written work he had to deal with, just to stay ahead in his daily grind. Consequently, there was little time left for family interaction.

In this environment, Zander, often left to his own devices, spent a lot of his time either reading books or, as most people did in those far off days, listening to the radio. His particular favourites were adventure yarns, tales of exploration and accounts of exciting deeds done on the high seas – even better if they involved pirates.

One visitor Zander always looked forward to welcoming was his mother's brother, Uncle Jim. With no other family, he took a great interest in his two nephews, particularly the one who was still young enough to listen to an old salt's tales. What this actually meant was that when Uncle Jim was not telling his younger nephew imaginary tales of sailing, the sea and sailors, he was filling the young lad's head with a travelogue of myths and legends interspersed with the occasional fact. The young Zander absorbed this information like a sponge. So strong was Uncle Jim's influence on him that whereas other boys wanted to be train-drivers when they grew up, Zander's only desire was to be a sailor and sail the romantic, fun-filled ocean blue and do what Uncle Jim had done.

George, Uncle Jim's older nephew, was an active member of the local rowing club, who firmly believed that if he was to 'get somewhere' in the Club – and possibly become Captain someday – he had to be seen to be someone who was always around, ready and willing to help anyone at the Club. This meant that any time Uncle Jim turned up, George was more than happy to leave his little brother in his care and get away to the Club on his own. This left the way clear for Zander to become Uncle Jim's favourite.

Before long, George became one of the club's top oarsmen. Consequently, his regime of practice and fitness training took up a good part of both his and Zander's time, so it was only natural that, this time in his brother's 'care', developed in Zander the essential attribute for any sea going man, immeasurable patience.

*

The Rowing Club's boathouse was located on the promenade of Edinburgh's seaside resort, Portobello. The club raced, 'jolly-boats' which had to be carried from the boathouse over a tidal sandy beach to the sea. Then at the end of the day, when everyone was exhausted, they had to be carried back there again.

In time, Zander progressed from sitting in the boat and being set down on the sand just back from the water's edge, to staying on board and going out to sea with the crew. There, contentedly sitting at the back of the boat, he would watch all that was going on around him. When he had grown tall enough to see round the heads of the crew, he was trusted with the steering – but only on training spins.

Soon, with experience, Zander became so good at controlling the rudder and calling out the stroke that he progressed to steering the boat on time-trials, until eventually, he became its Cox in full-blown competitive races.

As he grew up, Zander got bigger and put on muscle. No longer a spindly-legged teenager, he spent many happy hours in the boat, him steering, George at 'stroke'.

George's crew usually won more races than they lost. In rowing circles, it is a tradition that the Cox of the victorious crew is 'ducked', so as George's team won nearly every race, Zander was ducked a lot. For a few wet seconds, he was the centre of attention – and he loved every microsecond of it. Perhaps these frequent immersions allowed seawater to seep into the young Zander's veins and contributed to his lifelong attraction for anything and everything to do with the sea.

*

Towards the end of the Second World War, George was called away to serve his country. The day he left home was the day that Zander emerged from his older brother's shadow and took over his role at the Rowing Club.

By this time, Zander, in his final year at school, was no longer a slim, lightweight lad, but a strong, stocky oarsman and natural successor to his brother's role as stroke of the Club's number one boat. Even then, somewhere in his psyche dwelt a desire to be in the limelight. Consequently, anytime his Cox got ducked, – just for a laugh – Zander would end up in the water beside him; the girls watching from the shore loved it, and so did he.

2

When He First Put the Uniform On
Edinburgh

In a conscious attempt to compensate for their lack of family bonding, Zander's parents provided their sons with an excellent education by sending them to one of Edinburgh's prestigious fee-paying schools. This school's disciplined, scholastic regime, instilled in its pupils the fine moral principles and excellent manners, which would stand them in good stead in later life

At his school's entrance interview, Zander was excited to learn that the school had a Sea Cadet Unit and saw that by joining it he would be able to follow his Uncle Jim's example. However, by the time Zander took up his place at school, both of the teachers who ran the Cadets had become Naval Volunteer Reservists. With no Masters to lead the would-be mariners, there could be no Sea Cadets! Zander therefore had no option but to become a Cadet in the school's Army Corps.

To compensate for his disappointment, he also joined his local Sea Scout Troop. Unfortunately, his service there only lasted a few months. Characteristically, on joining up he worked hard at becoming a good Sea Scout. So well did Zander apply himself that at the end of his third month,

Aquila (the Scout Mistress who had taken over the troop from the Scoutmasters), announced that Zander and another boy were joint equals for the coveted title of 'Sea Scout of the Month'. This award brought with it a badge that the winner wore on his navy blue jumper for the whole of the following month. *Oh joy, oh rapture – as they would say in the Pirates of Penzance!*

Zander, with visions of wearing this shiny medal on his chest at troop muster, shore parade or just walking along the local streets on his way to troop meetings, just had to have it. Then everyone who saw it would know what he had achieved, adult approval would be a certainty and most importantly, he would be the envy of all his young friends.

Alas, there was only one medal and the very young, trusting and naive Aquila – still unaware of Zander's craving to win the prize 'dangling' so enticingly in front of him – told the joint winners to decide between themselves, who was to be Scout of the Month.

To resolve the matter in what the Scout Mistress believed would be a polite and courteous manner, she sent them into a side room. Almost before the door had closed behind the 'winners', Zander re-appeared saying that the other boy had agreed that he should have the medal. Aquila, in the act of pinning the coveted silver medal on Zander's chest, noticed the other 'winner' staggering out of the side room nursing a bloody nose. Instead of Zander winning the medal, he had to hand in his woggle, go home and never come back to the troop.

*

At school, Zander regularly attended the meetings of the Army Cadet Corps (the 'junior' service as far as he was concerned), and with no other social activities to distract him, he rose quickly through the ranks. By the time he entered his final year he held the exalted rank of Warrant Officer 1st Class and, on occasions when the band went out on parade, he was its Drum Major.

As the time approached for him to do his National Service, Zander submitted a request to serve in the Royal Navy. However, at that time, the Navy were not taking in National Service recruits, so he could only opt to be a soldier or a 'Bevan Boy'. Deflated but resigned to the inevitable, Zander, with no desire to work down a coalmine, chose the lesser of the two evils and became a soldier, believing that his wealth of soldiering experience would come in handy and that he would not have to start out from scratch.

However, to the real Army, the former cadet WO 1st class was just like every other new recruit, a very ordinary private soldier.

3

Soldier Sailor etc   Southampton

On the day he joined his training unit at Larkhill in Wiltshire, Zander asked for an interview with his Commanding Officer. Within a week, he was in the Regimental Office standing in front of his CO, a piercing-eyed youthful Captain whose opening question was, "Well, my man, what do you want?"

Zander's reply of, "I respectfully request to be considered for a commission, Sir!" made the CO look closely at the soldier standing to attention in front of him, eyes fixed on a point on the wall above and behind his head, and enquired,

"You're a National Serviceman, are you not, soldier?" and when Zander answered;"Yes, Sir," he went on. "It is not the policy of The War Office to offer a commission to short-term service recruits." Then allowing a well-rehearsed tight smile to lighten up his face, he added,

"It would be a different matter however, if you were a regular soldier."

Zander said nothing but thought dismissively, *a regular soldier! Three whole years? No thanks!*

The CO took a deep breath, then glancing down at the papers on his desk in front of him, his expression changed again. Snapping his fingers, to give the impression that he had suddenly had an idea, he searched through his in-tray and pulled out a letter. With a conspiratorial smile on his face he looked up and said,

"Mmmn, I see from your records you're interested in sailing. That could well be to your advantage. I have something here that might be just the thing for you. Then pausing for a few seconds, he went on,

"Southern Command Officers' Club keep a 'Moody 34' in Southampton Roads. It already has a permanent skipper but the chap who helps him out on board is due for demob. In a small unit like ours, we don't often get people through here who know something about boats. Would you be interested in trying out for his place?"

Zander could hardly believe his ears. His CO was offering him the keys to paradise, a berth on a 34-foot yacht; and it had all come about because he had asked for a commission. With his mind in turmoil, Zander took only a microsecond to compose his words of acceptance, and looking his CO directly in the eyes, he blurted out,

"Yes, sir! Thank you, sir!"

At which, the CO pointed to behind Zander, who on turning round saw, a red-faced soldier standing to attention and looking as if he was about to burst. The CO went on,

"Good man. Report to the Sergeant Major there, at the Guard Room at 1300 hours on Friday. Dismissed!"

A salute, an about turn and a quick march through the door, already being held open for him by the Sergeant Major, who as soon as it had closed behind them, hissed in his ear

"You're a jammy little b****** Duff. Just make sure you're not late."

*

At 12.55 hours on the following Friday, Zander, in his number one uniform, was sitting on his kitbag outside the RSM's office when the door opened.

"Right, you worthless little item of body waste, there's a van over there waiting to take you to Southampton. And remember, down there you'll be in the company of young gentlemen, so behave yourself."

*

At the end of a bumpy ride in the back of the van, Zander arrived on a Southampton quayside, where his driver pointed him towards his new berth.

Standing looking down on the deck of a tidy-looking 34-footer, Zander knew how important it was to be seen to know the ropes and to do the right thing, so affecting a posh, confident voice, he shouted down,

"Permission to come aboard."

When he got the OK, he threw his kitbag on deck, climbed a couple of steps down the jetty ladder and clambered on to the afterdeck.

Looking to where the voice had come from, Zander saw, framed at the head of the companionway, the top half of a ruddy-complexioned man wearing a white roll neck sweater,

"Right lad, I'm the skipper. Just call me Skip. Welcome aboard. Our young gents are not here yet but you can get below and make a start at getting the spuds peeled and the peas shelled for dinner."

Zander's jaw dropped and he looked at Skip aghast,

"But I'm here to crew the boat. I could have stayed in camp and done all that."

"Sorry lad, that's what you're here to do. That and run after the officers, then clear away after them and clean up the boat when they leave. They do all the sailing. Think yourself lucky that I do all the cooking. Just do as you're told and you'll be all right."

From then on, Zander's life became one of, "Do this, do that, hold this, hold that," ad nauseam, all day long.'

Particularly awkward in that respect was a Major Ruthven. A tall, sandy haired, red-faced tyrant from one of the Guards' Regiments, he bullied Zander way beyond the call of Queen and country. For him, everything had to be done, instantly – or even sooner.

Over the seven days they were together, Major Ruthven made Zander's shipboard existence a living hell. Nothing ever pleased him and at every opportunity, he tore strips off his little 'Snotcatcher' as he called him, for anything and everything. Even for things done promptly, properly, and perfectly, he still gave Zander stick. It is therefore understandable that Zander and this boorish officer soon settled into a hate-hate relationship. The other officers, even though keeping him in his place, showed nothing but consideration for their subordinate.

One of them, a medic, who had brought his bag of tricks with him 'just in case,' asked Zander to put it in a safe place for him, which Zander did. Later, while all the officers were on deck playing sailors, Zander looked inside the doc's little bag and noticed a bottle labelled *Laxative*. After reading the prescribed dosage, he leached off a good bit more than the recommended dose into a small glass bottle.

Back in Southampton after their week of sailing, the officers, already packed and ready to disembark, asked Zander to get them all a cup of coffee for the road. This was Zander's chance. It should now not come as any surprise, that one of the cups also contained the former contents of the little glass bottle.

*

After his week at sea Zander was again back in Larkhill camp carrying out general duties and on standby to crew the Officers' boat as and when required. One of his duties was to act as general handy man and message bearer for the CO's wife. The lady, impressed by this smart, well-mannered fellow, told her husband, that he was "Not the usual rough chap you send me dear. And he tells me he wants to be an officer."

*

Inexplicably, there was no further call for Zander's services at Southampton and since he was at a holding unit, within a few weeks was posted. He had hardly settled in at his new posting when a letter came ordering him to attend War Office Selection Board – possibly his former CO's wife had prevailed upon her husband to do something on behalf of her young message boy.

Thus, it happened that Zander, along with a number of other aspiring officers, participated in a few full days of intelligence and initiative tests. During which time, members of the interview board lived with the candidates, ate with them and subjected them to ongoing physical and mental assessment tests.

One of Zander's assessors was a certain Major Ruthven who, although showing no hint of recognition, knew who Zander was and knew that Zander knew who *he* was, etc.

*

Five days after completing the assessment and back in his unit, Zander received a summons from his new CO to hear the outcome of his visit to WOSBy. Dressed in his best uniform and all fired up with anticipation, Zander was informed by his CO that regrettably, he had been not been successful.

Both Zander and Major Ruthven knew exactly why.

4

Do It in Style Get Out Fast   Edinburgh

However, Zander if nothing else, was a resilient individual who, in the wake of his disappointment, worked extremely hard at being a soldier and just to make sure that he was noticed by the 'powers that be', volunteered for anything and everything.

On one occasion, by virtue of an unpredicted passage through the transit area of an airport in a war zone, the army awarded him a Campaign Medal for active service there. This went some way to make up for the one denied him by the sea scouts. In a service career littered with ups and downs, Zander did experience the occasional minor 'up', but principally major 'downs', the most significant down being his spell of two years National Service, that put his professional career on hold, just when it should have been blossoming.

By the time he was ready for demobilisation, he had advanced to the exalted rank of Lance Corporal. This promotion was 'awarded' only six weeks prior to his demob, when he volunteered to become the regimental clerk at a National Serviceman's 'back to civvies' Rehabilitation Unit. Although Zander was convinced that this promotion was merited, every soldier knows that Army

Regulations dictate that anyone who does that job, is 'handed a stripe' to give him the power of the NCO over the ordinary Private soldier.

There is also an unsubstantiated rumour that on the train going home to ' Civvy' Street, by the scrape of a razor and the careful application of a pen, Zander's kit bag was 'promoted' from Lance Corporal to Lieutenant Colonel i.e. L/Cpl magically became Lt/Col. He naturally thought it then reasonable to assume that, if his kit bag had been 'promoted', it followed that *he* too had been 'promoted'. Thus with a deft flourish of razor blade and pen, Zander had bypassed the non-commissioned ranks, as well as a number of commissioned ranks and been elevated to General Staff level!

Disappointingly, the tools responsible for the quickest rise in the ranks ever achieved by a British soldier, were lost out of the carriage window of the train taking him home – otherwise they might well have found their way into some regimental museum.

On his return, Zander tried to re-establish himself in what he believed to be the *right* circles, i.e. those of people he thought were of *his* social standing such as; titled people, high-ranking officials, ex-officers and the like. Consequently, in describing his military career to such people, he would emphasise the fact that his contribution had been vital to the survival of Great Britain as a Nation. Usually he would start misty-eyed recollections with one of his stock in trade 'British' quotes such as, 'When I was doing my bit for Queen and country, defending the Realm and the Empire etc.

In the course of conversation one day, a friend suggested that he should apply for a post in the Civil Service; to everyone's surprise, Zander did this and passed the entrance examination.

During the years that followed, in his quest for promotion, he worked hard for long hours so had neither the time nor the money for sailing.

In these early years, when things did not go according to plan, the words of his mother often returned to fortify him,

"Failure, my beautiful little man, is just one step along the road to success."

He will have many of those in the future, but he always continued to believe.

5

Out With a Bang   Harthill

To fulfil a mandatory element of training in becoming a Chartered Engineer, one of Zander's early jobs, was as a site-based Engineer on the M8 at Harthill, Scotland's first motorway. As the new man and the most junior on the supervisory staff, he got the job no one else wanted; looking after the explosives store and responsible for the checking, re-checking and the checking again of every item of explosive issued on site. In addition, because it was at the time of a nationwide threat of IRA action, the control of explosives was very strict.

His on site contact with the blasting operation was Wee Johnny the shot-firer. Johnny, a local, was a few years older than Zander. His pallid complexion and yellow-toothed grin showed the effects of years of heavy smoking and his greying blonde hair made him look older than he was. Wee Johnny immediately took Zander under his wing and in no time at all, they were getting on like a house on fire, to the extent that when they knew there was no immediate call for explosives they went to the local pub together.

Over a pint on one of their early lunchtime visits, Wee Johnny invited Zander to his house for lunch. There, his new pal's younger sister, Betty, gave them a slap-up meal and only charged him for the ingredients. This proved to be so much better than eating in the noisy site-canteen or the transport cafe to the west of the office that thereafter Zander went home with Wee Johnny almost every day. As a result, Wee Johnny's house became his mid-day haven away from the job. On top of that, Betty looked after him so well, that he began to think optimistically; *Nice girl, I might get lucky here.*

This lunchtime ménage lasted for four months until, one morning Wee Johnny did not appear at work. Around coffee time, Zander saw through the window of his Portacabin office, a police car drawing up in the car park. The driver got out, put on his helmet, and spoke to a second officer sitting in the back, beside another figure that Zander could not quite see properly. Officer number one walked over to Zander's office, knocked sharply on the door and without waiting for an invitation, thrust his way in. The perplexed Zander was now face to face with a large, ruddy faced police Sergeant.

"Morning, Mr Duff."

"Morning, Sergeant. What can I do for you?"

"You're in charge of explosives here, yes?"

"That's right," Zander replied, his mind racing, "What's up?"

"We caught a man breaking into a jeweller's shop in Edinburgh last night and the explosives he was carrying have been traced back to your office. Can you explain that, sir? And while I'm here I'd like to have a look at your records."

Zander swallowed hard. *How could that be? Every item of explosive he handled, he personally signed for and docketed. His books were up to date and he was certain that there were no gaps in his records.*

"I don't know how that can be, Sergeant, I check everything personally." he said, as he stood up, got his stock book down from the shelf and handed it over.

"Do you mind?" the Sergeant said, pointing to Zander's desk and sat down at it to read the vital records.

After a few minutes, he slapped the page in triumph.

"That's the sticks there," he said, pointing to an entry.

Zander looked over the sergeant's shoulder; the entry was about two weeks old and had Wee Johnny's mark against it. "There must be some mistake!" he blurted out.

"No sir, no mistake, the numbers are the same. Wait a minute!"

With that, the sergeant went to the door and beckoned towards the car. After a few seconds, he stepped back into the room followed by a constable who dragged in a shamefaced Wee Johnny.

"Do you know this man, sir?"

"Yes, but...."

Wee Johnny's voice cut across him,

"Ah'm awfy sorry, Mr Duff!"

*

Six months later, working head down at his desk, a timid knock on his office door broke into Zander's thoughts.

"Come in." he called out.

In came an even paler, thinner version of his former lunch mate.

"Hullo, Mr Duff Ah'm back. Ah'm awfy sorry aboot a' the fuss thon time."

"Hmff." was all Zander could manage in welcome.

"Ah've dun ma time an Ah've got ma job back, but noo Ah'm jist laborin'."

"You know, you are a great disappointment to me, Johnny."

"Sorry Mr Duff! Nuthin personal, ye ken. Ah wus just dae'in whit Ah hud dun fur years."

"But I don't understand. How did you manage to get the explosives?"

"Well ye see, Ah jist used hauf o' the charges Ah signed fur in the holes, an' knocked aff every second yin."

"But surely you can't pinch detonators for them, the holes are counted and the firing is always checked."

"Och, Ah didnae need them; yon wee devil fire crackers work jist as weel. It says on them, 'light the touch paper and retire' an Ah did that bluddy quick Ah can tell ye."

"Mmph, I see! But after the police took you away from here, I went to your house to speak to your sister and a neighbour told me that she had gone away."

"Course she did, if she had a bin caught, the polis wud have dun her as weel."

As he absorbed this information, Zander paused,

"How did they catch you?"

"Weel it wis like this, she'd been goin oot wi the night watchman at this jewellers fur a week or two. He wis supposed tae skip off an meet her, and then she'd keep him away fur a while, until Ah did the joab, but he got sick an niver telt her. They pit someb'dy else oan in place o him, an' when he saw me, he nabbed me an called the polis. Caught rid handed, Ah wis."

"But your sister, how was she involved?"

"She had a different jeweller felly every few months, an every so often, Ah did a job where he worked."

"And I thought she liked me!"

"Aye she did that."

"But she never went out with me," said Zander.

"Aye but you're no a jeweller, ur ye?"

6

Asleep on the Job   Edinburgh

Another little escapade on the bumpy road along Zander's career path happened when he was supervising the refurbishment of a hotel owned by an oil Sheikh.

It was Christmas Eve and the site was winding down for the festive period. The Sheikh had arranged an after-work party for the Contractor's staff to keep them happy. When the workers saw the food and drink arriving just before morning tea break, they yielded to temptation and had helped themselves throughout the morning consequently,not a lot of work was done.

As Site Supervisor, Zander felt duty bound to lead by example and tried to ignore what was going on. Nevertheless, as the men got noisier and noisier, drunker and drunker, he came to terms with the situation; and to show them that he was really quite a good chap, he joined them for one wee drinkie. What did happen though was that he had a few more 'drinkies' than originally intended.

The party had been in full swing for more than an hour, there was no food or drinks left but because their pay packets had not arrived yet, the men were still hanging around and beginning to get a bit edgy. It was mid-afternoon before Zander saw the Foreman coming in with their wages. At last, the workers would get their money and go home.

With everyone paid, the Foreman, in company with a small group of workers, went back to his car and few minutes later brought in the Contractor's contribution to the party.

Not more booze! Zander thought, but it was – and lots of it.

Just when he had believed that his troubles were over, Zander – already feeling fragile and just managing to keep his end up – saw this new arrival of alcohol as a potential disaster. The workers understandably, took an entirely different view and continued from where they had left off.

Without losing face, Zander – who still had to come back after the Christmas break to supervise these same men – did not want to be the odd man out of the party? Was left thinking, *what should I do?*

In the clamour of the celebrations going on all around him, Zander could hardly hear himself think, and decided, *what I need is a bit of peace to sort this out!*

Turning to the Foreman, he said,

"I'm just going to my office to tidy up a few things. I'll only be a couple of minutes."

Back in his office, Zander sat down at his desk, blew out his cheeks and said to himself candidly, *Wow, I have had a bucketful. If I just rest for a minute, I should be all right.* Putting his arms on the desk, he settled his head down on them. One minute became five, then ten and soon he was sleeping like a baby and the sound of contented snoring was purring through his office.

It was pitch dark when he woke up; his mouth tasted like the bottom of a budgies' cage and his head felt fit to burst. Listening intently, he could hear no sounds of partying.

Great, he thought, *everyone has gone home.*

When he tried to stand up his elbows scraped against walls on either side of him, his chair would not move back and his face was right bang up against a door. Feeling for the handle, he tried to turn it, unsuccessfully. *Has my office shrunk? Where am I?* With some difficulty, he looked at his watch and its luminous dial was showing three forty five. *Was that am or pm?*

"Help!" he shouted and listened for a reply. There was none. He shouted again and once again his voice came straight back to him, confirming that, horror of horrors, somehow he was entombed in a confined space.

Outside of his little box, a deathly silence prevailed. His confused brain began to take in his predicament and kept coming up with some morale sapping facts. *By now, there was no chance that any of the men would still be here and the night watchman would have gone off on holiday too. The whole site would have shut down for the festive season hours ago. What am I to do? When will I get out of here? It might be days. I have no water and no food. If I don't die of starvation, I'll die of dehydration, but which will come first?*

Desperation then clicked in and he shouted for help until his voice box could only raise a throaty squeak, but still he heard nothing but silence. Frightened, in total despair and suddenly feeling very tired, he slumped back into the chair, let his head fall onto his chest and again slipped back into the soothing comfort of sleep.

*

A rustle of sound brought him immediately awake, dry mouthed and confused. He heard a scraping on the outside of his box then an anxious voice called his name. "Mr Duff, talk to me, are you all right?"

Someone was working on his tomb. Relief surged through him like the life saving charge from a defibrillator.

"Keep still, we'll have you out in a jiffy."

At last, a twinkling chink of light hurt his screwed up eyes, almost immediately followed by a dazzling burst of fluorescence as the door in front of him burst open. Anxious hands helped him to his feet, brushed him down while their owners offered profuse apologies.

Once his eyes had adjusted to the bright light, he recognised his rescuers as the Foreman and three of last night's drinking pals.

"We really are sorry. You were a wee bit the worse for drink last night and when we found you, you were fast asleep. We could not wake you up, so for a bit of fun we wheeled you into your stationery cupboard and locked you in. We did mean to let you out before we left, but with one thing and another and the effects of too much whisky, we forgot all about you until we woke up this morning."

"What's the time?" asked Zander weakly.

"Half past nine in the morning. And by the way, A MERRY CHRISTMAS!"

THE CHARTERS

Farewell to Lismore

7

A Skipper with No Boat   Edinburgh

The mature Zander has lost his younger Tony Hancock look-alike appearance. Now his grey blue eyes are set in a craggy weather beaten face that retains the beetle brows and the upside down, but mischievous, smile. It is only when he is perplexed or angry that this expression changes, his shoulders hunch, his eyebrows crunch down over his eyes and his lower lip protrudes petulantly. Fortunately, he has a forgiving nature and a good sense of humour, so his belligerent side seldom shows.

His clothes now have a well lived-in look, with each garment giving the notion of closing in on its expiry date. However, to him, they are comfortable to the extent that, should anyone criticise what he is wearing, he will show them the designer labels and dismissively admonish them with one of his favourite quotes, "You have to remember, it's the quality that counts."

On the few occasions he goes out with Jane, his wife, she makes sure that our ugly duckling turns into a well-dressed, immaculately groomed swan, almost unrecognisable to all but his closest associates.

However, right now, he is not a happy man. He has no boat and is on the beach, again. Emerald his beautiful boat had been sold – the one he named after the World War II destroyer on which his boyhood hero Uncle Jim served. In addition, without asking and without saying anything to him until after the event, Jane had lent the proceeds of the sale to her brother. When asked why she had done this, her 'dare to contradict me' response of "because the money was lying there doing nothing" – had left him speechless.

Consequently, with his 'boat fund' tied up – and knowing his brother in law, tied up for longer than he cared to think about – he no longer had the wherewithal to buy Emerald's replacement. Faced with no other option, he stifled his anger at his wife's gut wrenching *fait accompli*, shrugged his shoulders in surly acceptance and resolved never to put any large amounts of cash into their joint account again.

To date, last year's sailing season had been lost and a new one was almost upon him. He took some consolation however, in knowing that it was still winter – a season of shorter, colder days when most boats are out of the water and little or no recreational sailing is done in Scottish waters.

However, with the approach of spring and the weather beginning to show signs of improving, owners were starting to get their boats ready for the coming season. On any weekend, weather permitting, hulls are scraped and painted, and maintenance work done on parts that are only accessible when the boat is up on the hard.

Meanwhile Zander's career path had changed. His civil service employer had farmed him out to a major civil engineering contractor working on a multi-million pound Government infrastructure project. His job title was 'Controller of In-house Standards'. When he first heard about this appointment, it looked to him like being a good move, but in reality, it turned out to be a disappointing and thankless task. His new colleagues saw him as the gamekeeper – who interfered in their world of poaching – and treated him accordingly. Zander's position did not inspire a great deal of respect and because of its 'snooping' duties, he was universally ignored.

The job's principal advantage however, was that he was his own boss and as no one monitored his movements or lodged any reports about his performance, he could, within reason, do as he pleased. At the times when he should have been with his Principals, he would tell them he was with the Contractor. When he was supposed to be with the Contractor, he would say that he had been with his Principals, when in reality, he was with neither; the ideal circumstances for him to slope off unnoticed whenever he chose. Unfortunately, with no boat, he had nowhere to go.

8

The Captain's Wife   Edinburgh

Jane is Zander's long-suffering but very capable wife; she is also his lover, confidant, friend, auntie, sister, nanny, treasurer, etc. who has learned to live with and accept most of his little idiosyncrasies. She, with her well-honed ability to anticipate Zander's problems, is quite happy to paddle along in his wake and take the necessary steps to avoid them. Jane therefore is never around when Zander gets up to mischief or lands himself in trouble.

She also acts as his communicator and since the loss of Emerald, has kept in touch with the wives of two of Zander's former shipmates, Gilbert and Grunt. Emerald's third crewmember Murdo, had not been so easy to keep track of; divorced, a free spirit, of no fixed abode and at all times, very difficult to trace. It was possible that he spent a few weeks with one female cousin in one place, before moving in with another one in another place for a few weeks, and so on.

*

Perhaps the only time that Jane was actually involved in one of Zander's little boo-boos and did not see it coming, was when they spent a two week holiday in the Morar Hotel.

For the first week, they enjoyed wall-to-wall sunshine, sunbathed on the beautiful pure white sandy beach and swam in the clear, but not too warm sea. It was glorious. On their second week, the rain began to drain the heavens and showed no sign of ever letting up.

In those days, Morar was a small village and for two city dwellers, there was not a lot to do. They had seen the loch, looked for Morag (Nessie's rival), and watched fish jumping over the dam or swimming up the fish-pass. As far as they were concerned, they had already seen and done all there was to do here and anyway, these are not the sort of things to do in that sort of weather.

One dreary, wet evening Zander was sitting in the lounge when he noticed the local minister cycling through the driving rain towards the hotel. He stopped outside the front door, came in, took off his hat and coat, shook them and hung them in the porch before striding into the hotel.

Zander, always a bit of a Nosey Parker, called to him as he passed the lounge door, "Come away in here and get something to warm you up."

The minister, tall for a Scotsman and thin, all knees and elbows, looked in, smiled and washing his hands in a Shylock manner, said, "Thank you, I will."

A short chat with the minister served to inform Zander that he was here to check up on the catering for the following evening's whist drive in the church hall.

One thing led to another and Zander could not resist a little kite flying, "You know my wife has played a bit of whist and at some really big whist drives in Edinburgh. She has even played in New Zealand and she's won some prizes."

The minister's eyelids dropped and a sly smile formed on his thin lips,

"Why don't you come along tomorrow night then and help to make up the numbers?"

Thinking, *In for a penny in for a pound*, Zander said, "Yes, why not?"

The following night after dinner, Zander and Jane, hunched under an umbrella, braved a short hurried walk through the pouring rain down to the church hall. Inside, the minister who had clearly been looking out for them, came forward to meet them and introduce them to his flock as, "The fine city gentleman and his lady wife who have played whist all over the world." With an imperious nod and a wave Zander acknowledged the ripple of applause, the smiles and the warm greeting, all the while thinking, *the locals look like a lovely god fearing lot. How nice.*

Had he really thought about the minister's spurious introduction, he might not have been so patronising. Even if Jane did feel a bit uneasy, she saw nothing to worry about in a church hall.

Everyone sat down at about 20 card tables arranged in a ring around the hall, leaving two seats vacant for their visitors.

Before sitting down the minister made an announcement, "Remember it's progressive tonight. The winning pair picks up the table stake and moves clockwise, the losers stay where they are and renew the stake money. Let us begin! Hearts are Trumps!"

*

A disastrous night ensued as Zander and Jane did not win a single hand. To cap it all, when they played the minister, he and his partner took all 13 tricks, and, although he apologised profusely there was a gleam of triumph shining in his eyes.

*

Next morning at breakfast, an elderly man, a long time resident and a retired driver of the Jacobean train – now known as the Hogwarts Express – came over to Zander and Jane's table.

"How did you get on at the whist drive last night?"

Zander replied with a grim look on his face, "We were taken to the cleaners."

"Pity you didn't speak to me first. Did you not think that the table stakes were a bit high?

Tell me if I am wrong. There were two trestle tables covered with 'valuable' prizes, one for the raffle and one for the Tombola. You bought raffle and tombola tickets did you not? The tombola ones were all duds, weren't they?"

"Uh huh."

The draw for the raffle is next week and they took your name and address to send on any prize you won.

"Uh huh."

"Everyone sat down and there was one table left empty for you."

"Uh huh."

They told you that, just to make it more interesting they always play for table stakes.

"Uh huh."

"You didn't win a game all night and lost a fair sum of money."

"Uh huh."

With a smile of satisfaction the old chap went on, "The table you sat down at was the one with the pack of marked cards. You were the only ones who actually lost money; the others just play for fun. And by the way, you can tear up your raffle tickets, the stubs from that book never got into the draw."

"How do you know all that?"

"Because I know that the locals use the whist drive as a way of raising money for the new church roof. They catch a lot of passing trade from hotel guests and other overnight tourists. At the height of the season, if they have more than one pair of visitors a night, more marked decks means that just like you, they all lose. You might think that their little scam can't amount to much, but they put what they do get into Premium Bonds and so far they've done very well."

9

The Captain's Crew   Edinburgh

Zander, now with a lot of spare time, was badly missing his boat. It had been nearly eighteen months since last he and his Emeraldeers (their adopted name from their earlier yacht Emerald) had ventured out on to their own particular sea of mishaps. Back then, they had been a happy band of misfits enjoying each other's company and no matter what, things usually ended up in a mood of contented comradeship. However, there were times, when an opportunity arose, that showed they had no inhibitions about 'dropping each other in it' and then taking great delight in watching their victim's discomfiture.

Gilbert is the mate, only because when he first joined them, he bought their drinks – a practice he had long since given up. An ex army officer, of medium build with a small moustache but with not a lot of hair left on top of his head. What hair he still has he keeps neatly trimmed with the dedication he applies to everything else. Gilbert was a late addition to the crew and grateful to be a part of it, so he tends to be a background man, and only occasionally gets involved in the fray. He nurtures aspirations of becoming an inshore skipper but to achieve this, he first has to obtain a Competent Crew Certificate; something he works at with unswerving dedication.

Murdo, mainstay of the crew, is the chief deckhand. What he does not know about boats and sailing is not worth knowing. Murdo is a wiry, 'pint-sized' chap, who was formerly the best poacher around Loch Ness and incongruously, at the same time, a former Highland Regional County Councillor. Industrious and not overly sensitive, he is devoutly loyal to his skipper and shipmates. Everywhere he goes, at least one of his remarkably large harem of female 'cousins' appears 'out of the woodwork' to look after him.

The other deckhand, Grunt is an old school friend of Zander's. He is an easy going, six feet tall lump, who, in his younger days, was an athlete of some note, but is not a natural sailor and only goes to sea as a favour to his friend. Through long and hard-earned experience Zander has come to accept that, because Grunt is good at lifting heavy objects or pulling things around, it is better to overlook his bone-idle deficiencies and just take him along.

During last summer's sailing season, with no regular berth, Gilbert and Murdo had resorted to going down to the yacht club to plead with anyone who would listen, to take them on, either to race or just to help out for the day. On the odd occasion when these speculative pleas did pay off, they discovered that it was never as much fun as when they had sailed as Emeraldeers. Apparently, none of these boat owners had any of Zander's, often unwitting, aptitude for 'adventure'.

Grunt is the only one of Zander's regulars who had not missed being on a boat. The previous year he had enjoyed a lazy summer doing very little but doing it very well.

On the few occasions when Jane invited the Emeraldeers round for a beer, they reminisced about their past adventures and talked about the fun they had shared on their previous voyages together. Nostalgia not being what it used to be, they remembered the good bits with relish and forgot all about the bad bits. Any incident involving stupidity or lack of common sense was always someone else's fault.

At their last meeting, it was obvious that Zander had become desperate because as they left, he held Gilbert back at the door. When the others had gone out of earshot, he suggested that as he was the only other member of his crew who might be able to afford it, he should help him to buy a new boat. However, Gilbert choked and spluttered, as he said "Not on your life!" An emphatic refusal that closed off any hopes Zander might have had in that direction.

Gilbert knew only too well how expensive a mistress a boat can be; ever present in the background, regularly calling for costly maintenance, forever demanding lots of loving care and attention and always needing expensive new accessories. In other words it was a big black hole into which you pour your hard earned money.

With that door slammed in Zander's face – and what had seemed to be a good idea emphatically blown away, he was left wondering what to do next.

Will I ever get my Emeraldeers together again?

10

Wooing a New Mistress   Ardfern

The clocks had sprung forward to British Summer Time. All around Scotland the harbours, marinas and moorings were bustling with activity. Cruisers, yachts and all sorts of other small boats were being prepared for the coming season. Sad to say, this year Zander would not be part of that buzz of excitement and anticipation.

For their spring holiday break, he and Jane had rented a cottage in Ardfern, so for a whole month, Zander would be near the sea and around boats. From his window, he enjoyed a panoramic view of the marina and, spent a lot of time enviously monitoring the comings and goings of the fleet of boats based there.

Against the backdrop of white sandy beaches and small tree-covered islands, one boat in particular stood out from all the others, a big, tall masted dream of a boat that sat on a mooring well inside the bay. It had not moved since the day Zander got there and, he had not seen anyone go anywhere near it. Through his binoculars, he read that this beautiful, sleek, ocean-going yacht's name was Fast Lady. Running his binoculars over her, he became more and more impressed. Fully kitted out with roller-reefing sails, power winches, an enormous steering wheel, GPS, self-steering gear and radar, she looked fabulous. In fact to him, she was 'the full Monty'. From the moment he set eyes on her, Fast Lady haunted Zander's dreams. She was the ideal vessel to carry him out to St. Kilda or the other exotic landfalls he longed to visit.

An enquiry at the Marina Office confirmed that Fast Lady had been sitting on her mooring for much of the last two years and in that period, had only been out a handful of times. This set Zander thinking. *What a waste. How can this happen? If she were mine I would really look after her and certainly would not leave her lying there looking abandoned and neglected.* Jane as always, reading her husband like a book, tried to find out what she could about Fast Lady and her absentee owner. It did not take her long to determine that Fast Lady's owner was an Edinburgh entrepreneur who, because of business pressures, seldom had time to sail her. Coincidentally, and conveniently perhaps for Zander, that morning the owner had telephoned the Marina to say he was coming up at the weekend to take her out.

Jane passed these tit-bits of information on to Zander, and suggested that when the owner arrived, he should nip down to the marina, introduce himself and see what happens. "He may just welcome some help."

At breakfast on the preordained morning, Zander saw a big station wagon with Edinburgh licence plates turn into the marina car park. The driver and his single passenger got out. Zander watched them go to the dinghy compound and manhandle Fast Lady's tender towards the water. His time to act had come. With his mind racing uncontrollably, Zander got up in such a hurry that he tipped his chair over and spilt his porridge all over the table. Naturally, he left this for Jane to clear up.

Once outside, his stubby legs broke into a hop, skip, and walk action as he hurried down to the shore to make contact. Moving in for the 'kill', he allowed himself a little smile of satisfaction as he thought; *there are only two of them so they are bound to need help.*

Sure enough, as he scuttled into the marina, the tender heading out towards Fast Lady had only two people on board. It was only then that he noticed two more cars with Edinburgh license plates, were parking adjacent to the first one and that people were getting out of them.

As he watched, they unloaded a number of baskets and boxes, holdalls and rucksacks, items of wet weather and other gear. It was now clear that the owner had come with a full complement of crew and passengers, so it was unlikely that he would need anyone else to help him. This was a bitter blow to Zander. He had already convinced himself that the owner would be a rich novice who would welcome him on board to be the skipper of his beautiful boat. What Zander had just witnessed, appreciably slowed down his scurrying progress. People were now piling up gear on the pontoon ready to be loaded onto Fast Lady. The beautiful yacht came alongside and when all the packages were stowed away, everyone climbed aboard.

Zander took stock. What he now knew put a completely different complexion on things. After mulling over the new situation for a few a moments, he decided to take a different tack, still unaware that during his telephone conversation with the marina manager, Fast Lady's owner had been presented with chapter and verse about him.

With his heart pounding wildly, Zander approached the pontoon where two of the group were preparing to cast off.

"I'll clear the lines for you," he offered.

"Thanks," a voice from on board called back.

In response to the owner's signals, Zander slipped Fast Lady's moorings, whereupon with her motor smoothly purring up to a higher pitch, she slid off the pontoon and motored out into the bay.

Now that he had seen Fast Lady close up, Zander saw that she was even more beautiful than he had ever believed possible. With a look of longing admiration, he watched her stately progress over a slightly rippled sea, until she had disappeared from view.

Zander then spent the rest of the day sitting in his window seat, reading and keeping a weather eye open for any sign of Fast Lady coming home. As day ran on into evening a sickening thought struck him, *Horror of horrors, she might not be coming back at all!*

*

It was late evening, with the light almost gone, before Zander spotted Fast Lady coming home. Silhouetted against the deep yellow sun setting over the horizon behind her, she looked the picture of all he had ever desired. By the time she was running in, he was waiting for her on the pontoon and doing his best to appear as if he just happened to be there. Catching the mooring lines, he made her fast and as he locked on the last line, he heard someone calling,

"Would you care to come aboard?"

Zander looked up to see the owner beckoning to him. *Wow*, he thought, but replied calmly, "Thank you, I don't mind if I do."

During the course of their initial conversation, Zander found his host to be not only a knowledgeable sailor but a good listener as well. In addition, by occasionally throwing in the odd probing question, bit-by-bit Fast

Lady's owner winkled out more and more, about what made Zander tick.

Meanwhile, Zander discovered that his host had bought Fast Lady three years ago with the intention of retiring and sailing her round the world. Unfortunately a few weeks before the date set for his retirement, his younger business partner, recently brought into the practice to take over from him, had quite suddenly died. Of necessity, he cancelled his retirement and thus delayed any plans he had nurtured of long distance sailing.

Although retirement was still a possibility, so far, it had not happened. He loved his boat and lived in the hope that someday, in the not too distant future, he would sail her off into the sunset. For the time being though, Fast Lady just had to lie here unused, waiting for the day when his circumstances improved.

This was music to Zander's ears. *Opporchancity, come to daddy!*

Doing his best to keep the tremor out of his voice, Zander played the opening gambit of his little game by saying,

"If you like, I could keep an eye on her for you. My job leaves me with a bit of spare time. I sold my boat a while ago and I'm still looking for a replacement. Meanwhile, until I find one, I'll be staying up here quite a lot, so if you like, I could help you out."

As it turned out, Zander need not have worried. Fast Lady's owner was shrewd enough to have seen this coming and throughout their conversation, while assessing his guest, he had already decided that Zander would be a handy yacht sitter. In fact, whichever way Zander had played his pieces, Fast Lady's owner, had been ready to checkmate him. Zander, the habitual biter, was now on the point of being well and truly bitten himself.

"Really, you would do that for me?" was the owner's innocent sounding reply.

"Certainly," enthused Zander "and I also have a fine crew available who I'm sure would be only too happy to help."

The unsuspecting victim was now put through a pseudo interview, during which enquiries were made about his certification, his crew's competence and their general all round experience; most of which the owner already knew. In spite of what he had heard about Zander, Fast Lady's owner saw this appointment as a fairly small gamble, knowing that the watertight agreement his lawyers would draw up would cover any risks.

In outline, Zander was to look after on-board maintenance, keep everything shipshape and make sure that Fast Lady was, at short notice, always ready for the owner's use.

In return, Zander and his crew could stay on board whenever they chose and take Fast Lady out on short trips as often as they liked. However, any visions Zander had about getting her out to St. Kilda were promptly dashed when he was told that, for the time being anyway, the owner could not permit voyages lasting for more than a couple of nights; because that would not be covered by his insurance.

In mulling this over, Zander had an idea,

"If I am to be covered by your insurance, perhaps you could pay me an agent's fee for any charters I manage to arrange, on the understanding that I would be skipper and could use my own crew."

Fast Lady's owner smiled a satisfied smile "Yes, that sounds workable. I'll have my lawyer make the necessary arrangements". Then thanking his new boat sitter, he confirmed that, provided his lawyers approved that the last particular option would be part of terms of agreement, he would have it drawn up.

With the general principles of the arrangement in place, a handshake sealed the informal agreement.

*

In due course, the principals applied their signatures to a bit of paper, officially putting the formal agreement in place.

Zander could not believe his luck; finally, he had a new boat – and a cracker at that.

11

The New Mistress Succumbs   Ardfern

The day Zander took 'possession' of Fast Lady, Jane sent letters to Grunt's and Gilbert's wives to tell their husbands to come to Ardfern the following weekend to see Zander's new yacht – and to bring their sailing gear with them. In Murdo's case, a letter marked for his attention was pinned on the notice board of the Yacht Club at Granton.

Fast Lady was certainly no ordinary vessel; she was an impressive, beautifully appointed forty-five-footer, built for comfort and set up for luxury sailing. She was a stately yacht that rode well in the water and whose mast-tops stood aloof over every other yacht in the marina.

Zander was her 'master', however temporarily, and living in luxury on board his spiritual heaven. With 'his' yacht moored to the pontoon, Zander would sit in the wheelhouse; book in hand, a glass of wine nearby, looking down imperiously on the world of Ardfern, its marina and its inhabitants, advertising to all and sundry, just how important a person he was. While playing his self-satisfied part to the full, he would deign to acknowledge, the presence of anyone passing by or sailing past with a condescending wave; something he did frequently.

*

On muster day, Gilbert and Grunt set out early from Edinburgh and got to the marina around midday. Zander, leaning nonchalantly out of the wheelhouse, a can of beer in hand, welcomed them aboard. Both were slack-jawed with amazement at everything they saw and dying to hear how their skipper had pulled off such a coup.

The prospect of sailing on such a fine craft, overjoyed Gilbert as he just stood and took in the grandeur of the unbelievable yacht. Grunt meanwhile, although grudgingly admitting that it was all very nice, was more interested in booking the best bunk for himself, hurried below. When he pushed open the door of the stateroom-like main cabin, the un-made double bed and litter on the floor told him that Zander had already bagged this one; he also noted in passing, that it had a television, cocktail bar and en-suite facilities. *Pity I didn't get here first,* he thought and went to look elsewhere. With little to choose between the other equally well-appointed cabins, Grunt dumped his stuff in one of them and went back up on deck to hear Zander's story. Later Gilbert would bag another one.

When Murdo turned up, he would bunk up in his preferred residence – the forward sail locker. This cosy cabin, away from the trafficked areas of the boat, has a handy deck access hatch, through which sails are manhandled on and off the deck. Here he enjoyed independence and freedom of movement, particularly when it came to smuggling a female cousin on board without disturbing his messmates. According to the local jungle telegraph, Murdo was already somewhere in the vicinity and naturally, staying with a cousin.

It was mid-morning of the following day before Murdo appeared, and, after making all the right noises about Zander's new boat, he cheerfully set about tidying her up. In a short space of time – the result of a sustained effort by Murdo and Gilbert, a bit less from the Skipper and hardly any from Grunt – every part of Fast Lady was put to rights and by the time they were finished she was gleaming like new.

After lunch, Zander and his re-assembled Emeraldeers took Fast Lady out on a shakedown sail and soon had a fair idea of how she handled, how to operate her enormous powered roller-reefing sails and exactly what her other labour saving switches did.

By the time they tied her up that evening, her skipper and crew had convinced themselves that this magnificent craft, which drew admiring glances from everyone who saw her, was truly theirs.

*

Over that summer, The Emeraldeers enjoyed a series of weekend trips on Fast Lady, but they still hankered after longer voyages to tantalising places, as yet unvisited. Zander meanwhile, longing for some open-water sailing, kept hoping that a charter would come along. Here was a comfortable ocean-going yacht that was crying out to sail out to the Hebrides or up to Orkney or Shetland and perhaps even brave the Atlantic out to St Kilda.

As luck would have it, even though Zander had advertised Fast Lady's services, up until now, there had been no takers. By early autumn, he had almost given up hope, when completely out of the blue he received a telephone call from one of the Twins, a former shipmate from his time on the Puffer, who told him that he and his brother now owned a yacht charter company and had heard that Zander might have a boat for hire, at short notice.

The Twin then revealed that a large engineering organisation had offered his brother and him the option on a week's charter to entertain eight on-board guests. The only yacht the Twins had available could only take four or five, so they needed another good boat to take the rest of the party. They were due to rendezvous at Ganavan Bay just north of Oban, where they would pick up the passengers. If Fast Lady was available and Zander and his crew could operate it, a deal might be possible.

Zander immediately got on the 'phone to Fast Lady's owner who, on hearing the generous terms offered, readily agreed. Zander then confirmed the matter with the Twins and he and his delighted Emeraldeers began to look forward to the coming voyage, hoping against hope that it would involve some real sailing to some fascinating new and far-away places.

12

The Mistress Pays Her Way   Oban

Fast Lady's crew of former Emeraldeers got to Ganavan Bay the day before their passengers were due to arrive. The trip there had been like a holiday and they were now ready, able and (considering Grunt was on board) willing to do whatever was required of them to make a success of this new venture.

The first light of a new dawn blanching the night sky, revealed two yachts moored line astern alongside a pontoon, both appearing to be afloat on a mirror-like sea.

Today's weather forecast promised a bright, seasonable autumn day. Already there was warmth in the sun and gentle breezes were pushing light clouds across a clear blue sky. In addition, the long range forecast indicated that the fine weather would continue for at least the next two days. After that, the weather pattern already pushing in from across the Atlantic, was less certain and might just bring some rain. Conditions seemed perfect for what they were about to do.

Anyone who has sailed the waters of the Western Isles knows that at any time and without warning, the weather can change dramatically; so to make the most of this promise of good weather, the charters would get under way as soon as all of the guests were on board.

The Twins' yacht, Merryman, was a Fisher 38, and as her classification suggested, looked like a fishing boat. Her crew had called themselves the Merrymen but whether copying or mocking Zander's lot is not known. Zander and his Emeraldeers made it known that, if anything, they were to be referred to by their former collective identity and certainly not as the 'Fast Ladies'. Grunt underlined this point by telling the Twins that he would hold them personally responsible for any lapse that they or their Merrymen made in that direction.

When Zander got a copy of the prospective itinerary, his spirits fell. There would be no visit to the Outer Hebrides, let alone St. Kilda. Initially, the flotilla was going to Lismore to pick up one of Merryman's crew, before heading up the Sound of Mull to spend the night in Tobermory. A circuit of Mull would follow and if conditions allowed, the passengers would take a shore trip to Iona for a 'bit of culture' at the Abbey there. Their next overnight stop would be either in Loch Spelve or in Lochbuie, before finally re-crossing the Firth of Lorne to return to their starting point. Whether any actual sailing would be possible would depend on the weather. However, if the winds remained light, non-existent or blowing in the wrong direction, they would motor sail when they could, or at worst, motor all the way.

Grunt apart, when Zander's crew heard where they were going, their faces fell. They were going to do the 'same old, same old' and still get no trip to St. Kilda.

No matter how disappointed Zander felt, he believed it was up to him to rally his troops, so he smiled and said,

"Never mind, the main thing is that we're afloat again and this time we are getting paid for it!"

13

A Rival   Granton

The Twins knew that their client Steve Francey, managing director of a large building organisation, was an old rival of Zander's, but they conveniently forgot to tell him about Zander's involvement. Neither did they risk letting Zander know who his employer was. In these busy, end of season weeks, when every other suitable boat in the area was already booked up, getting hold of Fast Lady had been a last desperate resort; let's face it, they had been left with no alternative.

Francey, a certificated skipper in his own right, kept a boat at Granton on the East Coast and was a member of the same yacht club as the Twins and Zander and his crew. Francey had known Zander for as long as either of them could remember. As youngsters, they had lived in the same area and later, as budding civil engineers, had attended evening classes together. They had always been acquaintances rather than friends and observed the bare minimum of social grace towards each other. Zander's departure on National Service had broken their chain of regular encounters that only resumed when Zander submitted an application to become a member of the yacht club. What Zander did not know was that Francey was one of the first to support his application, a gesture that in time, he would live to regret.

Within the club environment, Zander soon realised that Francey was perched well above him in the club's pecking order. Furthermore, Francey's professional career had blossomed, whereas Zander's had suffered the stunting effect of being absent for two years in the army. Francey was the only civil engineer in the club, so, as far as engineering matters were concerned, he was the club's technical oracle, that was until Zander turned up. At first, Zander listened to Francey pontificating, always keeping his opinions to himself and only raising an eyebrow when he heard something that he did not agree with.

It was bad enough that Francey had all sorts of things that he did not have but what fanned the flames of Zander's resentment, was when he overheard Francey boasting about how he had cheated at his pre-services medical and thus avoided doing compulsory military service. From the moment Zander found out that Francey had sidestepped National Service, and in doing so allowed him to get on with his career, his whole attitude towards him took an about turn and he let his personal bitterness become obvious. One way this change manifested itself was that he now met any debatable issue in Francey's diatribes with argument and outspoken contempt. All that remained now was a grudgingly thin veneer of civility towards one another, but only if there was someone else around.

This illustrates an example of how the effect of some apparently insignificant matter, can have a huge impact on personal relationships. Both of them were now engaged in a game that neither could win, so the final score was likely to end up as 0-0, i.e. No brains each!

14

Who Will Win Fair Lady's Heart?
Ganavan Bay

As his principal means of marketing, Francey entertained prospective clients by taking them on luxury sailing trips. Usually using his own yacht to take them round the harbours and islands of the Forth Estuary and the East Coast of Scotland, while providing them with as much of the very best of food and liquid refreshment as they could – or sometimes could not – handle.

Francey took a lot of satisfaction from this ploy, which killed two birds with one stone. Firstly, the breaks got him away from the office and secondly they were tax deductible. By using his own boat, he could legitimately offset some of his outlay to business expenses.

In setting up these little jaunts, his policy was to invite guests who were not sailors and consequently unfamiliar with the ways and means of boats and sailing. Then, by his way of thinking, as the undisputed captain, he could impress them by showing off his familiarity with boats and his general on-board competence. Francey was into the power game and when he played that game, he played it to the limit.

Whenever Francey felt like cruising in an area not conveniently accessible to his own boat, he would charter one in his area of choice, preferably one with its own crew. This current charter with the Twins was one of those. Francey had heard many tantalising stories about the wonderful sailing to be had in the West Coast of Scotland and wanted to experience it for himself.

The Twins had assumed responsibility for the distribution of passengers and knowing that Francey was a skipper in his own right (and likely to want to be in charge of Merryman), they did not want him on their boat. The charter of Fast Lady had given them the perfect solution; Francey and three of his guests would go with Zander.

Francey, in the act of throwing his sea-bag on to Fast Lady, came face to face with Zander, who was standing poised in a catching position with a welcoming smile on his face. The smile froze instantly. For a moment or two, the pair just looked at each other. Then in the awkward silence that ensued, exchanged sullen nods and with a resigned shrug acknowledged that there was little either of them could do about it; Francey because he did not want to make a scene in front of his guests, Zander because he had no choice.

Zander glowered in the direction of Merryman and caught a glimpse of two pairs of eyes hurriedly looking away, confirming that their owners knew they had given him the sticky end of the toffee apple.

Francey, once he had got over the initial shock of finding Zander on board, realised that things might not be as bad as he had at first thought. He was the one who was paying, so Zander was his hired man. As sponsor and honorary skipper, he would naturally take command of Fast Lady. The more he thought about this the more he liked it, so he decided to waste no time in establishing his authority over Fast Lady's crew.

Zander on the other hand had gone below decks to mope. As he saw it, this development was bad news; here on his boat, was a man for whom he felt nothing but contempt and he was stuck with the nauseating prospect of having to spend the next few days with Fancy Boy – as the Emeraldeers called him. The thought of it made him sick to his back teeth. Worse still, he knew perfectly well that if anything went wrong, Fancy Boy would take great delight in telling the Twins it had been his fault.

The more he thought about it though, the better he began to feel, *Whose boat is it? I am the skipper, so by right I am in command.* However, still lurking at the back of his mind was the worry that he would have to keep a close eye on Francey just to make sure he was given no excuse to tell tales.

If ever there was a recipe for disaster, the ingredients were together on Fast Lady and it was not long before the cooking began. Knowing of the animosity that existed between the pair, it may seem strange that the Twins had put Zander and Francey on the same boat; but it all came down to their own self-interest. They knew that, if Francey sailed on their boat, there would be one too many skippers on board, and that could lead to misunderstandings and potential problems. As far as the Twins were concerned, it was their show and they would run it their way. The result was that Zander got Francey.

The Twins never had any doubt about which of them was in command on Merryman and, depending upon circumstances, either or both would take charge. They had been born to it, grown up with it and were used to supporting each other at all times. However, by assuming that Zander and Francey while acting as certified offshore skippers under maritime law, they would forget their petty squabbles and behave like responsible people – shows just how poorly they had misjudged the protagonists. At the outset of the voyage, an incident occurred which demonstrated just how mistaken the Twins had been.

It happened like this; at dawn in a deserted marina with no one stirring onshore, Fast Lady was coupled up to the services' bollard on the pontoon, taking on water and recharging her batteries. Under a clear blue sky, or as clear as it gets now that it is often criss-crossed with condensation trails, Merryman had already slipped her moorings and set off. Francey in the wheelhouse, waiting for his last guest to arrive, was filling in time by familiarising himself with Fast Lady's controls and other gadgets. Zander on deck was keeping an eye on the services' lines and with little else to occupy his mind, up to no good.

After Fast Lady's last trip, her owner had left a lot of booze on board and Zander had already helped some of it to 'disappear' into the safety of his own secret spaces. With Fancy Boy on board, the last thing he wanted was to get his private supplies mixed up with the guests' stuff, so, with Fancy Boy otherwise engaged, Zander took the opportunity to see just what goodies had come on board. Then if he knew what was there, and where it was stowed, he could arrange for some of the better stuff to find its way into his private hidey-holes!

Glancing ashore, Zander saw no signs of anyone approaching so, believing that he had plenty of time went below to carry out an 'inspection'. What he found brought the green light of envy to his eyes and a hollow feeling of greed to his stomach. *I'll say this for Fancy Boy,* he mused, *He certainly does know how to look after his guests,* followed by, *I wonder how much of this can safely be made to disappear?*

Unable to resist the temptation, Zander did what he should not have done and took a number of Francey's bottles of refreshment 'into care'. Chuckling quietly, he added these 'gleanings' to his own booze cache. Then the most satisfying of thoughts struck Zander, *Fancy Boy is providing me with all this alcohol, is this not fantastic?*

Meanwhile on deck, shortly after Zander's head had vanished down the companionway, Francey welcomed his last guest on board and thought, *Right we can get away now, I'll show Zander who is boss,* and switched on the motor.

The sound of the engine brought some of the other guests on deck to watch their departure. At the stern Murdo was tending the mooring line while Grunt was dealing with the one up at the bow. Zander, still busy below was oblivious to what had happened above. Yes, he had heard the engine starting up but thought, *that will just be Fancy Boy playing himself,* so unconcerned, he took no notice.

Topsides, Francey called out the orders,

"Cast off forward, cast off astern." which the crew did.

Slipping the motor into gear, Francey eased Fast Lady off the pontoon, then, gradually picking up speed, moved her out towards the open waters of the Firth of Lorne.

She had travelled hardly any distance before one of the guests offhandedly said to Francey, "What's that we're towing?"

Down below Zander felt the boat move and still under the impression that when the time came, Fancy Boy would rely on him to take Fast Lady out, muttered to no one in particular, "What's going on?" and started up the companionway to get back on deck. When he reached deck level, he saw that Fast Lady was already off the pontoon and dragging what looked like a water skier behind her.

In that sickening instant of revelation, both Francey and Zander knew exactly what they were towing and their troubled expressions changed to ones of wide-eyed panic; the un-ladylike Lady had ripped the services bollard – to which she was still connected – clean off the pontoon.

Horror-stricken at the magnitude of what had happened, both Zander and Francey slipped into damage limitation mode, which depended heavily on their immediate combined action; so for once working as a team (and possibly never again), they did what they had to do.

Francey closed the throttle, put the engine into reverse and slowly backed Fast Lady up. Zander picked up a boathook, pulled the wayward service bollard aboard, uncoupled the shore side service lines and dropped the lot over the side. Then after coiling and stowing Fast Lady's service lines, sat down in the afterdeck and assumed an air of casual indifference. Meanwhile at the helm Francey, ashen-faced and flustered, ignoring the geyser of water spouting from the severed water pipe on the pontoon, gently re-engaged forward gear, and to peals of laughter from his guests and the barely suppressed sniggers of his crew, he took Fast Lady out to sea at full throttle.

Possibly too aware of their own shortcomings to make anything of the other's failure, neither of them ever referred to this incident again.

15

The Wetting of the Pipes   Lismore

During their short voyage from Gallanach Bay to Lismore, the guests experienced a gentle introduction to life at sea. The winds stayed light, the sea was calm so motor sailing was the order of the day. They had amused themselves by reading or taking in the breathtakingly beautiful scenery, an encounter made all the more enjoyable by their regular consumption of copious amounts of food and drink. Everyone took advantage of the relaxing surroundings to get used to life on board – and as a bonus, no one was seasick.

That evening, Merryman and Fast Lady were 'rafted' together for their overnight stop. The guests, after disposing of further large amounts of fine wine with their evening meal, were sitting around, contentedly watching the sun sinking behind the purple hills to the west, its last golden gleam gently rippling over the water and making a shiny pathway towards them.

The Twins had gone to Port Douglas to pick up their missing crewmember from the ferry, but he did not turn up. They had scanned the dribble of passengers coming off the later ferries, until the last one berthed and its passengers had dispersed, but still their man had not appeared.

Not in the best of moods, the Twins got back to Merryman where a call came in on the 'ship to shore' telling them that their missing crewmember had gone to Oban by mistake and would meet up with the party in Tobermory. The journey to Lismore had been a waste of time and as a result, tomorrow Merryman would be sailing short-handed.

As far as the guests were concerned though, the trip had not been a waste of time. They had enjoyed a relaxing voyage and taken full advantage of Francey's generous hospitality.

After dinner, Francey brought out his bagpipes and while the sun was setting, he entertained them with a selection of jigs, reels and Strathspeys. During the performance, Zander, still smarting from the embarrassment of this morning's departure, and convinced that it had all been Fancy Boy's fault, attempted to recover some of his lost authority by miming Francey playing, stuffing his fingers into his ears and pulling faces.

It was while he was fooling around, that his resentful little brain hatched the embryo of a plan to even up the score. Taking Murdo aside, he asked him to find out if Fancy Boy knew the piping tune 'Farewell to Lismore'; if he did, he could then suggest that it might be appropriate for him to play it for his guests as they sailed off in the morning.

In a no time at all Murdo was back. Yes, Fancy Boy did know the tune and had already decided to do just what Murdo had suggested. Zander smiled and called his Emeraldeers into a huddle. When he told them what he had planned for the following morning, they nodded their approval then, smirking in anticipation, went back to doing what they had been doing.

That evening, just before lights out, Fancy Boy called his guests together and announced, "Tomorrow at daybreak, as we sail away from Lismore, I'll be on deck playing the well known air, '*Farewell to Lismore*' on my bagpipes. Come and hear me. Perhaps, in the future, you will even remember this appropriate and momentous occasion as being the highlight of your voyage."

*

In the morning, a clear blue sky tinged with the brilliant yellows of a newly risen sun and showing streaks of gold over the green hills, was the perfect backdrop for Fancy Boy's performance. To make things even more picturesque, there was just enough wind for the two yachts to slip their moorings and sail silently away together on an almost flat calm sea.

The early rising guests had gathered on deck their imagination fired up by the idea of hearing the bagpipes played on an early morning sail-away. They were not to be disappointed. With Fast Lady leading, the two yachts, under full sail, slid seawards over the gold-flecked waters and presented them with a wonderfully romantic visual spectacle. Behind and on either side, purple tinged hills rose out of the sea before gently rolling ever higher up to the grey mountains in the distance. Not a single cloud broke the blue mantle of the sky.

The stage was set and Francey would add the sound track. His expectant guests were going to experience something they were unlikely to forget. Francey was already on deck tuning up. He had never played on a moving vessel before and soon found that the boat's slight rocking motion made it difficult for him to concentrate on piping and still maintain his balance.

Zander looked on with interest and when he judged that the time had come to put phase one of his plans in place, he nodded to Murdo. Murdo went over to Francey, suggesting that if he got up onto the cabin roof and leant back in the shallow pocket formed by the close-hauled mainsail, he could balance there, and be able to apply himself to his piping. Francey thought about this for a second or two then did just that.

Poised above his audience, lying back on the mainsail, his eyes closed in concentration and playing his heart out, Francey was in his element. He had the stage to himself; he was feeling great and thoroughly enjoying the undivided attention of his guests.

Meanwhile, on the tiller, Zander had been biding his time. Now he was ready for phase two.

Giving Murdo another nod, and and getting one in return told him that everything was in place.

Zander called out, "Ready about! Lee ho!" and spun the wheel hard over.

Francey, with his drones growling in his ears, did not hear a thing and even if he had, could have done nothing about it.

The mainsail boom swung across the deck and thwack, Francey was catapulted straight overboard! In flight, he just had time to give out a prolonged, panic stricken cry of, "Waaaahhh." before the loud Splash shut him up!

Even before Francey hit the water, Zander had shouted, "Man overboard", whereupon a loud cheer rang out from the guests who, after a heavy night of drinking, now gave voice to their true feelings about feeling obliged to be up before dawn.

Zander was now in sole control of Fast Lady and gave his first command,

"Man overboard! Merryman, will you please pick him up? He should float – he and his bagpipes are full of wind!"

16

Airing Grunt's Goonie   Tobermory

A couple of Christmases ago, Grunt's well meaning wife Lucy, who was somewhat clueless about her husband's tastes, gave him a present of a long, maroon striped flannel nightgown. And, if that was not bad enough, it had come with a matching Wee Willie Winkie nightcap, tassel and all. He had no idea why she had bought him this, because he always slept *au naturel*. Was she trying to tell him something?

Every time she saw him packing for a trip she would remind him that it might be cold and damp on board, and insist that he take it with him; just in case. Grunt being Grunt hated the soppy, girly type outfit, although sometimes he grudgingly did find it useful when the cold conditions encountered at sea got through to him.

At such times, Grunt always waited until he was safely out of sight of the other Emeraldeers before putting his goonie on, so he still believed that none of them knew anything about his embarrassing item of night attire. However, in the close confines of a small boat where there is little room for privacy, his messmates knew all about his little secret and had done so for some time now. The matter was in the pending tray waiting for a suitable opportunity to let them show their 'appreciation' of his effeminate contribution to their otherwise macho world.

*

For the run up to Tobermory, as a temporarily replacement for her absentee crewmember, Grunt was transferred to Merryman. This gave his fellow Emeraldeers just the opportunity they had been waiting for. On their approach into Tobermory Bay, as both yachts rounded Calve Island, Murdo attached Grunt's nightcap and goonie to the main halyard and ran them up to the top of the mast. Then, with these very personal flags of convenience flying proudly at the masthead, Zander contacted Merryman on the ship-to-ship radio and asked if they would like to join them in a salute to the Isle of Mull by raising a pennant or some other such tribute on their masthead.

When the call came in, Grunt just happened to be near the radio and heard the message. Puzzled and not a little curious, he went on deck to see what had prompted this unusual request. It only took him an instant to recognise what was flying from Fast Lady's masthead, and he hollered out some uncharacteristically rude expletives at his pals aboard her.

When his guests asked Zander what the strange flag they were flying was, he put them in the picture and, pointing to the figure jumping up and down on Merrymaid's deck shaking his fist, identified their owner. Grunt's antics only serving to draw attention to what was going on, thereby adding to the Emeraldeers' and his audiences' enjoyment.

All round the bay, on boats and walking along Tobermory's busy waterfront, people were watching Fast Lady's approach, pointing and chuckling at the incongruous sight of a full rig of nightwear fluttering high on her masthead.

Seething with embarrassment, but for the time being powerless to do a thing about it, Grunt's next few minutes were taken up in wondering whether to blame Lucy for giving him the blasted things or his messmates for giving them such an embarrassing public airing.

As soon as both boats were alongside the pier, Grunt stormed off Merryman and on to Fast Lady. There, to a round of applause from the guests and the smug smiles and raised eyebrows of his messmates, he hauled down his embarrassing night attire, went below to the comforting solitude of the lower deck where he solemnly swore that some time, someday he would have his revenge.

17

The Wee Wee Waterfall   Tobermory

As first boat in, Merryman had bagged the last remaining public berth alongside Tobermory's main pier, leaving Fast Lady to tie up temporarily on a private berth immediately behind her. Later when the berth's owner arrived, Zander had to give up that place and go out into the bay. There he dropped anchor not far from where the 'Galleon Florencia', a refugee from the Spanish Armada -and reputedly still full of treasure – lies buried deep in the mud.

With Merryman's missing crewmember safely back on board and Francey and his guests ashore for a meal in the Western Isles Hotel, the off-duty members of both crews had arranged to meet up for a drink in the Mish Nish. Then after a pint or two there, go up to the same Hotel for a meal.

Topographically, a significant part of Tobermory lies on the high ground above the harbour and it is there that the Western Isles Hotel occupies a prominent site. The hotel's position allows its guests to enjoy magnificent panoramic views from Tobermory down the Sound of Mull. Access to the hotel is via the Back Brae, a road that doubles back on itself up a steep hill. To landward, the road cuts into the side of the hill, while a concrete retaining wall holds its seaward edge in place.

*

The rain came on just as the Emeraldeers got into the dinghy for the short trip to the pier. On their way ashore, the rain got heavier and heavier so, as soon as the dinghy bumped against the stone jetty Zander, Grunt and Gilbert jumped out and made a dash for the pub, leaving Murdo to tie it up.

The Mish Nish bar is a popular haunt of the sailing fraternity, tourists and locals and is usually crammed full to the doors. Nevertheless, both crews managed to fight their way to the bar counter for a drink or two before going on for dinner. When they got to the pub, it had been broad daylight and raining heavily, but when the combined crews left to go to the hotel, it was dark and no longer raining.

In spite of his outward show of camaraderie, Grunt was still smarting from the goonie-hoisting prank and when he saw the Big Brae's almost vertical retaining wall up ahead of him, an idea came in to his head, of how he could get back at his messmates.

When the Emeraldeers got to the foot of the five or six metre high retaining wall, Grunt issued a challenge.

"It's a long way round by road, what about a race up the wall?"

His shipmates, their faculties somewhat diminished by alcohol, took a look at the wall and stupidly allowing pride or bravado, call it what you like, to take over from common sense and reality; chorused,

"Right ho!"

Grunt then drew his victims further into his trap. "I reckon I can even give you a ten second start and still beat you to the top." and knew they had taken the bait when Zander said,

"You wait there, and remember no cheating! Don't you start until you have counted slowly to ten.

"OK, off you go then," said Grunt to his messmates, who had already started up the wall.

The Twins and their crew, wanting no part in this, carried on walking up the road towards the hotel.

Grunt however stood looking up, waiting.

When the climbers reached a height where jumping down would present a problem, Grunt took off and sprinted up and round the bend in the road, ignoring the "chicken" shouts directed at him by the climbers.

By the time he got to a point directly above the climbers, he had caught up with the Twins and the others, who were leaning over watching the climbers' progress. Grunt stood alongside them, unzipped his flies, and shouting, "You know what this is for!" released a cascade to rival the flow of the Mare's Tail waterfall (a natural feature that plummets down into Tobermory Bay).

That single hose piddling down from the top of the wall became five, as his former Merryman messmates entered into the spirit of things by contributing to the flow. After all, he had been one of them, even if for a short time.

In the spirit of inter-crew rivalry, there was no way that they were going to let this opportunity pass without some input/pissing.

The five streams were not aimed directly at the climbers but onto the surface of the wall, a metre or down so from the top where, as their waters spread out, they relentlessly headed down, towards an immobile Zander, Gilbert and Murdo.

With eyes sticking out like church coat hooks, the three climbers took stock of their situation and their instinct for self-preservation kicked in! To the cheers of the group at the top of the wall, they scrambled back down the way they had come.

A few bumps and scrapes later, the would-be alpinists ended up in a tangled heap at the foot of the wall.

While they were sorting themselves out, they heard the triumphant catcalls coming from above suddenly change to howls of anguish. When they looked up, they saw another deluge of water, considerably greater than the previous one, pouring straight down towards them. This time though, they had the time and space to get clear.

Unfortunately for them, none of the sprinklers above – intent only on doing what they were doing and laughing at the results – had not noticed that on the road behind them there was a big deep hole full of surface water. And, although they did hear the sound of a car coming, they were far too busy enjoying themselves to appreciate just how vulnerable they were. Too late! A wave of dirty, cold water swept up and over them.

Meanwhile the trio at the foot of the wall, looking up to see what had caused the second shower, saw that a car heading for the hotel, had passed behind their erstwhile tormentors, now all standing in open-mouthed shock, gasping for breath and soaked to the skin.

Grunt's petard had been well and truly hoist – again.

18

Francey Rations the Rations   Tobermory

Much later that evening when the Emeraldeers were singing their way back to the boat, as they walked past Merryman, Francey, sitting in the wheelhouse, invited Zander to join him on board. Zander, a little the worse for wear, whispered a theatrical aside, "Why does he want me to join him? Is he coming apart or something?" Giggle, giggle. Had he but known what was in store, he would not have taken the summons so lightly.

Francey started by saying, "According to the shipping forecast, sometime over the next day or two the weather is likely to turn nasty. This means that there will be no circumnavigation of Mull, or visit to Iona." Then he went on to tell Zander that when his guests had heard this, three of them had jumped ship and boarded the bus to Craignure to catch the ferry back to Oban and their parked cars. With fewer guests, he had no further use for Fast Lady or her crew, which meant his remaining guests would now be staying with him on Merryman and, weather and conditions permitting, they would just do some local cruising.

In the blink of a disbelieving eye, Zander's good mood evaporated. *Only halfway through the charter and Francey had ended it! I do not believe it!*

Worse was to come however when Francey told him that the Twins had already recovered all the provisions from Fast Lady. The now sorely distressed Zander thought *Calamity of calamities, all that good stuff has gone; this is not how it was supposed to be.* Nevertheless, that was how it was. There was nothing he could do about it.

Going back on board Fast Lady, his crew were sitting round the saloon table when he broke this terrible news to them. Glum faced he asked, "What are we going to do now?"

It took some time, but gradually their intrepid spirits revived and their brooding mood of depression turned to thoughts of reprisal. *How can we take Francey down a peg or two and show him up to his precious guests?* Whatever it was, they would have to do it before they took off to go back to Ardfern.

After a number of suggestions were put forward and rejected, a plan began to take shape; however to make it work, Merryman would have to be unmanned. They were sure that the remaining Corporates would spend most of their time tomorrow ashore, but, whether Francey would go as well, remained uncertain. Similarly, the Twins who normally followed their own agenda would no doubt go ashore at some point during the day and if they did, you could be sure that the crew would slip ashore as well.

As none of these factors were in the Emeraldeers' hands, they would just keep watch, bide their time and hope that everything would fall into place for them to pull off their little stunt.

Next morning Tobermory was a miserable place to be. The rain was spattering down on the Fast Lady's deck and everything was dripping wet. Grunt, who was tucked down under the hatch cover to watch the comings and goings on Merryman, did not have long to wait before, as predicted, the few remaining Corporates braving the weather, clambered ashore and made a dash for the Mish Nish. Shortly afterwards when the rain had eased off, the Twins and their crew climbed on to the pier and disappeared ashore, heading for places unknown. By a process of elimination that left only Fancy Boy on board.

Things are going our way.

Zander picked up the ship-to-ship radio mike and called Merryman. When Francey answered, Zander, in a voice full of congeniality said,

"Before we take off have you got time for a wee dram in the Mish Nish? There are one or two things about the charter I'd like to sort out with you." and after a short pause added, "I'm buying! Over." The very fact that Zander was paying for the drinks was the bait that set the trap.

Francey confessed to himself that he did not have a lot to do, so even the doubtful pleasure of Zander's company was better than just sitting around. Besides, he would get a most unexpected free drink out of Zander. So he readily agreed and replied,

"I'm on my way now, over"

"See you on the pier, over and out,' said Zander, smiling to himself as he hung up.

Francey had been tempted off Merryman.

While Murdo was ferrying Zander to the pier, the rain stopped. Fancy Boy, who had been watching Zander's progress, was standing alongside Merryman waiting for him, so they went straight to the pub.

Quickly turning the dinghy round, Murdo went back to pick up the rest of the raiding party. Earlier in the day, in preparation for their visit to Merryman, the Emeraldeers had been busy filling empty whisky bottles with tea, which were, along with a collection of various other liquid containers and a few necessary small tools, loaded into the dinghy and ferried over to Merryman.

Lashing the dinghy on to Merryman's seaward side, the Emeraldeers-turned-privateers boarded her unopposed. Grunt, already familiar with her layout from his recent spell on duty there, was thus able to direct them straight to the lockers and cupboards where all of the goodies were stored.

Eight bottles of whisky were substituted for eight containing cold tea, and passed down into the dinghy.

The next target was Fancy Boy's personal stock of fine wines.

Because red wine comes in coloured bottles, it is almost impossible to tell the colour of the liquid the bottle contains. Thus, by easing off the foil sleeves and removing the corks, the privateers poured the lovely red wine into the receptacles they had brought with them. Then by refilling the bottles with water, putting back the corks and sliding the foil tops back on again, no one would be able tell the difference; or so they hoped.

Substituting white wine is a different matter altogether; it usually comes in clear bottles and white wine is yellowish. Fresh water is clear, is easily identified as not being wine, so what readily available natural source of liquid can be used as a substitute? That alternative just does not bear thinking about. Anyway, the boarding party were not interested in white wine, so most of it stayed where it was.

On the way out, Gilbert looked in the fridge; sitting on the top shelf was a yard-long pork pie. He was certainly not going to let that go past him. Cutting it in half, he wrapped his bit in a tea towel and tucked it under his arm.

Murdo, standing on deck ready to go, noticed the pie and asked where it had come from; Gilbert told him.

"Hold on a minute," Murdo said and disappeared below again. A minute later, he came back with the other half of the pie tucked under his arm and lugging a crate of beer behind him.

"Here, give me a hand with this." he said in mock mitigation." A good pie needs a good beer to wash it down."

Grunt meanwhile had skimmed off all the other edibles he could find and loaded them into the dinghy. When no one came to disturb them, the looters recklessly helped themselves to even more booty. Enthusiasm and greed had replaced their earlier modest ambition. So much so, that they began to wonder why they had gone to the trouble of disguising the whisky and wine? Temptation had overwhelmed them and they knew it would not be long before their chicanery would be discovered.

Such was the quantity of their plunder that when the foragers added their own weight to the dinghy, its freeboard was close to zero. If the dinghy and its valuable cargo were to get back to Fast Lady without overturning, they would have to be very careful. Consequently, speed was not their first priority; however, they breathed a collective sigh of relief when they felt the gentle bump of the dinghy against Fast Lady's hull. The risky part of their raid was over. With all the goodies stashed away on board all they had to do now was get Zander safely back on board and escape.

The pillaging expedition had gone off without a hitch and the results were way beyond their expectations. Never before had the Emeraldeers been so well provided for.

When Zander came back on board and saw their haul, he turned to his Emeraldeers and said,

"I think we had better up anchor and away before anyone finds out what you've done.

The smug-faced Emeraldeers took up their departure stations and as soon as the anchor cleared the water, under minimum sail, they took Fast Lady out into the bay.

When they were far enough away and silence no longer mattered, her motor kicked into life and Fast Lady – living up to her name – beat a hasty retreat away from Tobermory and down the Sound of Mull.,

For the next hour, the fugitives ran on the motor, each man boasting of just how well he had done in the evening's escapade and grinning with satisfaction at the thought of Fancy Boy's dismay when he discovered his loss.

Murdo again seemed to find the right words,

"What's the use of Fancy Boy being on a floating gin palace, if there is no gin on board?"

19

You Must Know My Granny   Duart Bay

Even though the threat of bad weather still hung over them, thanks to their raid on Merryman, Fast Lady was home to a happy crew. Life had never been sweeter. For the remainder of this trip, they would eat and drink like kings, and still have enough left for one or two trips in the future. The fact that Fancy Boy had shortened the charter and 'sacked' them was enough to reassure the Emeraldeers that their act of piracy had been well within their rights and that it was only what he deserved. Especially as when Merryman's crew had cleaned out Fast Lady, they had taken much of Zander private stores with them. At the end of the day however, the stuff the Emeraldeers had pilfered was more than enough to make up for what was lost from Zander's hidey-holes and enough to stock up his cottage well into the foreseeable future.

Right now though, Fast Lady's crew needed to put as much sea room as possible between themselves and Fancy Boy. If the poor weather did come, they would run straight back to Ardfern but if nothing changed and the stormy weather failed to materialise – as often happens in this part of the world – they would just potter around for a day or two.

A breeze had sprung up and although overcast, it was good to be out on the water. Fast Lady's flight from Tobermory proved to be uneventful and consequently demanded little of either boat or crew, so they made good time.

During such periods of inactivity, idle thoughts sneak into the minds of idle people. Consequently, every subject of conversation they entered into was even more ridiculous than the last; someone even suggested rounding Mull and taking that long sought after run out to St Kilda. Although this was an attractive proposition and one that they had enough provisions on board to do, when they realised that they had no information about the tides or the weather to make it feasible, common sense prevailed. At least these were the reasons they clung to when they talked themselves out of it.

Often in the past when Zander and his crew had pottered around the southern end of the Sound of Mull, they had considered going ashore to have a look at Duart Castle, ancestral home to Clan MacLean, but so far, they had not done so.

With St. Kilda a non-starter Gilbert suggested that they could tick Duart Castle off their list of places to visit. When put to the vote, Murdo was the odd man out; he was not at all interested in going to see what, in his opinion, was just a pile of old stones built up on great lumps of rocks.

Zander, who had a grand aunt whose maiden name had been MacLean, had always believed that he came from good, aristocratic, highland stock. He also knew that she had been born on Tiree, MacLean Clan territory. Perhaps he was the one who should be living in that noble pile.

Undeterred by Murdo's views, Zander made an executive decision and declared that Gilbert, Grunt and he would visit Duart Castle and that Murdo would stay on board to look after the boat.

Zander, Gilbert and Grunt took the dinghy to the shore and tied up to a small landing place from which a rough path led off to the east, in the general direction of the castle. Reasonably satisfied that they were not trespassing, and in a mood of expectation, the trio made their way up what they took to be the Castle access. Sure enough, as they came over a rise, the castle's roof came into view. Further up the path the whole castle appeared. It was a magnificent old structure built on an imposing site and enjoying picture calendar views in all directions. However, there was no sign telling them how to get in.

An elderly man, dressed in a faded tartan shirt, its sleeves rolled up showing his muscular, tanned forearms, was digging over a flowerbed at the foot of the castle walls. His 'lived in' corduroy trousers were tucked in to thick stockings that disappeared down into stout muddy boots. As there was no one else in sight, Grunt went over to him and asked how to get into the castle.

The man leant on his spade and knuckling his forehead, just as the Emeraldeers had seen gardeners do in old movies, said,

"Go round that corner, young sirs, and there you'll see a big gate. Beside the big gate is a little gate. Go through that little gate and someone will be there to help you."

As he spoke, he had held out a hand to direct them. To the Emeraldeers an outstretched arm with an upward facing palm meant just one thing; a tip was expected. Like synchronised pocket billiard players the Emeraldeers poked around in their pockets. Gilbert lost out by finding his money first, and after dropping a few coins into the elderly fellow's outstretched hand, he thanked him. Strangely enough the moment Gilbert had paid up, Grunt and Zander found their money – so their coins slipped down into their pockets again.

Now with the small matter of the gratuity attended to, Zander felt the urge to get his oar in; and took the opportunity to try to make a favourable impression on the stranger.

"I feel like I'm coming home," he started. "I'm from fine, old MacLean stock myself. My maternal grand-aunt was one of the MacLeans of Tiree." Before he could launch into his own version of the clan history, the others dragged him away, allowing the old chap to get on with his gardening.

By following the directions that Gilbert had paid for, they found the big gate with the little gate next to it and on going through, saw in front of them a door marked *Entrance* and just inside that, a desk displaying brochures and postcards.

They hung around the desk for a minute or so, but no one came; the few politely muted coughs they tried met with a profound silence. Then Zander, in his best 'officer's' voice, bellowed a "Hello," that echoed round the castle walls; but still no one took any notice; there seemed nothing for it but to go on an unescorted walkabout.

The visitors' route was well signposted throughout the castle apartments and by following it they took a floor-by-floor, room-by-room, upward tour, until finally, by climbing up an unlit narrow stone stair they ended up at a small iron studded wooden door. Pushing against the doors' stiff hinges, they stepped out on to the bright sunlight castle roof.

Squinting to recover their day-vision, they were astonished to see that the old gardener chap was already up there, sorting out what appeared to be stone roof tiles. With a cheerful wave, he acknowledged their arrival and beckoning them over, gave them a thoroughly enlightening and interesting description of what they had just seen in the apartments below. He then went on to give them a brief account of the family history that included a short list of the high costs associated with the ongoing maintenance of the castle building.

Hardly pausing for breath, he told his attentive audience about the disastrous effect that the Battle of Culloden had brought to the Clan, exacerbated later by the resulting eviction of the clansmen from their island territories.

He then waxed lyrical about the visit of Samuel Johnson and James Boswell to Inchkenneth, a little island on the west side of Mull, on 17th October 1773, where the then chief of Clan MacLean, Sir Allan MacLean and his daughters entertained them. At that time Duart Castle lay uninhabited and had for some time before that been neglected and fallen into a poor, ruinous state.

His audience then noticed a misty gleam coming into the narrator's eye when he told the story of how one of the Clan chiefs, who as a boy had sailed past the roofless ruin, and then later in life had gone ashore to inspect his birthright. Standing before the ruin and appalled by its ruinous state, he vowed there and then to restore it to a condition fit to resume its rightful place as the home of the MacLean of Duart. This, in due course, he did.

Thoroughly entertained by the elderly retainer's eloquence, the trio felt duty bound to place a further monetary contribution into an outstretched hand that was politely waving them downstairs. This, with a wry smile, was accepted. Grunt paid the gratuity this time because Zander had found something interesting on a wall behind him and Gilbert stood by smiling, knowing that he had already made his contribution.

*

On their way down, the trio revisited the Sea Room and in the light of their recently acquired information, they found it much more interesting second time around. This encouraged them to take another more enlightened look at some of the other public areas.

When they got to the ground floor, an elderly woman joined them and, pulling aside a heavy wall tapestry revealed a door and invited them to go through. Leaving the stone corridor via the hidden door, they stepped into a large comfortably furnished sitting room, dominated by an impressive sculptured stone fireplace, in which a log fire was burning. Directly between them and the fireplace was a huge, high backed armchair, so vast it was impossible to say whether or not, it was occupied; however a thin puff of blue smoke rising from the chair, told them that someone was sitting in it, smoking.

The woman walking ahead quietly announced them,

"There are three gentlemen here to see you, My Lord."

The visitors hesitated. The smoker stood up, turned to face them and they were dumbstruck; standing smiling at them was their earlier acquaintance, the elderly gardener!

The significance of the introduction 'My Lord' now struck home. This was the Chief of Clan MacLean, MacLean of MacLean, Lord of Duart Castle, and Queen's Messenger etc, the immediate descendant of Sir Fitzroy Donald MacLean, 10th Baronet of Morvern, KCB, DL, etc, the man who had restored the Castle.

Red faced, the discomfited trio apologised profusely, and trying desperately to recover their composure, explained they had assumed he was an employee rather than the owner and Clan Chief!

Zander felt particularly relieved since, earlier, he had almost declared his own outrageous claim to the title of Chief of the Clan by treating the real Clan Chief to his own garbled version of the MacLean clan's history. Fortunately, for his visitors, the real Clan Chief was a true 'gentleman' who, by a few kind words and pacifying gestures quickly put the uncomfortable Emeraldeers at ease.

With a twinkle in his eye, he apologised for playing them along and admitted that, when he saw them coming up the path, he had taken the opportunity to enjoy a little diversion in what for him, had been a quiet day. Then taking Gilbert and Grunt 'gratuity' from his pocket, he handed it to the elderly lady, told her to put it in the shop till and to bring tea and buns for his guests.

After what turned into a very pleasant afternoon tea and a long chat, the latest fans of the Chief of Clan MacLean took their leave of 'Himself' and Duart Castle and headed back to the boat.

*

When Duart Bay came into view, they expected to see Murdo fidgeting around on Fast Lady, waiting for them to come back. There was no sign of Murdo, but more worryingly, there was no dinghy tied up to the jetty. Most worrying of all though, Fast Lady was not where she should have been! Alarming thoughts ran through their heads, *Where's the dinghy? Where is Fast Lady?* Then almost as an afterthought, *and where's Murdo?*

Racing down to where they had left the dinghy, all they saw was a big stone with piece of paper sticking out from under it. Zander lifted the stone and picked up the piece of paper. With his mouth, suddenly dry and his pulse pounding in his ears, he read the message so clearly meant for him,

YOUR BOAT IS IN CRAIGNURE.
ENJOY YOUR WALK.

There was no signature or any other indication as to who the 'boat-nappers' were. Three sinking feelings came into three stomachs. *It could not be Fancy Boy, could it? No, he was miles away.* They feared the worst.

With no other option, the Emeraldeers took the advice and started walking

"Craignure is nearly three miles from here, that's about an hour's walk," muttered Zander. "The sooner we get started, the sooner we'll find out what's going on."

*

It took a full hour for Craignure Bay to come in sight and when at last it did, to their overwhelming relief they saw Fast Lady tied up alongside the pier, looking deserted. At least they still had a boat.

Picking up pace and heading downhill towards her, there was still no sign of life on board; nothing was stirring not even a Murdo! Fast Lady was like a ghost ship.

Where could Murdo be?

Uneasily the trio of Emeraldeers approached their boat and Zander called out, "Ahoy, Murdo," his voice revealing his apprehension. There was no response. *Where is he?* And climbing aboard shouted again,

"Is there anybody there?"

Eventually he heard the sound of someone mumbling coming from below, following which Murdo, still rubbing sleepy eyes, appeared at the hatchway.

"What's all the shouting about? What do you want? What's the matter?"

Then looking shore wards he said in a hurt voice,

"How on earth did we get here? You might have told me we were moving."

A heated discussion went on for some minutes, during which time adjectives like lazy, stupid and worthless were among those heard, but poor Murdo could not explain how Fast Lady had got here. What his messmates could not understand was that, whatever had happened to Fast Lady, Murdo had slept right through it all.

Who could have done such a thing?

Although Fancy Boy was still the main suspect, he was supposed to be taking his remaining passengers around Mull, so how could it be him. Even after weighing up the facts – and there were few – Zander came back to his initial thought that Fancy Boy, hell bent on vengeance might just be the culprit.

Then an even worse thought struck Zander and his men, one that had them falling over each other to inspect the larders and lockers where all the food and drink had been stowed away. The longer they looked, the more frantic their search became until finally, they were forced to admit that what they feared most, had happened. The booze had gone, the food lockers lay empty and the larders were completely bare. As Zander went round his little hidey-holes, he was mortified to discover that the raiders had taken away his stuff as well.

Fast Lady was now an abstainers' paradise. There was neither a drop of booze nor a scrap of food left on board, and Murdo had slept right through it all!

The ship-to-ship radio suddenly crackled, indicating an incoming call.

"Hello, Fast Lady, Hello, Fast Lady, Merryman here. Are you receiving me? Over!"

With these words, the Emeraldeers now knew exactly who was responsible. Looking out to sea, sure enough in the middle distance, they could see Merryman heading up the Firth of Lorne back towards Tobermory. Zander picked up the handset,

"Hello, Merryman, Hello, Merryman. This is Fast Lady, receiving you loud and clear. Over!"

"Hello, Fast Lady, Skipper Francey here. Can you tell me where the nearest supermarket is? We need to stock up on a few things. Over!"

Sod it, thought Zander! *That pain in the nether regions is showing off again.* However, the last thing he was going to do was acknowledge that Fancy Boy had put one over on him. Unfortunately, right now, neither he nor any of his disconsolate crew could think of a suitable reply, so his pathetically futile response was a sullen and insincere,

"Hello, Merryman, Sorry, can't help you. Over and out!"

However, before he could switch off the radio, Francey got the last word in,

"Hello Fast Lady, we don't really need any help. We are perfectly capable of helping ourselves. Do have a drink on me! Over and Out."

The radio went dead.

A gloomy silence followed the click of Francey switching off the radio, and as if on cue, the Emeraldeers heard a knock on the hull and a loud voice demanding,

"Is there anyone on board?"

Gilbert went up on deck to see who it was and what they wanted. A few minutes later, grim faced, he came back below.

"It's the Harbour Master. He's saying we've run up a bill for berthing fees."

Zander spluttered out, "What?"

Gilbert held up a hand to discourage any further comment,

"There's more. He said that the skipper of the yacht Merryman, who brought Fast Lady in, told him that we were the flotilla's lead boat and would pay all of the costs when we picked up Fast Lady."

Gilbert raised his hand again to stop another of Zander's outbursts.

"And that's still not all; we have to pay Merryman's berthing fees as well. The man says a credit card would be fine."

Misery heaped on misery. Zander could only pay up; knowing that if he did not, the Port Authorities could impound Fast Lady.

*

With all harbour dues now paid the disconsolate crew of Emeraldeers, conscious that mooring fees are charged hourly, cast off and got under way as quickly as they could. Their unscheduled shore trip had cost Zander an arm and a leg.

All they could look forward to now was the dismal prospect of a miserable return trip to Ardfern with no food on board and nothing to help them drown their sorrows.

For poor Murdo it was an even more miserable trip back; everyone blamed him for the current state of affairs, so no one would talk to him, leaving him thinking,

Just because I had a wee kip!

20

Zander Jilted   Ardfern

All the way back to the mainland, Fast Lady's hungry and teetotal sailors' morale was at low ebb. So next morning, when they tied up at Ardfern, a tremendous feeling of relief washed over them.

In a moment of uncharacteristic weakness, coupled with his desperation to get home, Zander invited the crew to his cottage for breakfast. In their haste, thinking only of the culinary delights Jane would rustle up for them, skipper and crew dispensed with the post-sail clean up and took off post haste for Zander's cottage.

Jane being Jane took the surprise invasion in her stride, so her husband and his little sailor boy friends were hardly through the cottage door before, as if by magic, they each had a dewy can of cold beer in their hands. Then, once she had heard about their plight, in no time at all they were tucking into a hastily prepared, but deeply satisfying, full Scottish breakfast.

Later on, Jane put a few letters on the table in front of Zander, suggesting that he read the top one first. It had arrived two days ago and because she re-cognised the writing, she knew it was from Fast Lady's owner.

When Zander opened it, its content hit him like a hammer blow. The owner's brother, a Zimbabwean farmer, had decided to get out of farming, and Zimbabwe. He and his family were coming back to Scotland to sail Fast Lady around Britain. Would Zander make sure that Fast Lady was ready to sail away when he got to Ardfern? The real pain though came when in the next paragraph he stated that the party were arriving the following weekend. Zander shocked at the thought of the imminent loss of his fine yacht, could not face up to doing much about it right now.

As he read the earth-shattering letter, a brighter thought flitted across his mood of despondency,

Maybe the brother will need a skipper or a crew. First thing in the morning he would 'phone the owner to find out what was happening; meanwhile he and his crew would finish their meal, go to the Ardfern Inn for a beer or two and then, tidy up Fast Lady.

*

Unknown to Zander, the brother and his party had arrived at the moorings only an hour after Fast Lady tied up to the pontoon, saw her there, gone on board and found her in an appalling state. Brother went straight to the marina manager who had immediately hired a group of locals to do a thorough clean up, fully stock her with provisions and replenish her fuel and water.

The minute this was done, the brother and his family boarded Fast Lady and sailed her away.

*

Following a good night's sleep in the cottage and feeling much better in mind if not in body, the Emeraldeers headed for the marina to get on with putting Fast Lady to rights.

They were halfway along the pontoon before they realised that Fast Lady was not there. All they saw, lying alongside where they had tied her up, was a pile of kit bags and other miscellaneous bits and pieces.

Zander's first knee jerk thought was, *Not Francey again*, before the more rational part of his brain kicked in with,

Brother! Cruise! This week! Surely, not already?

A shout broke his train of thought. It was the Marina Manager. "Zander, there's a message here for you."

The Emeraldeers picked up their belongings and, trooped over to where the manager was standing. Zander took the folded note and opened it. It contained a stark message:

> *To whom it may concern,*
> *I have 'phoned my brother about the*
> *disgraceful state I found Fast Lady in*
> *today. He has authorised me to discharge*
> *you forthwith.*
> *He will be taking the matter up with you*
> *personally, in due course.*

Not only had the Emeraldeers' beloved Fast Lady sailed off into the setting sun without them but they did not even get the chance to say goodbye.

The marina manager again interrupted Zander's musings by handing him a second piece of paper and adding, "The guy told me to give you this as well." Zander took it. *What could this be?* When he read it the colour drained from his face and his nerveless fingers let both notes flutter to the ground.

Gilbert picked them up and read out the devastating news about Fast Lady to the others.

Then holding up the second note, said,

"And this is an invoice from an outside contractor for cleaning up and servicing Fast Lady. It is marked for the personal attention of Mr Alexander Duff. So thankfully, it's no concern of ours."

21

Francey's Knickers in a Twist   Glasgow

Less than a month later, the formal dinner of Zander's professional institution was to take place at a Glasgow hotel. The principal speaker would be no less a personage than the Lord of Duart Castle, MacLean of MacLean, Chief of Clan MacLean and Queen's Messenger, etc.

When Zander heard this, like a child in wide-eyed anticipation, he could hardly wait for the auspicious day to arrive. *Not only will I renew my acquaintance with my Clan Chief but I'll be doing so in front of my professional colleagues, particularly that b ******Francey.*

At formal dinners in Scotland, a high proportion of the guests wear highland evening dress so, to ensure that a higher than usual proportion of those attending would be 'properly dressed', a note on the gold edged invitation read,

'*As a mark of respect for our principal speaker, guests are courteously requested to wear the kilt.*'

On the evening of the big event, in line with the note on the invitation, both Zander and Grunt turned up in full highland dress. The tartan of Zander's kilt was that of his maternal grand aunt, the MacLean of Duart, while Grunt's, which he had bought second hand many years ago and had seen a lot of service while he competed in Highland

Games, was the MacDonald. However, he was comfortable in it and wore it with some swagger. Both of them also wore short silver-buttoned, Prince Charles evening jackets complete with wing-collared shirts and a full complement of accessories such as a furry sporran, a skean dhu, long white socks with flashes and brogue laced shoes.

As soon as Zander walked in the door, he could not help but notice Fancy Boy standing with a group of people, holding forth about something or other. By Scottish standards, Fancy Boy's outfit was over the top. With its garish, tartan kilt and silver buttoned, peacock blue short jacket with Paisley Pattern lining, jabot, lacy shot cuffs, and oversized horsehair sporran; he looked like an old Scottish Music Hall comedian. Francey had no clan connection, but reluctant to be out of things, he had hired this flamboyant full highland dress outfit and was wearing the kilt for the first time.

Zander, a big grin lighting up his face, joined the group and on catching Francey's eye, complimented him on his 'picturesque' uniform, and turning to walk away, he smiled sweetly and enquired, "Are you breaking in these legs for a seagull?" Grunt at his shoulder, not to be outdone, offered advice in a loud stage whisper, "Remember to feed your sporran or it might have to go round the tables scavenging for food". Francey, red faced and furious but stuck in the middle of a giggling group, could do nothing but try to smile.

Zander 15 – Francey love! Fancy Boy certainly did stand out from the crowd.

*

After dinner, the Chairman stood up, tinkled a wine glass for attention and addressed the assembled company,

"Members and esteemed guests, before the more formal part of the evening we will now have a short interval. Please be back at your tables within half an hour." Much to Zander's chagrin, the top table's officials and principal guests were spirited off to the committee room before he got anywhere near his chieftain 'friend'.

After failing to achieve his prime target, Zander with Grunt in tow, filled in time by wandering round the tables, chatting to old colleagues. This meant that by the time they got to the toilets in the main lobby, a long queue had formed, to 'spend a penny'. Progress was frustratingly slow and when Fancy Boy joined the end of the line, a good few places behind them, Grunt looked at his watch and said, "There's only a few minutes of the interval left." confirming what Zander already knew and there were still a lot of men waiting in the queue ahead of them. Increasingly feeling the effects of the amount of liquid still inside them and knowing that they would never manage to get through the speeches without having to make an embarrassing exit, something had to be done. When a man has to go, a man has to go, and in their case, quickly.

Grunt, ever the opportunist, had been keeping an eye on the adjacent Ladies' toilet, and had noticed that, in all the time they had been standing there, no one had gone in there. Nudging Zander and nodding towards it, he indicated his intentions. Then with legs crossed, he minced over to it and went in. Zander was right behind him.

Not long afterwards they came out, obviously relieved. Francey, who had watched their little ploy with interest, decided to follow their example. As he disappeared though the door, a giggly gaggle of high heeled, high spirited, short skirted, young ladies clearly 'out on the town', pushed their uninhibited and noisy way through the hotel's revolving door and spilled out into the hallway. This horde of 'bevvyed up' harridans, clearly not connected with the formal dinner, spotted what they were looking for and piled in through the door Francey had just gone through. The door swung shut behind them.

Zander and Grunt, who had been following their brash, noisy progress through the hotel lobby, winked to each other and sauntered back towards the still closed toilet door to see what they hoped was about to happen. Then, as if all their birthdays had come together, the 'Ladies' door burst open and, admist a tirade of verbal abuse – including expressions such as 'dirty old devil' and 'perv.', a figure flew out, its kilt whirling, its limbs out of control and frantically struggling to protect its modesty.

Francey, in full view of everyone in the hallway then suffered a further volley of verbal abuse from the 'bevy of beauties' at a significantly coarser level of eloquence than would normally be heard in this very posh hotel.

Doing his best to ignore his abusers and the catcalls, wolf-whistles and ironic applause coming from the line of men he had queue jumped, Fancy Boy adjusted his unfamiliar outfit, indignantly turned on his heel and self consciously stomped back to the main dining hall.

However, unfortunately for him, what he was not aware of was that, his unfamiliarity with highland dress was there for all to see – as were his polka dot underpants. The back of his kilt had caught up in his knickers-elastic revealing to all and sundry, that he was not a true Scotsman.

*

Back in the main hall, the principal guest rose to his feet to deliver his speech. Zander perked up. Until now, whilst everyone else had applauded a speakers' wit, his response had been the tiniest of smiles and a listless hand patting on the tabletop. Now though, everyone nearby was embarrassed as he laughed too long at the his clan chief's anecdotes, nodded over-enthusiastically at the points he made and when he sat down, continued to applaud, long after everyone else had settled down. Unfortunately, all of Zander's attention-seeking activity proved to be of no avail, because the principle speaker's eyes never strayed in his direction.

In the less formal period following the speeches, Zander, dragging Grunt along for support, made a beeline for the top table, plonked himself down in a vacant seat beside the principal guest and in a simpering voice said,

"M'Lord, you may remember us, we had tea with you; at Duart Castle a few weeks ago."

The MacLean recognizing the tartan of Zander's kilt smiled and for a little while anyway, gave Zander the benefit of his undivided attention.

"Was it only a month or so ago that we mistook you for the gardener?" Zander went on, unnaturally loudly, all the while looking around to see if Fancy Boy or anyone else he knew was within earshot. However, no one was paying the least bit of attention to him. Furthermore, we will never know if his Chieftain would have remembered them without prompting, but then, epitomising the fine breeding of the true Gentleman he was, he smiled and took Zander's gushing attempts at familiarity in his stride.

Normally, good manners dictate the limit of time that any individual should hog the company of a principal guest, but Zander paid no attention to this – or to Grunt tugging at his sleeve. His Chieftain, anxious to spend some time with his hosts, and hoping that Zander would take the hint and leave, finally stood up, only to find that Zander did not take any such hint. Tagging along, like a well-trained dog, Zander followed his Lordship who as a last resort, was heading for the committee room. It was Francey – a committee member – who prevented Zander – not a committee member – from following him in. At which time the grateful principal guest took that opportunity to mutter a goodbye. Whereas Zander, reluctant to lose contact with his Clan Chief could think of nothing more eloquent to say than,

"See you later then, My Lord."

Unfortunately, his speculative invitation went unheard and was the last ever exchange between Zander and his clan chief. Francey meanwhile, with a smug, well-satisfied look on his face, shut the door firmly in Zander's face, thereby effectively and positively ending Zander's brief encounter with his noble Clan Chief.

POLITICS AND PARTY

Murdo's Hat

22

Love Me and Leave Me   Edinburgh

Before the start of winter, Zander was back in Edinburgh, a sailor without a boat and with nothing to fill his long leisure hours, fed up to his back teeth. It was now that the fickle fingers of fate set him off on a new voyage, one that at first appeared to be an attractive proposition that would with time, see him plagued by what for the present, were unforeseeable problems.

Fate's messenger came in the guise of an invitation to an afternoon drinks party in a luxury hotel in the Murrayfield area of Edinburgh. How was he to know that it was not exactly a party, more like the launch of a Finance House's Unit Trust, hoping to attract new investors?

The gilt-edged, beautifully scribed invitation read,

".......... *seek the pleasure of the company of Mr Alexander McLean-Duff BSc.,C Eng, Euro Eng, FICE, FI Struct E, FIHT, FIWEM to an informal gathering of like-minded, distinguished citizens and influential people.*

Zander, particularly impressed by the quality of the invitation card – especially the hyphenation of his name and the listing of his professional qualifications – accepted the invitation at face value. With nothing of interest on his immediate horizon, he decided to go along just for fun.

At least it should be good for some posh grub and a drink or two.

On the appointed day, Zander dressed in his faux 'country gentleman' ensemble; elegant tweed suit, yellow foxes' head motif tie fastened to his check shirt by a gold tie pin in the shape of a horseshoe and whip, suede boots and a battered dark brown, soft felt hat, he thought he looked like a million dollars.

When Jane saw this outfit, she observed dryly,

"You look as though you're off to a weekend shoot or a house party, rather than some stupid meeting. What you should have on is a dark business suit, plain shirt and sober tie." Zander, in spite of her sensible advice, stuck to his guns and insisted that he wanted his look to be 'country affluent'.

Feeling like the 'bees knees', Zander strode up to the hotel reception, presented his invitation and climbed up the thickly carpeted stairway to the first floor. There, along a wide corridor, he saw flowers arranged outside a room with wide-open double doors.

Taking the proffered glass of wine from a waiter standing just inside the doors he went into a function room. One of the hosts' meeting and greeting people introduced him (passed him on) to a small group of other guests, each one eying him up with curiosity and all keen to find out how he might fit in with their own agenda.

Zander, equally tuned in to take advantage of the slightest hint of an opportunity to advance his social, financial or other standing, went about the business of mingling with his fellow guests.

As was his way in such situations, Zander was 'talking up' his own technical expertise to anyone with the patience or good grace to listen, all the while emphasising his personal contributions to many of Scotland's engineering wonders, and for that matter all over the rest of the world.

To his delight, one of the most distinguished-looking guests – introduced to him as the Hon. Somebody-or-other – seemed to take an interest in him and apparently enjoyed his company. When the 'party' assembled for the 'presentation', he sat beside Zander to discuss the opportunities offered by their hosts' new venture.

After the presentation, Zander was standing enjoying a final coffee with a group of fellow guests when his new acquaintance joined him. Greeting him like a long lost brother, he clamped Zander around the shoulders and said,

"I'll walk you to your car."

On their way to the car park, the Hon. Somebody-or-other, still tenaciously hanging on to Zander, handed him an ornate gilt edged, business card that showed him to be

Staff Procurement Consultant

to

Internationally Famous Companies.

With a wink that seemed to emphasise confidentiality, he told Zander he was looking for one or two very special people to fill top-line jobs.

"Perhaps I could arrange for you to meet my clients to see if anything can be set up to our mutual advantage?"

Zander thinking, *nothing venture nothing gained*, replied with a vague,

"Yes, why not?"

The long and short of it was that this new found friend arranged a meeting for him with three men, introducing them to him as fellow members of a prestigious Edinburgh club.

Even though Zander was not looking for work, he made two fundamental tactical errors; firstly, he turned up for the meeting and secondly, showed a polite interest in what was said.

The 'team' worked on him like time-share touts, relentlessly drawing him in, until Zander believed that, not only was he the ideal candidate for the post, but the job was just what he had been looking for. He was even reckless enough to sign a form that stated that he would accept a post should he be offered it – another tactical error!

The recruitment team sent him on his way with an assurance that they would do everything in their power to convince their client that Zander was just the man for the job. They knew they had him. So thoroughly was he manipulated, that by the time the 'touts' released him back into the real world, he was worrying that he might *not* be offered the job.

There followed an anxious few days before confirmation came that he had indeed been successfully presented for the vacancy and would be expected to take up post within the next few weeks.

*

That he had actually been headhunted – or so he believed – appealed to Zander's sense of self-importance. He could not stop himself drooling as he thought about the guaranteed terminal bonus he would get at the end of his four-year tour, the equivalent of 50% of the already generous salary package. The whole deal was too good to be true, but by now, Zander was a believer.

Unfortunately, in order to reap these benefits, Zander had to accept that for the period of his tour, he would have little opportunity to participate in his first love, sailing (his second love, if Jane was around). However, when he weighed everything up against the huge carrot dangling in front of his mind's eye i.e. that he would earn more than enough to buy a fine new boat and retire – he 'bit the bullet' and accepted the job.

To the new recruit it was a tremendous comfort to think that at the end of this posting he would have enough money to be able to sail every day and to enjoy all the comforts of the good life.

*

The last time Zander came back from an overseas appointment he vowed never to be tempted to work overseas again and until now, he had remained faithful to that vow. Although he was not too happy about leaving his beloved Scotland again, he was conscious that because formerly he had been in engaged in a series of short-term jobs, he had not made any real provision for his retirement. This package would provide him with a pension plan that would assure his financial future.

Right now, he was dry washing his hands while dreaming about what he would do with his 'guaranteed' astronomically generous salary. Later, he would not be so pleased when he discovered that the Hon. Somebody-or-other's introduction fee was taken out of his first pay cheque and in each of the following months a fair slice of his salary went the same way.

If the truth be told, before fate took Zander by the hand and led him to the Hon-Somebody-or-other, he had been trying desperately to fill that particular post for months and been close to writing off the possibility of earning any fee out of it at all.

Someone had done well on the deal and it was not Zander!

23

The Party's Over   Edinburgh

Now that Zander was heading off to pastures new, he arranged for his Emeraldeers and their wives to join him for a farewell dinner and overnight stay in an Edinburgh hotel! Murdo, a bachelor, said he would bring a *cousin*.

*

Before joining their partners at the Caledonian Hotel in Edinburgh's West End, the men met up for an aperitif in the Royal Overseas Club further along Princes Street. This select establishment is not the sort of place they would normally dream of going into, but Zander, always game for a taste of the good life, had prevailed upon Grunt to get one of his old school friends to sign them all in.

However their sponsor, having weighed them up, signed them in, showed them where the bar was and disappeared. That first wee drinkie led to another wee drinkie so that by the time they left to join their womenfolk, they were well down the road to irresponsibility.

Back outside again, they strutted along Princes Street towards the rendezvous, four abreast and arm in arm. Their swaggering steps and occasional staggering missteps providing other pedestrians with a poor imitation of the silver screen's Three Musketeers.

Earlier that afternoon, Princes Street had been the scene of a big parade and a number of 'no-parking' cones were still lining its pavements. As the garrulous quartet neared the West End, Murdo decided it would be funny to use one of these cones as a hat, so stooping down he picked one up, and with a flourish, placed it on top of his head. Passing pedestrians however, were unimpressed and just put on the sort of tolerant smile they normally reserved for idiots and drunks.

Murdo's fellow fools, determined not to be outdone, put on conical hats as well so they too looked equally idiotic.

When they got to the front of the Hotel, they found their way blocked by a large crowd gathered in the hope of catching a glimpse of some film star who was currently staying there.

Undaunted by the press of fans ahead of them, the buoyant, cone-topped Emeraldeers eased their way into the crowd, which, on seeing the coned heads, parted like the Red Sea to let them through.

As is sometimes the way, Sod was not too far away, and tonight he was not playing for Zander's team.

The four 'mad hatters' reached the steps at the hotel's entrance where their partners had just arrived and – smoothing down skirts crumpled during the taxi ride – were waiting for the doorman to open the door for them.

"Hi girls!" Murdo shouted to let the women know that their escorts had arrived. Unknown to the Emeraldeers, but obvious to their partners and to the spectators, ominously tagging along behind them, loomed the presence of two of Edinburgh's finest uniformed, police officers.

Why else would the crowd have let them through? An authoritative voice ringing out from behind them, cut into their mood of well-being, by enquiring, "You were going to put these back, were you not, gentlemen?"

A cheer went up from the rubbernecking throng, sensing that in the police officer's demand lay the promise of a diversion to keep them amused while they waited for the appearance of their adored one.

In an instant, the expressions of the Emeraldeers' wives changed from tolerant smiles to, frowns of black-affronted displeasure. As one, they turned, flounced past the commissionaire – who was doing his best to keep a straight face – and strode into the hotel.

Taking stock of their situation Zander's little band of brothers decided that discretion heavily outweighed any outward attempt at valour. So, sheepishly removing the traffic cones from their heads they filtered back through the crowd of cheering spectators to join the waiting police officers. Then, in the embarrassing company of a police escort, the Emeraldeers walked back along Princes Street to put the parking cones back where they had come from and this done were finally sent packing with what sounded like parental advice,

"You should know better at your age. Go away and behave yourselves. Just think yourselves lucky that we're in a good mood tonight."

Retracing their steps to the hotel the red-faced Emeraldeers again had to fight their way through the melee of laughing, cheering fans, still hanging around waiting to catch a glimpse of their favourite. Even in the comparative sanctuary of the hotel doorway, the commissionaire, with an admirable display of trembling-lipped self-control, just managed to stifle his mirth until his guests had disappeared into the lounge.

According to Murdo, earlier, he had caught a glimpse of his cousin getting out of a taxi but when she saw what they were getting up to, she had climbed back into her cab and been driven off.

*

In spite of the Emeraldeers' earlier embarrassment, dinner that evening was a success, mainly because Zander had decreed that everything, including the accommodation would be his treat. For once, he had pushed the boat out. On the other hand, though and what no one knew at the time was, that in due course, he hoped to recover the costs from his new expenses' account.

Then again, not everything at Zander's dinner party was as it should be. While to a casual observer, the wives were doing that wifely thing of acting normally with everyone else, they were blatantly ignoring their men.

When the women had gone to powder their noses, Zander and his crew went out for a breath of fresh air. In expansive mood, they walked fifty or so yards along Princes Street. Zander allowing his eyes to roam along its length, taking in the floodlights on Edinburgh Castle, the Scott Monument and then beyond to the buildings of Calton Hill, while reflecting, *I am really going to miss all this!*

Back outside the hotel street entrance Zander stopped on the top step, turned to look at his little group of aficionados and with legs astride, arms extended on either side of a puffed-up chest, decreed in a voice poorly mimicking General MacArthur,

"I Shall Return."

As they swung through the revolving door into the reception area, the commissionaire's voice from the shadows said,

"If you ever do come back, sir, the management would prefer it if you did so without the police escort and certainly not with traffic cones on your head."

24

A Night on the Tiles   Edinburgh

By the time Zander and his little group had searched through the hotel's lounges and found no sign of their wives, they assumed that – to make a clear statement of their discontent – they had all gone to bed. Their husbands, still smarting from their frosty treatment at the dinner table, were now even more peeved to find that their true loves had abandoned them. Therefore, in a apathetic attempt to re-inflate their punctured authority they decided to stay up late and have a nightcap.

Comfortably ensconced in big leather lounge chairs, one nightcap became two and as is their way, each one fanned the flames of wifely injustice that in time inevitably lead them to thoughts of reprisal. In mulling over their problem, someone suggested they go out on the town and make a night of it.

Although it sounded like a good idea, it did present a problem; the sum total of their experience of this sort of activity was zero. *Just where can we go and what can we do?*

Gilbert was first to make a suggestion,

"What about going to a nightclub?"

So, like children testing the boundaries of what they could get away with, they all agreed. Then Grunt identified their next problem.

"Anyone know where the nearest nightclub is?"

"Don't worry;" said Zander, "I know what to do. Let's go!"

Without a care in the world – until their reunion with their wives – they left the comfort and safety of the hotel and ventured out to sample the exciting life of the big bad world.

At the front door, Zander in an imperious tone of voice demanded that the commissionaire get them a taxi. As soon as it drew up at kerb the excited Emeraldeers fell over one another to climb aboard, whereupon, Zander with someone's backside squashing his face down into the seat springs, spluttered out, "Driver! Take us to the best nightclub in town!"

A few minutes later, with order restored in the taxi, the eager miscreants were travelling along a poorly lit street. The taxi stopped and dropped them off in front of the blank mass of a tall building. Their driver, clearly uneasy, pointed to a dark passageway to their right, assuring them that this was where they wanted to go. Then as soon as the fare was paid, the taxi took off like a racing car and disappeared into the night.

The night-clubbers, hesitantly inching their way along the unlit lane almost bumped into two large 'slabs of beef' dressed in shiny dinner jackets, standing with arms folded and clearly guarding something.

"Yes, Gentlemen?" one of these beefy slabs enquired, looking at them as though they had just crawled out from under a nearby stone.

"My good man, we would like to gain admission to your fine establishment," said Zander in his best Oliver Hardy manner.

"OK, that will be twenty five pounds each. Pay the girl at the desk."

"Twenty five pounds?" echoed the prospective night-clubbers in disbelief. *That's a heck of a lot of money.* Then, seeing the unsmiling faces and threatening attitudes of the 'sides of beef' now glowering over them, the bold boys got the idea that backing out was not an option.

So collectively salving their consciences by thinking, *Well, we've come this far and if it costs that much, it must be good. We'd better go in.*

They paid the over made up, under dressed girl, were given a ticket each and told,

"Go down that corridor and a girl there will let you into the show."

Full of anticipation of the delights about to be experienced, the fully paid up night-clubbers hurried down the corridor where, sure enough, another scantily dressed young woman was standing beside a door.

The door remained shut until they all got up to her, and then warning them to "Mind the steps," she opened it to reveal a bank of dazzling lights and the sound of loud music. Concentrating on 'Minding the Steps' the blinded night clubbers stepped through the door and down, only to hear a bang as the door slammed shut behind them. The music stopped, the lights snapped out leaving them enveloped in pitch-black darkness and when they felt the chill of a light breeze; they knew were no longer inside a building.

Try as they might they could neither get the exit door open, nor raise any response. Gradually with their night vision slowly returning, they saw that they were in a narrow lane, almost identical to the one where they had gone into the nightclub.

By the simple technique of fumbling their way along the wall beside the door they had come out through, they got themselves back to the nightclub's entrance and the two 'sides of beef'. Zander, holding up his ticket, made to go in. The two enormous men closed ranks in front of him and in enquiring voices that clearly brooked no nonsense, asked,

"And where do you think you're going, mate?"

"Back inside," said Zander still flourishing his ticket.

"Sorry, sir," one side of beef advised him, "If you read your ticket it says that once you come out there's no re-admission," and with an air of finality, added,

"You went in, you came out, if you want in again, you pay again. Either pay up or hop it."

Zander now felt a presence behind him.

"What's going on here?" a voice said.

Turning round, Zander felt a surge of relief when he saw that two uniformed police officers had arrived.

As the first of Zander's saviours came up face to face with him, he switched on his torch, peered from under his chequer-banded peaked hat and said, "I've seen you lot before, haven't I?" Then his puzzled look became one of exasperation when he remembered exactly where they had met.

'Haven't you been in enough trouble already today?'

"But officer, we've been swindled here," Zander blurted out despairingly.

"How's that?" was the officer's patient sounding question.

"We've been thrown out without even getting in," Zander pleaded, "and they won't let us back in. See here's our tickets."

The police spokesman took the proffered ticket, put it in the beam of his torch, pointed to a line on the back, printed in uppercase letters and underlined in red, that stated,

NO RE-ADMISSION UNDER ANY
CIRCUMSTANCE

"All seems legal to me," he said before adding a word of advice,

"I've warned you silly old farts already today. Away home and behave yourselves. Any more trouble and it'll be a night in the nick for you."

25

All That Glistens!   In Limbo

It transpired that Zander's new job title was that of vice president with an American-registered company with a UK office in London. From there, he would act as their visiting liaison engineer with the Wali (head of local government) of Constantine, Algeria.

Zander's overseas visits meant him spending around twelve days a month in Constantine and the rest of the month living in at home. This was a bit of a bind but he kept reminding himself that, his silly-money salary – together with the more than generous terminal bonus and pension – would be enough for him to retire on comfortably, at the end of his contract.

His Vice Presidency though carried no company equity and it was not long before he discovered that it carried little or no weight in the organisation either. In time, he realised that everyone in the company held a grandiose title; and as far as he could tell, none of them was an equity holder either.

As it turned out, his 'faithful' Emeraldeers did not follow the path he had mentally mapped out for their future. Gilbert and Murdo seldom got out on a boat while Grunt just did what he always did – not a lot. The old sea dog Zander was now destined to a period of sailing-denial.

26

A Hapless Man   In Transit

Sitting in a first class compartment on a train to London to take up his new post, Zander thought back to another train journey he had taken a long time ago when he finally finished his two years of National Service. That trip though, was in the opposite direction and in far less comfortable conditions than he was enjoying now.

In the depth of winter, following two years of 'existing' under the strict regime of the British Army, Zander was at last going back to civilian life and all the comforts of home. Finally clear of the army and doing his best to act like a civilian again, he has dressed like one; wearing blazer and flannels, a cravat in his open neck shirt and was still finding it hard to believe that he no longer had to jump to obey the whim of every trumped up little tyrant he came across.

So far, his journey had not been without its difficulties; it had taken him a while to shake off a 'Geordie' he had shared an army transport lorry with on the way to Salisbury station. He too was going home, but only because – with his training completed – he was going on embarkation leave.

Had this chap had a better command of the English language, travelling with him might not have been too bad but, every time he could not bring to mind the word he was searching for, he substituted it with the 'f' word. At the top of his voice and with painful frequency, he used that word as noun, verb, adjective or adverb, and in a voice like a foghorn.

This imaginative stalwart could transform the simple sentence "The man has broken the switch," into "The f***ing f***er has f***ed the f***ing f*** switch!"

Zander, desperate to escape from the blasphemer before he got on the train at Kings Cross, had found his chance at Waterloo; where almost halfway down the escalator to the Underground he heard the rush of air as a tube train approached the platform. "Let's go!" he shouted and took off down the still moving steps. With only a light bag to carry, Zander was at a considerable advantage. His companion, dressed in full service marching order, weighed down with all of his possessions packed into a cumbersome kit bag and haversacks both front and back, could hardly walk, let alone run.

Zander dashed onto the platform, where the train was standing with its doors open. His jump on board coincided with the "Mind the Doors" announcement. Then making no effort to hold back the closing doors he watched his hot and breathless former travelling companion arrive on the platform, too late. Zander, looking through the window, put on a sad-face, shrugged his shoulders and watched while his former travelling companion slid slowly past. The last sight he had of the red-faced foghorn was his mouth forming his most frequently used word, but thankfully, the sound of it did not reach Zander's ears.

*

At Kings Cross Station Zander boarded the train to Edinburgh. In those early post war years, even on long-distance trains, much of the rolling stock had no corridors and once you were in a compartment that was where you stayed. The train was already quite full and, even though he would be sitting between two very generously proportioned women, thankfully he did find a seat.

For the first hour or two, everything went smoothly and with night closing in, Zander could see, through the dirty window of his compartment, a clear moonlight sky which at that time of year, carried with it the threat of frost.

Then, shortly after leaving Peterborough, all the lights blinked out and the train slowly ground to a stop. As the minutes passed Zander felt the compartment getting noticeably colder, and when the large woman on his left opened a window to hear what the guard outside was saying, she let in a blast of freezing cold air. Apparently, the lights and heating systems had broken down and all windows and doors had to remain shut, to retain what heat there was. By that time however, it was too late!

As the compartment got colder and colder, Zander, travelling in lightweight summer clothes, now discovered his middle seat had become the place to be. Slowly he snuggled in to the warm folds of flesh of the fat woman on his right, who had fallen asleep almost as soon as the train started and had still not wakened up. Things got even better when the other bountiful woman to his left, also fell asleep and snuggled up to him. Now he was the thin slice of meat in a very cosy fleshy sandwich.

It was some time before the train got going again and when it did, it went backwards into Peterborough Station. There, the in-train loudspeaker announcer said that all passengers for Edinburgh should board the relief train right away; it was the one standing directly across the platform.

Extricating himself from between his pair of warm 'Brunhildes' bookends, Zander braved the freezing outside temperature, crossed the platform and got on board the warm, well-lit relief train. This was a corridor train so he walked along the passageway to find a seat. After sliding open a few doors, looking in and finding the window seats already taken, he found one whose sole occupant was an elegantly dressed, good looking young lady, whose beauty, form and figure were at the opposite end of the spectrum from his 'Brunhildes'.

Taking the seat opposite her – half hoping that the heat on this train would go off to give him an excuse to snuggle up to her – he engaged her in conversation. He began modestly enough but before long, he had switched into his 'impress the people' mode, and was painting a verbal picture of his glorious achievements, high social position and excellent prospects. He did not mention the Army.

For about half an hour all went well and during this time, Zander's female companion patiently absorbed his overtures and even told him something about herself, which lead him to think. *I might well be on to something here.*

Up until now, life in this carriage had been good for Zander. It should therefore come as no surprise when, in the midst of his looking deeply into his companion's eyes and hanging on to her every word, the compartment door should burst open and standing framed in the doorway was his former travelling companion, pouring out a string of expletives.

"f****** Hiya f******Zander f******fancy f******
well catching up with f****** you again!"

Zander's former travelling companion then took off his
haversacks and other stuff and dragging them into the
compartment, dumped them on the empty seats or in the
overhead luggage racks, sat down beside Zander's
prospective female friend and – in his own distinctive 'blank
spaced dialect' – began to 'chat her up'. After suffering her
new suitor's advances for a few minutes, Zander's
prospective girl friend shook her head in exasperation, shot
daggers – more at him than at her new companion – stood
up, left the compartment, then disappeared along the
corridor. This left Zander to suffer an unsophisticated,
uninteresting and unwanted, one-sided conversation with
his soldier pal, all the way to Newcastle.

Who was it who said, "Those were the days!"

LANDLOCKED

Top Secret

27

Words and No Music   Edinburgh

Zander was learning to speak French. Not that he wanted to and indeed, nor was there a specific requirement for this ever mentioned at any of his early interviews. However, his employer had told him that to do his job effectively, he must have a reasonable understanding of that language or his position could be at risk. Left with no option he complied and straightaway enrolled on a crash course at a language school in London. This for him was a huge undertaking as since being at school, languages had never been one of his strong suits.

The language school provided a concentrated level of instruction by allocating one tutor for every five pupils. Zander, as a late entrant, got the last remaining place in a class of French-speaking Africans, who were there to learn to speak English. Ambiguous but true, their instruction books and tapes translated French into English, whereas his translated from English into French.

On Zander's first day, he found all of his new classmates were deeply tanned, heavily moustached Arab-looking men who gave no hint of where they came from. His tutor though did tell him that they were serving military officers, whose sponsor was an undefined dictatorial regime.

Apparently, they had to be able to speak English before they could go on a pilot training course.

His tutor was a beautiful, slim young French girl, with pale blue eyes and long, golden blonde hair. If ever there was a recipe for disaster, it was here! All four of Zander's classmates believed he was man's gift to womanhood. Each one of them was constantly vying for the nubile young teacher's attention and then making a blatantly obvious pass at her.

Zander, doing his best to understand and speak French was on a hiding to nothing. Every time he managed to attract his tutor's attention, one of his classmates, in a high-handed manner, would demand her immediate personal attention. As a result, in those first crucial early days of tuition, Zander received little or no assistance.

During his third week in class, Zander heard that following an incident involving one of his over-amorous classmates, his young tutor had refused to go into the classroom with them again. Her replacement was a heavy, flouncing middle-aged woman, clearly chosen with a view to dousing his classmates' ardour.

While puffing and panting her way around the small classroom, she had a disconcerting habit of using her hands and forearms to adjust the hidden structural underpinnings of her nether garments, a manoeuvre that reminded Zander of the late Les Dawson in drag. Zander saw her as the epitome of over-ripe French womanhood and when she leant over him to inspect his work, wafts of her pungent body odour assailed his nose and had him shrinking away in revulsion. Understandably, Zander now took great pains to avoid one to-one help and for that matter, so did his classmates. Never the less, in her zeal to dispense close attention to her little flock, she was not to be denied, so anytime she targeted someone to help, they just had to grin and bear it – and try not to breathe in too deeply.

These were just a few of the factors that contributed to Zander's failure to grasp even a minimal comprehension of the language and had his coach been the best tutor in the world and he had done all of his homework, the outcome would likely have been the same. A magazine article he read at the time, describing the diverse workings of the brain, offered him an excuse for his shortcomings by stating,

'Because of the way a brain develops, some people have a natural gift for language skills, while on the other hand, people who do not have such skills, often excel in other fields."

Zander's self-diagnosis convinced him that, during childhood, his growing brain had expended so much energy on the host of things he was now brilliant at, that it left no spare capacity for him to learn foreign languages.

Thus, despite the time and money spent on tutors, he still spoke French like the police officer in the television sitcom, 'Hello Hello'.

At the end of the course, Zander and the other four members of his class each received a certificate. This took the form of a beautifully written letter that did not refer to the recipient's language skills. All it attested to was that its holder had completed the course and that his attendance level had been exemplary.

Delighted with the documentary proof of their qualifications, one of his classmates took a class photograph, saying that if Zander gave him his address, he would send a copy on to him, which he did.

In due course, the photo arrived; accompanied by a letter on behalf of all of his classmates, thanking Zander for the valuable help he had given them all with their English and adding, "Without your help we would never have become pilots."

*

It was many years later, following the horrific 9/11 attack on the Twin Towers in New York, when photographs of the alleged perpetrators of this act of extreme terrorism were published, that Zander thought he recognised two of them.

Thinking back, he realised that the only connection he had ever had with anyone who looked like that had been at the language school; so looking out the old photograph, he saw in it smiling up at him out of the group, two faces uncannily like the ones now staring up at him from the newspaper.

A hollow feeling hit the pit of his stomach, his mouth went dry and with his brain in a spin, he thought, *no, not my former classmates. It couldn't be, could it?*

28

Mister Vice-President   Constantine

In his role as Vice-President of the North African branch of an American Corporation, Zander began commuting between the UK and Algeria. Yes, he really did hold that distinguished title, confirmed in black and white on the firm's letterheads.

However, even to Zander, the title rang a touch hollow; he knew that all he did was act as the engineering advisor to an Algerian Local Authority. True he did get some satisfaction from the title but what gave him significantly more pleasure was the astronomical salary that came with the job. When he thought of how little he had to do for it, *it's like taking sweeties from babes*.

Zander's work pattern meant that he spent one week, Monday to Thursday, in Algeria and the next week or so, in the office in London, then another four days trip to Algeria and back to the office and so on.

Even taking account of his recent intensive tuition, his ability to speak French would still hardly take him beyond the first chapter of a 'Teach yourself French in Three Months' book. Thus it came as no surprise that he needed the services of an interpreter, not because of his own language shortcomings, but because the business language of Algeria is a form of patois French. All of this left him wondering, *why then, did I spend so much time and effort trying to learn the language? However, it is not for me to reason why, and anyway I'm sure I'll find the services of an interpreter useful.*

The interpreter's name was Hubert Le Duc, a 'pied noir' i.e. a French-Algerian now living in France, who moved out before Algeria declared its independence. Zander got Hubert's telephone number and arranged to meet up with him in Paris on their way to Algeria.

When Zander first heard Hubert's name, an image of the other, Hubert, aka Grunt – one of his Emeraldeers – sprang to mind. However, in complete contrast, this Hubert turned out to be Zander's idea of what a typical Frenchman should look like; of medium height, of medium stature, immaculately dressed and with a melancholy expression only enlivened by the mischievous gleam that shone from his penetrating pale grey eyes. Right from the start, they got on well together.

Consequently, the pair soon developed a routine for their periodic visits to Constantine. On a Sunday evening, Zander flew from the UK to Paris where they would meet up in a Paris hotel. They would stay there overnight, then, early on the Monday morning, catch the Air Algerie or Air France flight from Orly Sud to Constantine.

29

On a Wing and a Prayer   Constantine

Zander's introduction to Algeria should have been a warning of what the future had in store for him. Flying in from Paris for the first time, accompanied by Hubert whom he had met the previous evening, everything went well until they stepped off the plane. It was then – as they walked from the baggage claim hall and tried to go through customs and immigration – that their troubles began. In front of them and barring any further progress was a row of trestle tables manned by an army of serious looking uniformed men.

The queue of passengers awaiting clearance looked to be a mile long. Luggage lifted on to the tables for inspection was sifted through by Officials, who when they were finished left the jumble of personal belongings partly on the tabletop, partly on the floor and made no move to do any repacking. A laborious operation that took ages to complete.

While apprehensively watching this performance, Zander noticed that some of his fellow Europeans had packed a bottle of whisky or a girlie magazine in their suitcase so that as soon as it was open it came into view. This, the official deftly removed and in the same movement struck a chalk tick on the luggage, rewarding its owner with speedy access to the next stage of the entry process.

As neither Zander nor Hubert had been advised to carry these 'access passes' their luggage was given the full treatment before eventually it earned a white tick chalk mark – next time, they would know better. Without pre-knowledge of the steps necessary to pass customs, this lengthy rigmarole sorely tried the patience of all incoming visitors to the county, but there was more to come.

Their luggage inspection completed, Zander then had to go over to a desk where he was handed a bundle of forms and, by sign language, told to fill them in.

Completing this bulky set of multi-page forms was a mandatory requirement for each non-Algerian National entering the country. These forms ranged from the pink one, on which any infirmity, along with details of diseases or ailments that he or his parents had suffered had to be declared, to a green one, by far the most important one. Within its pages, he had to write down, in duplicate, a complete inventory of the contents of his pockets and hand baggage, including a detailed description of his watch and any other item of jewellery.

On this form, there was also a space for him to account for all the money he was carrying, currency-by-currency and denomination by denomination. With Hubert's help, this tedious, time consuming task was completed, the form signed and dated, then handed to an official. After taking a long, hard look at Zander, the official stamped the form, separated the duplicate from the original and handed the duplicate back to him.

Hubert took great pains to impress upon him the need to keep this vital document safe, as on departure – even before he could get into the transit lounge – everything itemised on it was checked against the original and any item not listed, would be confiscated and stay in the country. Furthermore, he would have to produce a receipt for any currency he used during his visit.

Hubert also advised him that, any drawings or plans the Client gave them to take back to the UK, had to be a certified for export and signed off by a principal officer of the Local Government. Drawings brought into the country to be left with the Client also required a similar 'proof of receipt letter' before the pair could fly out

*

Fortunately, by the time of their second visit, they had become VIPs and from then on, an official met them on the tarmac and at breakneck speed, whisked them through the formalities.

*

Zander and Hubert were booked into the Cirta Hotel, one of the finest in the city, a relic of French Colonialism. Its public areas were magnificently proportioned and superbly appointed in a Moorish manner, but looking just a little tired. This initial bubble of grandeur burst as soon as Zander got into his bedroom where he found that the furniture and facilities were not all that they appeared to be. The furniture looked fine until he tried to use it. Only one drawer in a chest of drawers opened. The others although looking convincing enough turned out to be dummy fronts fixed onto a carcass. A similar surprise met him when he tried to use the wardrobe. As only one of its two sliding doors opened, the drawer section of the wardrobe was completely inaccessible and therefore unusable.

*

It was late in the evening before he and Hubert got to their hotel. Dinner turned out to be disappointing; most of the items on the menu were "off" and all that remained was a soup and a lamb couscous. When Zander asked what kind of soup it was, the Moorish waiter just shrugged his shoulders. Zander's question was answered later when the waiter arrived carrying a plate on the palm of his hand, his thumb hooked over the rim to steady it, his thumb deep in the soup.

Clearly, this was Thumb-of-Algerian soup, mused Zander. When Zander brought this little indiscretion to his attention, the waiter smiled, laid the soup plate on the table, sucked his thumb and retreated towards the kitchen. Zander, aware of what function the left hand performs in some countries, tried to remember which hand had carried the soup but could not, so his soup went un-supped.

In forking through the couscous, Zander discovered that any meat it may have contained once upon a time had long since gone.

"Café?" enquired the waiter putting down a small cup of black, viscous liquid in front of him and as before, was gone before Zander could say yes or no. The coffee was so thick he could almost stand his spoon up in it. He tried a sip. It was good – in fact, it was very good. Thank goodness, he could enjoy something of his first meal in Algeria.

Shortly after dinner, Hubert – who had suffered a similarly uninspiring culinary experience – tilted his head towards the stairs to the bedrooms and they both called it a day.

Back in his room, Zander closed the heavy brocade curtains and the gap between the curtains halved, with each of the halves moving from the middle to the curtain's outer edges. By the dim light of the partially covered window, Zander feeling exhausted after his long day, shrugged his shoulders, undressed, flopped on to the bed and fell fast asleep.

It seemed as though his head had hardly touched the pillow before he was again, wide-awake. The strident call of the Mullah was summoning the faithful to prayer and the sound of it was coming from a loud speaker about twenty metres away from his window. As he lay tying to get back to sleep, he watched dust motes waltzing around in the air, highlighted by beams of light shining through the outer gaps of the curtains.

When he got up in the morning, he discovered that his Algerian bathroom had another surprise waiting for him. Stuck to the wall with dried up crumpled tape was a faded notice stating,

Adaptors for electric equipment are available at reception.

At reception, the desk clerk told him that these adaptors were in short supply and that he must bring it back as soon as he was finished with it. Going back into his bathroom, he struggled to get the adaptor into the socket, but eventually he did. When he had finished shaving, the found that the adaptor was stuck in the socket and his shaver was stuck in the adaptor.

Were he not dealing with an electrical appliance, Zander might have been tempted to throw a bucket of water over the lot. (He had heard this works with coupling dogs.) Eventually brute strength prevailed and the whole lot, including an area of plaster, came away from the wall, exposing bare electrical wires. Although he did manage to extricate his shaver from the adaptor, he could not get the adaptor out of the socket. His problem now was, should he hand the whole lot in to reception or just leave it lying in a prominent position in the room?

In the future, any time he could not get his shaver out of adaptors or sockets, he just packed the whole shebang into his suitcase and took them home, where with tools, they were easily prised apart. Perhaps this was why these adaptors were in such short supply.

On their walk along Constantine's broad, tree-lined boulevards towards the Wali's office, the pavements around them were thronged with dark sun-tanned locals, a high proportion of them wearing a flowing Burnoose. The fair-complexioned Zander and Hubert, dressed in light coloured suits, stuck out like sore thumbs. Soon they became aware that there were very few women on the streets and that the men, quite unabashed, were walking hand in hand or with their arms about each other's shoulders.

Hubert had already told Zander that this was the norm here and they were either family or good friends, but Zander, more used to British social conventions, still felt a bit uncomfortable. However, in spite of the saying, '*When in Rome, etc*' he was certainly not going to put his arm around Hubert's shoulders nor even worse, take his hand!

30

Acclimatisation Constantine

Constantine, in spite of its many reminders of French and Roman occupations, remains essentially the City of Cirta and ancient capital of the Numibians. Perched high on a towering, rock plateau and surrounded on three sides by the precipitous canyon of the River Rhummel, it still gives the impression of being a fortress city.

The City takes its current name from the Roman Emperor Constantine whose conquest of North Africa did not get much further south than here. Roman remains are common in the area and a larger-than-life size statue of its founding Emperor dominates the entrance plaza to the railway station. Unfortunately, the country has in recent times gone through a spell of uncertainty, so sadly, historical artefacts are, by necessity, sorely neglected; the idea of conservation or archaeology is only now beginning to receive attention, but is still not at the forefront of Algerian interest.

During the long period of French-Colonial rule, Constantine was home to many French people, so to remind them of their native country, they constructed the buildings and other physical features in 'the grand style'. Due to its elevation, Constantine provides a more moderate climate than most other parts Algeria. To the French therefore, it was a home from home. Its abundance of fine buildings, beautiful, tree-lined boulevards, striking monuments and delightful parks mirror some of the best features of Paris. Sadly, since the War of Independence, many of these have suffered badly from a lack of maintenance.

*

Traffic in the city was heavy and to an astonished Zander, it moved with no sense of order. Priority goes to the bravest, who, ignoring the shouts of fellow road users, and apparently without a care in the world, travel in whichever direction takes their fancy. On top of which, even knowing how difficult it is to replace a dead battery, motorists given the least excuse, blow their horns excessively.

At the top end of the local business scale is an abundance of shops selling gold, their shining wares crammed into brightly lit windows. Residents cannot take gold out of the country, and neither can an outsider; it is therefore hard to understand who buys it, other than the wealthy for personal use. At the other end of the trading scale, live a horde of wide eyed, mop-haired child entrepreneurs who buy packets of cigarettes from street corner news/cigarette stands to sell on to passers-by, one or two at a time. Cigarettes are outrageously expensive which makes any duty-free packets brought into the country a useful 'gift' for officials etc.

Away from the city centre, in the suburbs or out in the country, where there are more women around, Zander had expected to see people carrying the traditional water jugs on their heads. Instead, he was amazed to see women balancing metal gas canisters there while the older or less able ones rolled them along the ground with their feet.

He was also struck by the unseemly speed at which funeral processions hurried through the city on the way to the grave. The deceased would be lying face uncovered on a bier and carried on the shoulders of a relay of running mourners to be laid to rest, before the sun sets on the day of their demise.

An even more disconcerting sight to an uninitiated Zander occurred on the day before the end of the Feast of Ramadan, when he noticed that everyone was leading a sheep around on a rope, as if it was a pet and the sound of bleating was heard everywhere. Next day, not a single sheep was seen, let alone the sound of a single b-a-a-a. Moreover at the bottom of its gorge, the River Rhummel ran bright red and everyone in town looked contented and well fed.

31

Just the Job   Constantine

In keeping with his role of planner and information gatherer, Zander spent much of his time either attending interminably long meetings with local government officials, or making time-consuming site visits to proposed development areas. Meetings took place in hot, airless rooms where the air conditioning was not only noisy, but made no appreciable difference to the room temperature. It is no surprise therefore, that Zander preferred the site visits, where at least he was out in the fresh air.

Zander's contract stated that he was engaged to assess the development potential of Constantine and to report on a number of proposed projects within the City and its suburbs. Then almost as an afterthought, he was required to carry out all of the local ground survey work and any mapping needed for such assessments. To assist him with this, the client would supply him with maps of the study areas.

These maps turned out to be the old French topographical surveys of 1927, showing very little of what was on the ground now, so they were useless. Subsequent enquiries, both in Algeria and the UK, revealed that there were no modern maps available of any of the areas he was working in. He would therefore have to make his own. What had been an afterthought was now a time consuming and demanding task.

As Zander became familiar with the city and its suburbs, he began to appreciate the magnitude of the job facing him. Following in the wake of the recently resolved period of civil unrest – the struggle for freedom from French 'occupation' – it had become clear that the city's infrastructure had suffered from many years of neglect, with only minimal maintenance carried out. Almost everywhere he looked, something needed doing, and quickly. The existing urban road system was in a poor state and a significant number of essential bridges were crumbling towards failure. If the City was to match the country's vision of a New Algeria, then as well as fixing the existing problems, areas for development needed opening up and new infrastructure put in place to service them.

Almost at odds with the European idea of the Arab culture, Constantine was buzzing with anticipation about these new development proposals. Central Government was demanding that the Client (The Wali) produce a comprehensive programme for the maintenance and development of the infrastructure, as soon as possible. This led to the Client pressuring Zander into moving things forward with all possible speed. The carrot the Wali dangled in front of him was a hint that, if he succeeded in keeping the Central Government satisfied, the President would personally reward him.

A nice thought, but right now all Zander was feeling was pressure. It took Zander and Hubert only one visit to discover that there were no flights out of Constantine on either a Friday or a Saturday. Consequently, if they did not get out of the country on the Thursday mid-day flight to

Paris, they were stuck in Constantine over the weekend. This drove Zander to make sure that he always got enough work done by Wednesday evening, to be on that mid-day flight out on the Thursday.

*

Tight schedules, a heavy workload and travelling back and forth between the UK and North Africa took its toll on Zander, leaving him with neither the time nor the opportunity to do any sailing. On his weekend trips to Scotland, weather permitting, he would try to get out for a round of golf with his long time crewmember and friend, the imperturbable, lumbering gorilla, Grunt. However, right now that was little compensation for not being able to engage in his favourite pastime, sailing

Since he began to travel between Edinburgh, London and Constantine, a number of factors, (increased physical activity in a warmer climate, coupled with his abhorrence of North African food) left Zander a good bit lighter than he used to be. Pounds of flesh had rolled off him, his chin count had come down and his waistline had reduced significantly. While he still stood 5'7' in height, this bulking down made him looks younger and taller than before. His formerly florid complexion was now sun bronzed by his outdoor life and it gave him the appearance of rude, good health. So much so that, after the first few months, when he met up with some of his friends in Edinburgh, they did not immediately recognise him.

32

Location Location Location   Paris

On one particularly memorable trip to Constantine, things started to go wrong even before they had left Paris. On the night before flying to Constantine, Zander and Hubert met up in the departure lounge of Orly Sud Airport, deposited their bags in airport's luggage lockers – ready to be picked up before taking their early morning flight – and took the shuttle bus to the nearby Airport Hotel for dinner and a good night's sleep.

First light saw them heading back to the Airport on the shuttle bus. Rather than rush breakfast in the hotel, they had decided to eat in one of the airport's many restaurants, which at that time of the morning, were practically empty.

On their way to pick up their luggage, they heard the airport's usual early morning sounds interrupted by a terse multi-language announcement, demanding an immediate evacuation of the terminal buildings. This sent everyone rushing for the exits. Outside, another announcement said that security officers had found an unaccompanied package near the El Al departure gate and until the package was dealt with, everyone must stay well clear of the airport buildings.

For four uncomfortable hours, Zander and Hubert were left sitting on the grass in the hot sun, before the airport authority announced that boarding procedures would resume right away; adding that the Authority would make every effort to get all suspended flights back on schedule as quickly as possible.

Back inside the airport and again heading towards the left luggage area, Zander and Hubert went past the Constantine check-in desk, where already a heaving mass of passengers, mainly Arab women, of all shapes and sizes, were jostling for position, each one carrying at least two suitcases. The majority of these cases were in nearly throwaway condition, their contents bulging out from the gap between the two halves, held together by a belt or a bit of string. Hand luggage was mainly large red, white and blue striped nylon carrier bags, also stuffed to bursting point. The male passengers were lounging nearby, smoking and waiting to have their boarding cards brought to them. Their job was to look after the free 'cabin/hand baggage', in the form of car tyres, car doors and wheel arches, microwave ovens and sundry other small electrical goods, all of which somehow, had to go on board.

Anxious to retrieve their bags, Zander and Hubert hurried on to the left luggage area, all the while dreading the thought of joining that 'queue' and then be part of a second melee passing through customs and security before they could join their flight. Breakfast would now have to be pre-packed sandwiches.

Arriving at the left luggage area they found it deserted. Zander located the locker corresponding with the number on his key; put the key in the lock, but it would not turn. Zander's exasperation-driven curse brought a smile to Hubert's face as he put his key into his locker keyhole. His smile faded when he too experienced the same failure Zander had suffered only a moment or two ago.

Perplexed, they looked at each other. *Why will the keys not turn? Check the locker numbers with the keys!*

Each man flicked his eyes from key to locker. The key and locker numbers matched.

Obviously, their next move was to try the keys again, but still they refused to turn

What has gone wrong? What could go wrong?

Completely at a loss and starting to worry about not getting their bags – containing papers essential for their meetings – in time to catch their plane.

They tried again and with each twist and turn bringing the same sickening result, they became more and more frustrated. The time already spent here meant that there was now a distinct possibility that they would not get to the departure gate before it closed, and knowing the bureaucratic ways of airport check-in staff, brought home the seriousness of their situation. The still baggage-less pair checked their watches. With the flight time fast approaching, all thought of breakfast evaporated.

What could be wrong? What could they do?

Again, they checked their watches and it now seemed that time was ticking on faster than ever. The longer this pantomime went on, the more worried they became. Then from somewhere not too far away, they heard the clank of metal.

Turning sharply in the direction of the sound, Zander caught a glimpse of someone passing between the ends of the lanes of lockers. These lockers rose to above head height and were set out in a grid pattern, with alleyways between the rows and every sightline, apart from along the alley you are in is blocked out

Together the lost souls shouted,

"Hello!"

A voice replied. "Allo!"

Where was the voice coming from? They moved down their alleyway to the next intersection, but still there was no one in sight.

Another multi-echoed "Allo" rang round the lockers, but it was impossible to tell where it came from.

If Zander needed a brain wave, he needed one now. He called out,

"Do you speak English?"

"Yes".

"Do you know anything about these lockers?" Zander echoed back.

"Yes, I'm the locker attendant," was the response.

"Our keys will not open our lockers!" Zander shouted.

"Are the keys the same numbers as the lockers?" was the next tinny response from their invisible respondent.

It was now Zander's turn to say "Yes".

"OK, what lockers are you at?" was the next enquiry.

"2756 and 2754," Zander called out.

"Stay there".

A few seconds later, a small woman in a blue overall, carrying a mop and pail bustled round the corner of a block of lockers and came towards them.

"Show me your keys," she demanded.

The look she gave them would have melted ice. "These are blue keys! Can you not see these are red lockers? Did you deposit your luggage when you arrived into the airport?"

An indignant "Yes!" was the only answer that Zander could give her.

The woman, recognising the tone of Zander's reply, responded like a schoolteacher instructing a naughty child.

"Blue keys are for blue lockers; red keys are for red lockers. You are in the '*departure*' area. Your keys are for the lockers in the '*arrival*' area, upstairs!"

Zander looked at Hubert and pointed to a little red dot on the door panel beside the keyhole.

Then giving the woman their own impression of a Gallic shrug, they thanked her and hurried off upstairs. There they found the blue lockers and their little blue keys magically opened them to reveal their luggage.

Their mistake had lost them a lot of time and in full flight back to the departure level, they heard their flight's last call announced. At the check-in gate, the mass of passengers had disappeared and the desk was unmanned. Zander ran over to an adjoining Air France desk, pushed ahead of the line of passengers and asked the uniformed assistant if she could help them.

She picked up her desk phone and after a short conversation told him that, someone would be with them shortly. Sure enough, an Air Algerie check-in girl appeared, took their tickets and handed them boarding cards. She told them to go to Gate 30 as quickly as possible, as boarding had already started and since the baggage trolleys had already left to start loading, they would have to carry their own luggage. It would be a close run thing; they still had to get through security, between them and the boarding gate.

Fortunately, Zander and Hubert waltzed straight through an empty security area and things were looking good until just short of gate, they turned the last corner to find that a sea of Muslims kneeling in prayer blocking the passageway to the gate. The leader of this large group of the faithful had already identified the direction of Mecca and called his group together for one of a Muslim's five mandatory daily prayers.

In the blink of an eye, Zander and Hubert came from full pelt to a shuddering stop.

How can we get across this sea of devout, kneeling people?

Not far beyond the carpet of prostrated human beings, they saw the last of their heavily burdened fellow passengers filtering through Gate 30; car parts, electrical goods *et al.*

We have come too close to fail now, Zander said to himself and with Hubert following immediately behind him, he lifted his suit case above his head and with a solemn, respectful look on his face, did a hop step and jump tip-toe dance through the mass of devotees while acknowledging every misjudged step, with a deferential, "Excuse me".

With the last of their fellow passengers disappearing down the access bridge, they reached Gate 30. *Phew!*

On board, looking for somewhere to put their suitcases, they found that every nook and cranny of the overhead lockers was already crammed full of the most bizarre mixture of stuff you would not even expect to find at a car boot sale, let alone on a plane. In addition to enormous bulging soft-topped cases, there were enough car parts to build a whole car, and enough small electrical goods to furnish a few kitchens. On top of that, stuffed in amongst all of this, taking up all of the remaining space, were great big red, white and blue striped nylon bags. There was nowhere for them to put their luggage.

The flight attendant met Zander's sad faced appeal with an insincere, apologetic smile, said she was sorry, and then reminded him that they could not carry luggage on their laps or allow it to block the passageway.

A short time into the flight, matters took a further turn for the worse when, in three languages, the in-flight address system announced that due to the problems at the airport, the catering staff had not restocked the kitchen so regrettably, there would be no in-flight meals and only water to drink!

33

We Got Plenty of Nothing   Constantine

With their suitcases (fortunately not too big) uncomfortably stowed, one on the armrest and the other on the floor under their feet, Zander and Hubert tried to relax. It did not happen. During the flight, they suffered frequent scary moments as their plane bumped its way through a succession of air pockets over France, the Mediterranean and Northern Algeria until eventually landing in Constantine. By the time they got there, they were five hours late and completely knackered.

On *terra firma* again, they waited for an escort to whisk them through security. When no one turned up, the pair hung around until the airport police started to show an interest in them, which left them with no option but to go through the normal arrivals rigmarole.

(Later they discovered that someone had told the official that their plane 'had been cancelled'.)

Because they had no goodies for the customs officials, they had to endure exhaustive luggage checks and interminable form filling. Consequently, by the time they got through all of the formalities, the taxi drivers who usually meet an incoming flight, had either found a client or gone home. Zander and Hubert now had a problem, how do they get to their hotel?

Their rescuer came in the form of an airline worker heading for home at the end of his shift who with an eye on their aeroplane duty-free carrier bags, offered to take them to their hotel. An unnerving journey in a battered old Peugeot that coughed its way into town, seemed to have no springs and whose driver was a maniac eventually got them to main entrance of the Panoramic Hotel.

Their usual hotel, the Cirta, was full up, so staying in the Panoramic would be a new experience.

Going in through the revolving doors, they walked across the deserted hallway towards reception, their footsteps echoing back from the highly polished marble floor. From behind the desk, a uniformed receptionist/porter struggled drowsily to his feet. Hubert asked if the Wilaya's staff had booked rooms for Mr Duff's party.

"Yes, rooms have been reserved," the receptionist/porter replied, asked them to sign in then presented them with their room keys.

Leaving their luggage at reception (including Zander's duty free carrier bag – already lighter by a carton of 200 cigarettes) – Zander turned to Hubert and said,

"Let's go and get some food."

Hubert asked the receptionist/porter where the hotel restaurant was.

With an upside down smile, he looked at his watch and said, "I am sorry, Monsieur, the restaurant is closed."

Hubert then asked for room service.

The upturned smile straightened up and became tight-lipped.

"No, regrettably that is not possible."

"Can we get any food in the hotel at all?" queried a now exasperated Hubert.

A trace of a smirk crossed the receptionist/porter's face.

"Sorry, the kitchen is closed and locked up, the chef has gone home and he's taken the keys with him," obviously pleased to get a few back at the strangers who had disturbed his night's sleep.

The guests could now see that they were not going to get anywhere here.

What should they do now? They were both starving. The last thing they had eaten was a shared bar of chocolate sitting on the grass outside the airport in Paris. By relying on the in-flight meals and dinner in the hotel to keep them going, they had cut out breakfast. Now they were in a hotel with no food and ravenously hungry! Disappointment followed disappointment!

Hubert then gave the receptionist/porter a chance to add to his score,

"Is there a restaurant nearby?"

"Yes," was the oily, smiling reply," but it will be closing soon, because in town, all lighting is turned off early, to conserve energy. No one stays out as late as this on weekdays."

Stepping out onto the street, Zander and Hubert saw it was deserted and with only about one in ten of the lighting columns operating – and even then at a peep – it was quite dark.

Following the receptionist/porter's directions, the hungry men sallied forth to find some sort of food. To their left a dim *restaurant* sign was flickering on the solid grey mass of a building. Full of hope they walked towards it. Pushing through large double doors and into a big empty dining room, its stools upturned on the tables, it was immediately obvious that there was a problem here as well.

A large bushy moustachioed figure in a brown stained apron threaded his way between the tables towards them,

"Messieurs, ca va?"

Hubert took the initiative and asked if they could have a meal.

"Pas possible, ce soir. Nous sommes ferme!" the bushy moustache stated with a Gallic shrug.

Hubert persisted, "We've not had anything to eat all day. Is there anything you could let us have?"

With a sympathetic tilt of his head, bushy moustache relented. "Allors! Suivez-moi".

With their hopes rising, Zander and Hubert followed bushy moustache through the back door of the dining room, across the kitchen and into a dark room where a few men were drinking from tiny cups.

With an expansive gesture, bushy moustache pointed to a counter at the far end of the room, gave a slight bow, backed off through the kitchen door and with a sharp click of finality, locked the door behind him.

Zander and Hubert approached the counter, manned by another moustachioed man in a brown stained apron; his moustache however was a pencil-thin one. On the wall behind him, a menu offered three choices of coffee: black, very black and extra black. Realisation struck home; they were in a coffee shop so it was coffee or nothing.

"Have you any food at all?" Hubert enquired.

"Coffee comes with a biscuit."

It is not much, but it is better than nothing at all.

They ordered two coffees and a plate of biscuits. Within seconds, two tiny cups of what looked like treacle arrived and lying in each saucer was a small water biscuit.

Is that it? Are there no more biscuits?

Apparently, these measly little wafers were the last two. That **was** it!

Just as they were finishing their inadequate 'supper', every light in the room went out. The power had been switched off for the day and the rest of the night.

By the light of a few spluttering candles, Zander and Hubert went out into the street to find that they had walked into a blank canvas of darkness. Not only was it pitch black, but they had no idea of where they were. Yes, they were familiar with the streets around the Cirta, but up until now, they had never been anywhere near the Panoramic, so they had no idea what the streets around it looked like, even if they had been able to see them.

As their eyes adjusted to the gloom, they might have looked up to appreciate the brilliant night sky where the Milky Way cascaded across the brightly starlit heavens; but this was not one of those times. Therefore, resigned to not eating tonight, all they wanted to do now was get back to their hotel and sleep.

In complete contrast to the warmth of the evening air, a cold shiver crept over their skins and a flicker of fear gnawed at their bellies; here they were, strangers in a foreign land, not knowing where they were and with no idea of which way to go.

Hubert remembered that he had picked up a book of matches in their Paris hotel. Taking it from his pocket, he struck a match and with it set the others alight. A little flaming torch burst into life. Its short life revealed nothing that was of any use to them. As it burned down close to his fingers, he dropped it onto the pavement, where its flame guttered and died.

Just then, in the distance, their eyes picked up a small pinprick of light that got larger and brighter by the second.

As it got closer, they saw it was a motorcar with a little light on its roof, a taxi in fact.

Hubert planted himself squarely in the middle of the road forcing the driver to stop. Zander got into the cab and sat down, feeling his backside jagged by a broken spring. Hubert piling in after him said, Hotel Panoramic and joined Zander on the seat made up entirely of spring ends.

In the pale glow of the courtesy light they could see a puzzled look cross the driver's face, but Zander was not having any nonsense so, waving his hands in a shooing motion demanded forcefully,

"Allez! Allez! Vite! Vite!" Not for the first time his French would come back, particularly when he was scared.

The driver, shrugged, tilted his head and obeyed.

Relieved to be off the street, the occupants made themselves as comfortable as was possible – on seats with more broken springing than stuffing.

After a while, an uneasy thought replaced their initial relief, *surely, we've not been this far away from the hotel.*

When the driver eventually stopped and held out his hand for the fare, Zander, peered out of his side window and to his unbounded relief saw they were indeed outside their hotel and almost shouted,

"We're here!"

Their taxi driver demanded an exorbitant fare, but as neither Zander nor Hubert could see any basis for argument, it was a case of either pay up or shut up, so grudgingly they paid up.

At reception, lit by the dim light of a single low wattage bulb powered by an emergency generator, there was no sign of the receptionist/porter. So still unfed and exhausted, they, helped themselves to their room keys, felt their way up one flight of the grand staircase and by applying basic Braille techniques to heaven knows how many doors, found their rooms. The generator's bounty did not stretch as far as the bedrooms, so in total darkness, tripping over their luggage lying in the middle of the floor, stubbing their toes on furniture and banging their heads on other unseen obstacles, they fell into their respective beds and were instantly fast asleep.

34

Food Inglorious Food   Constantine

Zander's head had hardly hit the pillow, when he woke up to clanging and banging noises coming from just outside his window. Sticking his head under the pillow did little to reduce the audio assault on his brain. Exasperated, he got up to see what was going on, and with some difficulty, opened the French windows to see where his early morning alarm call was coming from. His bleary, half-opened eyes peered down at the street, one floor below.

There, on the other side of the street was the source of the morning chorus. At regular intervals along the road, men were sitting just inside their open doors, banging away with hammers and chisels on trays, plates, pots and pans, car bodywork panels, etc. In that instant, Zander knew that the Panoramic Hotel backed on to the metalworking area of Constantine. Yes, it was possible to see the beautiful panorama of the El Kantara Gorge and the Sidi Rached Bridge shown in the hotel brochure, but that was the view from a room a good few floors above his.

From first light until dusk, apart from siesta time – just as their forerunners had done for countless years before them – these artisan coppersmiths, silversmiths, goldsmiths and other general metalworkers plied their physically demanding trades.

Exasperated, but resigned to staying awake, Zander closed the window – again with some difficulty – and came back inside to see something that cheered him up. Standing on his dressing table was a beautifully arranged basket of fruit and beside it a bottle of wine. *Ins'allah*! These welcoming gifts must have had been there all night. If only he and Hubert had not been in such an all-fired hurry to go out and get some food, all of last night's problems would have been avoided. Even though he was not a great fan of fruit, it would have helped to stave off his hunger.

Zander got dressed and went downstairs for breakfast. By following the signs, he quickly found the dining room and was dismayed to see that it was deserted. Bewildered, he looked at his watch, *Surely, I am not too early for breakfast and I cannot be too late*. Just then, a door along the hallway swung open and the sounds of clinking plates and cups, made his ears prick up. Then, following these sounds, he found their source.

On the wall outside the door was a notice in Arabic, and under it on a small piece of paper a shaky hand had written in faded blue ink, *Salle de Petit Dejeuner* (one of the few French phrases he remembered) so at last he would get something to eat.

Pushing open the door took him into a large rectangular room divided down the middle by a wooden refectory-type table. Sitting on either side of it was a collection of Arabs and Europeans, already eating. At the far end, someone got to his feet and shouted

"Zander! Over here!"

Hubert had beaten him to breakfast and was pointing to the right and saying,

"Over there, that hatch in the wall. It is self service; get your food and join me."

At the prospect of eating,' Zander's expectations soared. However, when he saw what was on offer, they dived straight down to zero again. He could have anything he liked from a selection of dry, hard, wizened croissants, lard-like butter, watery apricot jam and thick black coffee. Frustratingly too, there was no member of staff nearby, to beg, borrow or steal anything better from.

Unpalatable though the menu was, Zander was starving, so he put some bread and thin, apricot preserve on a plate, poured himself a cup of coffee and sat down beside Hubert. Even although no member of staff was there to see it, his face did not hide his disapproval.

Even a cheerful, "Good morning" from Hubert did nothing to lift Zander's mood. As far as he was concerned, conversation was not on this morning's menu, at least not yet.

Still hungry, Zander got up to go back to his room to eat some of the complimentary fruit that had become slightly more appealing. Hubert had other ideas. Nudging Zander towards an exit door, he suggested,

"Let's have a walk in the sunshine. We're got a long day of meetings ahead of us, so some fresh air will do us good."

Reluctantly, Zander agreed.

The street outside was bathed in a glow of bright early morning sunshine and after basking in its warmth and breathing in some fresh mountain air for a minute or two, Zander grudgingly admitted that it was indeed, pleasant to be out here.

Idly, Zander kicked at a piece of cardboard on the pavement, did a double take, peered down to look at it more closely and saw it was a charred book of matches. It looked vaguely familiar and when he picked it up, it confirmed his suspicions. In his hand was the burnt out book of matches Hubert had dropped before they got into the taxi, last night. Now 'the penny' dropped as well; evidently that crook of a taxi-driver had picked them up at the back door of the Panoramic Hotel, driven them around for goodness knows how long before dropping them off at the Hotel's front door. No wonder they got that funny look when they had asked for the Panoramic Hotel, but it had not stopped the taxi driver from taking them for a ride – and an exorbitantly expensive one at that!

35

Falling Down on the Job Constantine

Still mentally and physically shattered, Zander and Hubert set off for their morning meeting with the Client's representatives.

Their contact man in Constantine, Patrick Rauser, a slimmer version of Peter Ustinov, met them at the Wilaya's offices.

Escorting them past security, he guided them through a series of spacious hallways and beautifully decorated rooms, their walls covered by enormous colourful tapestries and gigantic gilt-framed oil paintings. On the floors stood innumerable statues on pedestals and glass cabinets full of expensive looking antiques.

Zander had lost count of the ornately decorated doors they had walked past before Patrick stopped at one, and, indicating that they should wait outside, he went in to announce them. His soft knock brought an officious sounding command of "Entrez!" which he did. Moments later, he reappeared and signalled them to come inside.

The chamber they went into, had it not been for the four magnificent red marble pillars that supported its majestic painted ceiling, could easily have housed a badminton court. The ornamentation here was even more elaborate and sumptuous than anything they had seen so far.

At the far end of the chamber, bright morning sunshine was streaming through a great stained glass window. In front of this was a large rectangular boardroom table and ranged along each side of it, sat ten of what they correctly assumed to be Wilaya officials. A single elaborately carved chair bathed in the solar spotlight, its back to the window, occupied the far end of the table. At the near end were three empty chairs, clearly indicating that this was where they should sit. When Hubert, Patrick and Zander sat down, the sun was shining directly into their eyes.

A man immediately to their left, signalled for everyone to stand and then like a town crier, he made an announcement. The Wali – the Algerian equivalent of Mayor – entered through a door adjacent to his ornate seat where, with the sun behind him his face was in shadow. He had taken the high ground. He was middle-aged, of medium height, portly and dressed in a lightweight fawn suit. Exceptionally well groomed to the point of looking buffed up and polished and, clearly, a professional politician. With an elaborate, well-practiced wave, he signalled that everyone should sit down. Patrick then introduced Zander and Hubert to the Wali and the other officials present.

Introductions complete, the Wali, with imperious dignity nodded, indicating that the meeting should begin.

The days' business was conducted in a local form of French that Zander found it difficult to keep up with. Even though Hubert was translating for him, he quickly lost the thread of what was going on and allowed his attention to wander. Bored out of his skull, his mind in limbo, Zander tried to work out what was happening in a huge historical tapestry, partly hidden behind one of the room's large marble pillars. While leaning over to see past the pillar, he stretched just a bit too far and because his chair was poised delicately on two legs, lost his balance.

A rush of adrenalin surged through Zander as his chair slipped from under him and with a solid thump, his backside hit the floor. To add to his embarrassment, his chair skittered across the highly polished floor, banged into a table piled high with loose-leaf files, knocked it over and brought an avalanche a letters, files and folders crashing down onto the floor.

Every eye in the chamber turned on Zander. With his mind in a whirl and not knowing where to look, he crawled across the floor to repair the damage caused by his errant chair and to make matters worse, when he stood up holding some of the scattered papers he had gathered up, he bumped heads with one of the officials who had rushed over to help him. For an instant Zander's world was one of flashing lights, bright starbursts and whirling planets. They exchanged polite apologies and together gathered up the scattered correspondence and placed it on the main boardroom table.

The meeting resumed and for the remainder of the morning Zander managed to stay awake. However, to his immense relief, the Wali's body language eventually showed the unmistakable signs that the meeting was over. Zander gathered up his agenda and other bits and pieces, stuffed them into his briefcase, said his goodbyes and along with Hubert and Rauser left the meeting.

Back in their hotel after lunch, Zander and Hubert, sitting in the faded opulence of one of the hotel's large public rooms were feeling better now that they had a substantial meal inside them. Zander was drinking a small tumbler of cola while Hubert sipped a large glass of absinthe. When their drinks bill arrived, Zander expressed some surprise when he saw that Hubert's large alcoholic absinthe had cost a fraction of what his little glass of cola had. Hubert explained that locally made absinthe cost next to nothing to produce, whereas cola is imported and is highly taxed; Zander made a mental note of this, for future reference.

While Hubert and Zander were carrying out a post mortem of their meeting, Zander emptied out his briefcase to find some papers. Hubert picked up the uppermost letter from the bundle and asked, "What's this?"

Perplexed, Zander took it from him, looked at it and replied. "Never seen it before in my life,"

Taking back the letter, Hubert explained, "That's the Wali's headed notepaper and the red lettering across the top says Top Secret. You must have picked it up with the stuff that was on the floor. What are you going to do with it?"

"What do you mean? *What am I going to do with it?* We're in this together," was Zander's indignant response.

"We can't take it back and we'll never get it through customs," Hubert asserted, taking another book of matches from his pocket.

An amazed Zander watched Hubert walk over to the great baronial-type open fireplace, put a lighted match to the bottom of the document, hold it until it was burning his fingers, then drop it into the grate. Zander stood open mouthed, as he watched the document crumble into ashes in the hearth.

Turning back to look at Zander, Hubert said with some finality,

"What they don't know can't hurt us."

36

Toilet Tales   Constantine

If you know anything about the North African lifestyle, you will know that the men do not sit on toilets. A lifetime of practice has endowed them with in-built balance and the fine directional skills that allows them to stand on the raised metal footprints and with instinctive and unerring accuracy, hit the small dark, opening between their feet.

Since the French left Algeria, there was no longer a great demand for western 'khazis', so not only are they few and far between, but no one bothers to maintain those that do. Outsiders soon realise that the few European toilets they do find in Constantine's public areas still present a few built-in hazards. At first glance, they look safe enough but using them can give the lie to that initial impression.

Zander is unlikely to forget his first experience of 'needing to go' in Constantine, particularly as it happened on his first visit to the departure area in its busy airport.

After walking along a line of cubicles and finding that, each one contained an Arab stand-on facility, Zander opened the door to the last remaining cubicle and was relieved to see that it housed a European bowl toilet. At last, he could do what he had come here to do.

All went well until he pulled the chain. A surge of water flushed down into the bowl, sent a tsunami-like wave over the water surface, gathering up his recent deposits, swept them over the porcelain rim and discharged the lot over the front of his trousers and shoes.

Before returning to face the public, he cleaned himself up as best he could, but that sort of stuff sticks and smells. As a result, when he got back to the main departure area, his soiled trousers and frequent 'shaking-leg' step drew funny looks from passers-by. Unfortunately, as his suitcase, containing his spare trousers was already on its way to the plane, all he could do was try to ignore the problem, and go about his business as though nothing had happened. Zander and everyone within smelling distance of him would just have to suffer all the way to Paris, where he would recover his suitcase and his dignity.

In the wake of that uncomfortable experience, anytime Zander had to use a Constantine bowl toilet, he would do what he came to do, open the door and push the flush while at the same time taking a swift backward jump – but even then, he was not always successful.

Constantine airport's Arab toilet flushing mechanisms are not all that well maintained either, as Zander found out on his first and never to be repeated visit to a 'stand up and beg' toilet. Waiting in the queue to visit the rest rooms, he found that progress was slow.

As he got near to the front of the queue, the man who had just come out handed him an empty, plastic bottle. He had already noticed that whenever someone at the front of the queue got a bottle, he went to a nearby tap, filled it with water and rejoined the queue. Therefore, when it was his turn to get a bottle – still with no idea what was going on – he shrugged, took it, filled it and rejoined the queue.

When his turn came, he went into the cubicle, placed his bottle of water on the ground, stood on the raised metal footprints and went about his business. When he pulled the chain to flush the system, nothing happened. Now he knew the function of the water bottle. However, even this jewel of knowledge left him with a problem; did he fill the cistern on the wall in front of him and pull the lever, or just pour the water straight down between his feet?

Being civilised, or so he believed, Zander decided to do the former and with a flourish, he emptied his water bottle into the cistern. That was when the dreaded Algerian toilet demon struck again. A jet of water squirted out of the lower joint in the cistern's discharge pipe, soaking his trousers from the knees down to his shoes. *Does this always happen? If not, why only to me?*

*

On another unforgettable occasion when Zander got a touch of Algerian tummy, he rushed into the hotel's toilet, and sat down to do what he desperately needed to do. Sitting there with one foot on the floor and the other extended in front of him to keep the lockless door closed, he reached sideways for toilet paper while at the same time raising a cheek to affect his personal ablutions. Precariously balanced; with trousers round his knees, his body at 45°, one shoulder leaning on the wall, one foot on the floor, the other holding the door shut, he felt the bowl slipping sideways. At any second, the whole thing was going to go from under him and deposit him on the floor, amongst the deposit that used to be his. Panic-stricken and knowing that his already tenuous points of contact were becoming less secure by the nanosecond and desperately aware that time was against him, he thought, *what can I do?*

By some reflex action born out of his natural instinct for self-preservation, he took his foot off the door, put it on the floor, manoeuvred his elbow on to a little ledge on the sidewall and by delicately redistributing his weight, pulled his trousers up enough to be able to get to his feet. With the stabilising effect of his body taken away, the toilet bowl dropped to the floor with a clunk, swilling its contents all over its cracked tiled surface. Fortunately, the mess had drained away from where he was standing.

His technical curiosity aroused, Zander looked to see why this had happened. Scientific analysis was not necessary; the empty holes at the foot of the pedestal and the absence of bolts sticking up out of the floor bore testimony to the fact that the bowl was not fixed to the floor and never had been!

Zander did what he could to clean himself up, adjusted his clothes and – for once – walked off after a lucky escape.

37

An Arresting Situation   Constantine

One of Zander's seemingly endless tasks was to check on just how much of the infrastructure detail shown on the 1927 maps still existed on the ground. He would then need to update these maps to show what had disappeared and what had changed since then. In places where there were new bridges, roads, and roundabouts, he had to do some on-site survey work. Whilst this work was not too difficult to carry out in rural areas – where he could still find the old roads and there was little or no traffic, he made good progress. In the congestion of the city however, it was a different matter altogether. Taped measurements across busy roads were not an option, as it caused unacceptable traffic disruption. Therefore, to do this work, Zander used a modern optical measuring device.

In principle, this instrument allows the surveyor to stand on one side of the road directly over the kerb, focus the device on a point on the opposite kerb, turn a focussing screw on the side of the instrument's telescope until the two images merge and then from a scale on that screw, read the distance across the road.

Early in the day while the traffic was still light, Zander went out to measure road widths in the middle of

Not Again

Constantine. Fully engrossed in his work and making good progress, the telescopic images of the far kerb suddenly turned black. Opening his other eye to see why, he saw a large man in uniform standing almost nose to nose with him. Zander waved his hand dismissively to get the man to move out of his line of vision. He did not move. Zander sensing another presence behind him turned round and saw that another equally large man was standing directly behind him.

Zander's feeble language skills leapt to his defence. Waving his hand again, this time more vigorously he said, "Allez! Allez! Vite! Vite!"

All that happened was that the first man pointed to his instrument and demandad,

"Camera, Donnez le moi."

"Non, ce n'est pas un camera, c'est un (pause) distance finder."

After Zander's attempt at Franglais the man enquired unnecessarily, "Parlez vous Francais?"

"Non."

By now, the officials (at least Zander assumed they were) had taken up station on either side of him and grasped him by the elbows. It was clear they wanted him to come with them and from their grim faced expression, they knew that he was not going to refuse.

Zander thought, *what the hell, I have nothing to fear. They believe I'm using a camera, but I know I'm not. After all, how could they know that I'm working for the local authority and doing nothing wrong?* So, he decided to go quietly.

They hustled him along the road, through a small gate in a high walled enclosure that took him into a large dusty courtyard with a shaded colonnade. Pushed into a building,

Zander was marched along a long corridor and thrust into a small, barely furnished room.

One of his 'guardians' indicated that he should sit on the far side of the table in the middle of the room, which he did.

It was some time before an officious looking man in uniform came in, looked at him and demanded abruptly, "Passeporte, s'il vous plait."

This he could not do because, following Hubert's advice, his passport was in the hotel safe.

"Pas possible, c'est dans l'hotel," he improvised.

(It is amazing how, in a crisis, some semblance of long forgotten French phrases comes to mind). Zander's inquisitor shrugged his shoulders, made a dismissive gesture and producing some forms from a folder, laid them on the table. Miming a scribbling motion, he instructed Zander to fill them in and with that, left the room. Zander looked at the forms. They were in both French and Arabic, with spaces for the answers in French on the right hand side of the page, and spaces for Arabic, on the left.

At a total loss because his French was not up to the task and because he could not even read the Arabic, he could do nothing. He sat back, folded his arms and waited for the next move in this farce to unfold.

Time passed slowly. It felt like he had been sitting there for ages. *Maybe I will have to sit here to rot, or sweat it out, or whatever else happens to captives?*

Then, after what seemed like an interminable age, but was probably less than half an hour, the door opened and a thickset, uniformed official with a grand waxed moustache strode in. On his broad sloping shoulders were epaulettes splashed with an impressive amount of gold braid and his barrelled chest was covered with rows of medal ribbons.

Clearly, he was a high-ranking officer and in his hand was Zander's measuring device.

Sitting on a corner of table, one leg nonchalantly dangling not too far from Zander, he put a yellow notice on the table beside him.

One of Zander's few practical skills was the ability to read upside down and when he noticed that the page heading was the word **ARRETER** in bold capitals, panic spread through his being.

"Gulp!" *That means stop, or arrest or something unpleasant.*

"Anglais?" enquired 'Waxed Moustache' officiously.

"Oui." Zander's amazing fluency in the language had come back. (He did not try to complicate matters by offering, Ecossais or de Grande Bretagne.)

"Parle Francais, monsieur?"

Here we go again Zander thought, "Non."

The official banged the delicate measuring instrument down on the table, Zander wincing at its heavy-handed treatment,

"Qu'est-ce que c'est?"

By now, Zander was desperately wishing that he had paid more attention to his French schoolteacher rather than reading the Batman comics hidden between the pages of his French book.

With no common language, communication was nigh on impossible; the questions understood were few and the sensible answers, non-existent.

Zander, thinking about the horrifying tales he had heard about Algerian prisons, just knew that they were not the sort of place he ever wanted to visit.

Then Zander looked at the officer's rows of medal ribbons and noticed a cloth paratrooper's badge, sewn on above them. As a last resort, he mimed a parachutist falling through the skies while pointing to the officer's badge, all the while nodding and smiling. Waxed Moustache was clearly perplexed at first and stared at Zander as though he had gone mad. Then a light bulb suddenly lit up in his head and he twigged what Zander's demonstration was all about.

Pulling back his shoulders and straightening up to his full if short height, he stuck his medal-beribboned chest out and proudly asserted,

"OUI! Et vous?"

Nothing daunted, Zander replied, "Oui."

Well it was a half-truth; even though he had not actually jumped out of a plane, he had volunteered for and completed the ground-training course.

Encouraged by the smile lighting up the face of his newfound comrade in arms, and relieved that his inspired brainwave might well get him out of the frying pan, Zander felt his confidence flowing back.

It was then that Waxed Moustache remembered he could speak broken English – but significantly less broken than Zander's smashed French. Waxed Moustache also supplemented his newly remembered skill with typically expressive Gallic sign language. In a flash, the mood in the room changed and a more sympathetic and co-operative atmosphere was established.

Zander, took the opportunity to say, "Je travail pour le Wilaya." hoping this meant, "I work for the local authority." At last, he had the officer listening.

Officer: "Who for you work?"

Zander: "Le Wilaya, et aussi Monsieur Rauser."

Officer, " Aha! Monsieur Rauser?"

Zander: "Yes"

Officer: "I phone him, OK?"

Zander: "OK."

At this point, Waxed Moustache pulled a little black book from his pocket, found a number in it, dialled and then sitting down opposite Zander, leant back and waited. Zander, heard a tinny voice answering the phone. The officer tilted his chair back, put his feet on the table and proceeded to have a long spirited conversation.

It was clear the officer was on good terms with whoever was at the other end of the phone and after a lengthy conversation passed it to Zander.

"Hello, Zander, Patrick here. I hear you are with my good friend Robert, the Chief of Police. It **was** Patrick Rauser on the line. *Thank goodness,* thought Zander. Patrick went on, "Don't worry, everything is sorted out and, to oil the wheels I've taken the opportunity to invite Robert to your hotel for dinner this evening. Bye!"

Zander handed the phone back to Waxed Moustache, who he now knew to be Robert, who smiled, stood up and indicating that Zander should follow him, led him through a labyrinth of corridors until on opening a door they came out into the warm, welcoming sunshine beating down on a busy Constantine street. Robert handed Zander his precious instrument, shook hands and with a shooing movement indicated that he was free to go.

Zander took leave of his waxed moustached, newfound friend and erstwhile captor by calling out a relieved, "Au revoir."

Little did he know how prophetic, this casual comment would turn out to be.

38

Deja Vu!   Constantine

Much of the day had already been lost, but the work must go on, so Zander went back to taking street measurements and had only been working for a few minutes, before 'his collar was felt' again. This time by two plainclothes men, who were even less talkative than the earlier pair. They just grabbed him by the collar and the seat of his pants and frogmarched him back in the direction from whence he had just come.

He was marched through the same small door, into the same enclosure, under the same colonnade and along the same corridor, before being bundled into a different, smaller, barely furnished room. This time, a different uniformed man demanded his passport.

Again, Zander suffered a bout of questioning but this time his fractured Franglais replies only brought angry repeats of the questions, until in exasperation, he demanded,

"Laissez-moi parlez avec le Chef de Polis, Monsieur Robert."

The police officer did a bit of 'French shrugging' as if he did not understand what Zander was saying, however, when Zander persisted with his 'Chef de Polis' bit, eventually the dull eyes of the 'uniform' brightened up and with a flicker of recognition, and a further, different, sort of shrug, indicated that Zander should come with him.

They retraced their steps along the now familiar corridor, stopped outside a door marked Chef Du Polis and Zander's captor knocked respectfully on the door. A voice shouted, "Entrez."

Zander was taken in and both he and his guard stopped in front of a big desk.

Robert looked up, and looked surprised but when he worked out what was going on, his face turned angry. He sprang up from his chair, walked round his desk and prowled around Zander's escort. Then red faced, standing on tiptoes, his eyes looking directly into those of the unfortunate man, he burst into a saliva ridden tirade of curses that left the poor man in no doubt that he was not the flavour of the month. Zander, with a smug smile on his face, stood watching, relishing the sight of his escort's discomfort; and only sorry that due to his lack of the French language, he was unable to appreciate the finer points Robert was making.

Then, with a short, sharp open-handed but forceful clip round the back of the head, Robert sent the cowering Algerian copper grovelling out of the room.

Robert, straightening his uniform, turned and motioned Zander to sit down, reached into his desk drawer and with a raised eyebrow and enquiring expression, brought out a bottle of whisky and two glasses. These he set down on the table and poured generous measures into them.

This gesture took Zander by surprise. Algeria is a Muslim country and maintains a strict alcohol ban, so he knew that any Algerian – who did manage to get his hands on alcohol – would usually drank it in secret and even then only on special occasions. Here he was, being honoured and feeling grateful for his Patrick Rauser connection, which had unexpectedly turned out to be so fruitful.

Robert, outwardly relaxed, raised his glass to Zander, who raised his in return and said "Slainthe!"

A few minutes of pensive, silent sipping saw their glasses empty, Robert again guided Zander and his 'camera' through a maze of corridors before re-releasing him out into the tree dappled sunlit streets of Constantine.

Whereupon Zander, deciding he had had enough excitement for the morning, went back to his hotel.

39

Deja Vu Again   Constantine

Zander determined to do some more work that day but reluctant to go back to the area of his 'arrest', decided to work in an entirely different part of Constantine.

Enjoying the walk along the tree-lined boulevards of this beautiful, if neglected city, he got to his destination – a large roundabout – and started to take measurements.

The measuring device was hardly out of its case, before two men came up behind him, bundled him into the back of a car and it took off. As the vehicle accelerated, he felt the oppressive, odorous presence of the large men sitting on either side of him. *What next* he thought.

The car, siren wailing and taking most of the corners on two wheels, raced through the streets at break neck speed. So tightly jammed in was Zander, that he was in no danger of falling over, let alone making a break for it.

The car slowed to a crawl then, after a short pause, lurched forward again before screeching to a shuddering stop. Zander, squinting through a side window thought, *I know this place; I am back at Robert's office* and before he could muster any further thoughts, he was bundled from the car, into the building, frogmarched along a now familiar corridor then told to sit on a chair outside Robert's office door. One of his kidnappers, even more aromatic now after his exertions, went into Roberts' office and in the blink of an eye, was back out to help his cohort to drag his prisoner in to face Robert.

Robert, sitting at his desk, looked up and when he saw whom his 'prisoner' was, stood up, walked round his desk, shook Zander by the hand and apologised profusely. Even as that happened, Zander's abductors, oblivious to the error of their ways, stood by puzzled. Robert turned round slowly, gave them a look that would have soured milk, followed by a volley of abuse that reduced them to quivering shadows of their former selves. The arresting officers turned and fled, doing their best to dodge Robert's barrage of well aimed kicks and punches.

With his underlings dispatched and the door closed firmly behind them, Robert turned to Zander, gave his uniform a corrective downward tug, brushed his moustache with the back of his hand, turned to Zander and said, "Come with me."

Outside in the courtyard, Robert snapped his fingers and in the blink of an eye, a car and driver appeared. Seating himself in the 'senior officers' position, Robert asked Zander where he would like to go. Right now, Zander felt like going back to his hotel for a shower and a long drink, instead asked to go to back to where he had just come from. The car, siren wailing, making people jump out of its path, was there in no time at all. Robert got out of the car and told Zander that he would stay with him until he had finished his work.

Thanks to his new assistant, who, if the traffic was too dense for Zander to get a reading, stepped on to the road, held it up and cut off any protest with a dominating glare. As a result, with everything he needed jotted down in his little book, Zander was soon finished for the day.

Back outside his hotel as Zander got out the car he reminded his 'assistant' that this was where they were to meet for dinner that evening.

Dinner was a turning point in Zander's association with the Algerians; not only did he have the highest ranking surveying assistant that he was ever likely to have, but that assistant was also Patrick Rauser's brother-in-law.

STILL NO SAILING

Airport Taxi

40

Last Plane Out   Constantine

It was Thursday and as was their usual practice, Zander and Hubert were leaving Constantine on the mid afternoon plane to Paris. Thanks to Robert's intervention, Zander had done everything he had planned to do on this trip and a taxi was booked to take them to the airport.

By the time the taxi turned up, they were cutting it fine to get to the airport in time to catch their flight. At first glance, the taxi looked as though it was long overdue a visit to one of the scrap yards dotted around rural Algeria. With the second, it looked even worse, an impression reinforced by the noisy clattering coming from its tired engine.

To get hold of another taxi now was out of the question so, praying that this clapped out old banger would live long enough to get them there in time to catch their plane, Zander and Hubert climbed aboard.

The taxi lurched forward to begin the nine-kilometre trip to the airport and did manage to keep going until it was just clear of the city suburbs; it was there that its tired engine began to falter. Within fifty metres, the faltering had become a juddering and the taxi had slowed to walking pace. At the death, with an ear-shattering bang that drove a flock of pigeons in a nearby field swirling into the air in panic, the taxi ground to an expensive sounding halt. Unfortunately, where it had died was nowhere near the airport.

The driver jumped out, lifted the bonnet and was immediately lost in a cloud of thick brown smoke. Amidst a bout of coughing, he fought his way out from under the bonnet and with the now familiar Afro-French shrug, indicated the blindingly obvious fact, that their conveyance could convey them no further.

The occupants' hearts sank; here they were in the middle of nowhere without transport and in serious danger of missing their plane. The prospect of a weekend in Constantine was now looming large on their depressing horizon.

Almost simultaneously two taxis going back to town pulled up alongside them and both drivers got out and offered to take over the fare.

Phew, we may have a chance yet, thought Zander. Nodding to Hubert, they took their luggage out of the boot of the dead taxi and were about to throw it into one of the others when an argument broke out between the recently arrived drivers, about which of them was to take over the fare.

The vocal exchange developed into a girlie-type hand-bag-slapping match, escalated through one or two increasingly violent phases before finally erupting into a full-scale all in hair tugging, eye gouging, flesh biting brawl.

Zander felt a hand grip his elbow. He looked round and there, with a conspiratorial look on his face, was their original taxi driver. Picking up Zander and Hubert's luggage, he shooed them towards one of the other taxis, tossed the cases on the front seat, urgently indicated that they get in the back and jumped into the driver's seat. As soon as its doors had closed, their 'requisitioned' taxi, took off in a tyre-burning u-turn, to complete their interrupted journey to the airport.

Looking through the dirty back window decorated with a multitude of dangling ornaments, all Zander could see was a cloud of dust where the two taxi drivers were still battling it out, neither aware that a daylight taxi-jack had just taken place. Their own driver muttered something that sounded like a mixture of Arabic, French and English; the garbled content of which, Hubert translated as, "It's all right to borrow the car; it is his brother's."

With no alternative but to believe him, the passengers accepted that this was the only chance they had of reaching the airport in time, so they sat back and tried to relax.

When they pulled up outside the doors of the airport's departure area, Hubert grabbed their luggage, Zander paid the driver and together they ran towards the check-in desk. Horror of all horrors, the desk had closed. An enquiry to a passing airport official revealed that the plane was just about to board and because it was already full, that was that.

It now looked like the unhappy pair would be stuck here for the weekend and free to enjoy all the comforts of a 'five star hotel' – where from a top floor room, many more stars were visible through a hole in the roof. Even more depressingly, there would be nothing for them to do, because in Constantine no one did anything over the weekend; the place would be empty. Worse still, almost all of the guests had already checked out and gone away, so the hotel's limited menu would be even more restricted than usual.

Zander being Zander, quickly weighed up the situation and due to the unthinkable thought of being denied the comforts of home, his thinking process went into overdrive. Just what were his options?

With passport in hand ready for inspection, Zander then noticed like a beacon of inspiration, Robert's business card, shining out from between its pages. Was it possible that his newfound friend's power would stretch as far as the airport? His thinking was now travelling along the lines of,

When the barrel is empty, you may no longer be up to your neck in it, but you are still in deep doo-doo, so do-do something! Anything was worth a try.

Acutely aware that the situation was fast running away from him, Zander showed Robert's business card to the helpful airport official; and using sign language, asked if the official would contact that person for him. Yes, the official agreed, that was the least he could do. With Zander desperately praying that Robert would be there to take the call, the official dialled. When the call was answered, the official snatched it away from his ear as though there was a venomous spider lurking in the earpiece. A screeching metallic voice berating the poor official with words and phrases Zander had last heard during the police officers' dressing down; and which, even from some distance away, delivered a clear message. The official picked up the passenger list ran his finger down it until his finger stopped. Putting the phone on hold, he switched to the airport announcement system and in Arabic, his voice boomed out over the public-address system.

With his message delivered the official switched back to the phone and with some snivelling and grovelling, did, in a few words, tell his story and accept Robert's thanks. As the official put down the phone, he saw a motorised buggy passing by. Bundling the driver out, he commandeered it and told Zander and Hubert to get on. Then with the buggy's squeaky horn beeping continuously, the white knuckled official/racing car driver carved a path through passengers and staff alike, towards the departure gate. Driving with the buggy's drive pedal flat on the floor and flashing his identity card, they sailed through every control point on the way to the boarding lounge.

In the few minutes it had taken to get there, the lounge had cleared, the plane had boarded and all that remained were two airline officials and two sad looking men with their hand baggage at their feet, each of them holding a boarding card in his hand. The buggy driver screeched to a halt beside them, snatched their boarding cards, handed them to Zander and Hubert and in the same movement, pointing to the plane, pushed them out of the airport building and as they sprinted across the tarmac, they heard his voice shouting, "Vite! Vite! Bon Voyage!"

Safely on board, this time with their luggage stowed in the overhead lockers, Zander sat back and thought, *if I had not been arrested I would not have met Robert and I would be spending a dreary weekend in Constantine. Instead, of which, thankfully, I am on my way to Paris and then home.*

Next time he went to Constantine, some cigars and a bottle of whisky for his new friend Robert would not go amiss.

41

Pick a Pocket or Two   Constantine

It was evening and Zander was feeling down in the dumps. Some dignitary or other was visiting the Wali so work had come to a standstill. Zander had nothing to do and had all day to do it in. When he had something to do, he did not mind doing nothing, but he could not abide having nothing to do.

Constantine in Algeria is not the place to be without having some sort of diversion to hand. He had tidied up his logbooks in the afternoon; dinner had taken up the early part of the evening but now – nothing.

He had the choice of either of the two channels on Algerian television, the first in Arabic, the other the same programme but with French subtitles. These 'programmes' took the form of a succession of news items with 'talking heads', interspersed with intervals during which the screen is filled with a portrait of the Premier accompanied by rousing martial music. Yes, there were cinemas but the films were all old French black and white ones with Arabic subtitles or vice versa. Since the French had left, theatres just did not exist.

His only remaining choices were, to take a sightseeing walk amongst the hand-in-hand, predominantly male population or stay in and read a book, until the power was cut-off.

If he was going to read, he would do it in his bedroom because, if he sat in the hotel lounge too long – or any of the other public areas for that matter, a succession of English speaking members of staff or locals looking to improve their conversational English, would try to engage him in conversation. To Zander, this was not a desirable recreational pastime. On the occasions when he could not avoid this unwanted fraternisation, he would meet the offending conversationalist's eyes with a blank stare, say nothing and hope that the ensuing silence would embarrass them into going away.

On this particular evening, Zander decided that a walk was the lesser of the two evils, so he called on Hubert to see if he fancied coming with him. Hubert who was in a similar frame of mind agreed to go.

Earlier in the day on their way to one of the construction sites, they had noticed a place not too far away in the souk area, that looked interesting. It was called the Rue D' Echelles (Road of the Ladder), which as its name suggests, is a steep, narrow alleyway with overhanging houses, running from the top of the town all the way down to the river.

Ten minutes later Zander and Hubert were part of a mass of people of all ages, principally male, many soldiers in uniform, passing up and down this narrow street. Some of the houses had a red light over the door, the old French sign, telling the world that it was a house of ill repute. Many of the soldiers were milling around the metal grilles on the ground floor windows of these houses, where a free peepshow of its merchandise is on display to anyone wanting to look before they bought.

It was directly outside one of these places that Zander noticed a youth in front of him, behaving strangely. The youngster appeared to be dancing with him; when Zander moved left or right, his face-to-face partner was still there, standing in his way.

Zander's hand instinctively clutched at his back pocket where he kept his cash. The pocket was empty! Spinning round quickly, he saw that the crowd had opened up immediately behind him. Between him and the space three youths were looking directly at him, their eyes wide open in surprise. Zander glancing down saw that his instincts had not failed him as there, lying on the ground, were three of the four banknotes he knew, had been in his pocket.

Someone had picked his pocket!

What followed happened in a flash; two of the youths fled down the steep alleyway, jostling and barging their way through the crowd of pedestrians. The third stood his ground, but Zander noticed that he was standing awkwardly.

Knowing that he had to act now or not at all, Zander bent down to pick up his money and as he did so, he lunged head first into the youth's midriff, knocking him flat on his back. Where the youngster's foot had been, was the missing fourth banknote. The crowd parted, the youth got up and ran, and in a flash, the crowd had swallowed him up. Hubert, still unaware that anything untoward had happened was blithely wandering on, but when the youth rushed past him 'Pell Mell', he came back to Zander to see what was going on. The events of the past few moments had shaken Zander, who whispered tremulously,

"I've just had my pocket picked."

Hubert looking around saw that everyone was going about their business as usual and that everything looked quite normal. There were no signs that anything had happened, so in an enquiring tone, said,

"Are you sure?"

"Yes," the indignant Zander replied, "some youngsters tried to steal my money."

"But it's still there in your hand," the unimpressed Hubert said.

Exasperated by his companion's lack of either sympathy or belief, Zander gave up on the discussion. Hubert, still determined to have the last word, underlined his disbelief by stating emphatically,

"They don't do that sort of thing here. If they're caught, they get a hand cut off."

Zander thought, *oh ye of little faith*.

Nevertheless, even he, who had been so intimately involved, wondered *with it all over so quickly, had it really happened*.

42

Japanese Breakfast   Paris

As time went by, a chilling wind of doubt drifted into Zander's mind when he thought about the irregularity with which his salary cheques arrived. On top of this, there was always a significant item in his salary statement quoted as 'Commission to the Hon. Somebody-or-other'. In time, when Zander discovered what this item was, he would think of him as the Hon. Mr So-and-bloody-So.

True, he had built up a healthy pot of Algerian dinars in his bank in Constantine, because 60% of his salary went directly into an account there, accordingly while he was out there, he had plenty of money in his pocket. What he needed now though was to find a way to transfer more of his money out of Algeria to somewhere accessible. Unfortunately, for him, under Algeria's strict currency control regulations, his Algerian bank would only transfer 20% of his salary, in sterling, to the UK, and even then, only by direct instruction from the Government.

When he sought advice from his UK bank, the smiley, smug faced manager told him that UK banks will have nothing to do with dinars and that he knew of no bank in the world that did.

Zander now knew that if he was to get any money out of Algeria and into the UK, he would somehow have to exchange the Algerian dinars for some other negotiable currency, but how or where could he do this? With customs controls being what they were, it was impossible to get anything readily convertible, like gold, out of the country. Even the cabin staff on Air Algerie flights did not accept Algerian dinars for in-flight goods and services!

When he approached Patrick Rauser with his problem he was assured that, towards the end of his contract, when he had all of his money ready to exchange, all he had to do was take a trip down to the gas fields on the Northern edge of the Sahara desert. There a big International Contractor, who needed dinars to pay the wages of its large number of local workers and staff, would change it for him.

Zander, a stranger in a foreign land and a trusting soul, took this assurance at face value. Perhaps he should have found out a bit more about this system.

*

Eleven months into his contract, Zander was sitting at home; enjoying his morning coffee and reading about what was happening in the big world. Only half listening to the television news and mentally discarding most of it, one item made his ears prick up.

"The people of Algeria went to the polls today to elect a new leader."

Zander's brain immediately switched from unfocussed listening and avid reading, to intense listening and not reading at all. He lowered his paper to look at the television screen where a talking head said,

"A report from our North African correspondent will provide more details later in this newscast."

Zander sat watching the television through a series of mindless reports and vacuous news items that underlined the lack of news to report on that day, and was probably the reason why the item about Algeria appeared at all.

When the announcer eventually got to the promised report, it was hardly worth waiting for; the only additional information Zander got was the name of the new President.

He then began to wonder if this new regime would have any effect on his job. Not much, he supposed; he had a cast iron contract with the Wilaya. Patrick had told him that the Wali had held the post for years and would stay on well into the predictable future, so Zander should be all right. Next week, when he went out there, he would find out more.

As usual, he would meet Hubert in one of the Orly airport hotels. On this particular occasion though, he could not get a room in any of them, so he booked himself into one of the larger hotels in the centre of Paris and arranged to meet Hubert later, at the airport.

On the morning of departure, Zander went down to the restaurant early to have a leisurely breakfast, before he took the shuttle bus to the airport. Outside the dining room, he found the queue had already spilled out into the hotel lobby. The queue, composed entirely of elderly Japanese tourists, was not moving.

When he joined the end of the queue, each successive group in front of him ushered him forward, everyone chattering, giving him a little bow and gently nudging him on until he found himself right at the front. *Very polite these Japanese,* he thought.

It soon became obvious why he had received such preferential treatment. The pre-packed breakfast trays were stacked up on a framework of shelving and the guests who had breakfasted earlier had taken all the trays from the lower shelves. The remaining full trays were on the higher ones and none of the Japanese was tall enough to reach them.

At such an unearthly hour of the morning, there was no member of staff anywhere in sight. *Does this only happen in Paris? What was he to do?*

Although not particularly tall Zander was certainly taller than the Japanese guests were, consequently he could reach the upper trays, which he started to dish out to them. With each tray he handed out he was rewarded with a broad smile and polite bow; a gesture he felt duty bound to return.

When there was no one left to serve, Zander took down a breakfast tray for himself, sat down at a table and started eating. He would have finished a lot quicker had each of his beneficiaries, their meal over, not stopped at his table to thank him again. With every polite bow he got, Zander felt obliged to get to his feet to respond in kind. With his breakfast finished and on his way back to his room, he found his way barred by a throng of Japanese travellers, *what now?*

One tiny, smiling Japanese woman took him by the hand, led him over to the group now lining up for a photograph, placed him in the middle of the front row and presented him with a large bottle of champagne. Then for the group photograph, everyone except Zander said the 'Japanese equivalent of Cheese! Cheese! Cheese! (An apology to W.S.Gilbert)

The tour interpreter then told him that the group had kept their bus waiting to allow them to show him their gratitude. The interpreter then took a souvenir picture of Zander on his own, which he would give to each of his passengers at the end of the tour. Once again, Zander ran the gauntlet of handshakes and bows before he was free to head for the airport.

Later, when Zander told his story to Hubert it had become a saga about how he had single-handedly fed an enormous group of starving Japanese, probably some large trade delegation or other important diplomatic group. And, from the way he told the story, he alone had been instrumental in improving Japanese/French/British relations.

An unconvinced Hubert, with a Gallic shrug, just said, "Et alors?"

43

It Had To End Sometime   Constantine

Little did either Zander or Hubert know when they got off the plane at Constantine, that a new Wali was already in post and that the resulting re-arrangement of local government staff had changed their future operations in the country of Algeria.

The first intimation they had of any problem was at the Arrivals area. *Strange, there is no one here to meet us.* It was also strange how airport officials – who normally stood back, smiled and saluted when, as VIP guests, they waltzed through the formalities – had forgotten all about this courtesy.

Just as they had feared, and with no 'presents' in their luggage to ease their way through, these same officials subjected them to the autocratic treatment meted out to ordinary travellers.

Consequently, it was almost dark before they were free to enter the country and then, had to fight their way into one of the last remaining taxis to get to their hotel.

At the hotel the receptionist recognising Zander, took a letter out of a pigeonhole and gave it to him. He opened it. It was from his friend Robert. It did not say much, but intimated that all of their former contacts in Government had moved on to other jobs and that when he reported to the Wali's office tomorrow, he should ask for General Le Minestral of the Department for the Interior.

Next day, with Constantine bathed in the bright sunlight of a summer morning, Zander and Hubert left their hotel for the short walk along the familiar tree-lined avenue to the Wali's office. At the front desk, Hubert, as instructed, asked to see General Le Minestral. Following a telephone call, they were escorted upstairs and shown into a large ornately furnished office. As soon as they got through the door, a small bustling man with a large waxed moustache, dressed in a freshly pressed uniform, at least one size too big for him, rose from behind an enormous desk and said,

"Ca va, Monsieur Duff!"

The uniform had changed but the medal ribbons and paratrooper's badge were just the same. It was his former assistant surveyor and friend, Robert!

Zander suffered the usual French air-kissing embrace – which he always found embarrassing – then watched Robert pull a bottle of whisky and three glasses from the bottom drawer of a filing cabinet, pour out drinks and signal for his visitors to sit down.

Robert pressed a button on his desk whereupon a young lady came in, smiled and told Hubert that she was an interpreter and would interpret from Arabic to French; Hubert would then translate from French to English and vice versa.

Thus through the interpreters, Robert got down to business.

He informed them that in about an hour's time, Zander would meet the new Wali and it was Robert's impression that the contract with Zander's employer was about to be terminated. Robert hoped that Monsieur Duff would not take offence by his telling him this, but he thought that he would want to know about the situation as soon as possible. Again, through the interpreters, Robert explained that whenever a new Wali came to power, he brought his own people with him (sisters, cousins and aunts and their male equivalents). Clearly since Zander's last visit, it had been 'all change'. Zander would not know or be known to anyone now holding a senior post in the Offices of the Wilaya. Although a few of Zander's former associates were still working there, they were no longer in positions of power, influencers or decision-makers. Robert had been lucky. As the new Wali's former comrade in arms, he got promotion.

"What happened to the former Wali?" Zander asked. "I thought he had no political opposition?"

Robert's answer, delivered through the two interpreters, was,

"Unfortunately for him, his department lost some highly sensitive, top-secret documents!

Hubert looked at Zander and Zander looked at Hubert, but not a word passed their lips.

*

At the formal meeting more than an hour later, Zander did not even get to meet the new Wali. Instead, a thin, serious-faced minor official took them into a tiny, barely furnished room, and without preamble said,

"His Excellency the Wali of Constantine regrets he is not available to meet his most esteemed guests this morning, but a pressing matter has come up that requires his personal attention. However, he has asked me to express his gratitude to you for all the valuable advice and assistance that your organisation has given, not only to Constantine but to Algeria."

He handed Zander a letter and went on,

"His Excellency also told me to give you this formal notification of the cessation of your contract; consequently, as of now, that contract is terminated."

The Wali's aide stepped past the Wali's former employees and holding the office door wide open for them, cocked his head, swept an outstretched arm towards it – a clear indication that the interview was over – and that they should now be on their way.

Then added as they went through the door,

"There's a car waiting at the front door to take you to your hotel and from there on to the airport. Seats have been booked for you on the mid-afternoon flight to Paris. Good day gentlemen."

Pointedly perhaps, there was no, "Au revoir."

In the taxi back to the hotel, Zander ripped open the letter and began to read. Skimming over the first few paragraphs, his eyes focussed on one that read,

With regard to outstanding fees, 40% in dollars will go into the company's bank account in London. The remaining 60% in dinars will go into the company's account in Constantine.

Zander thought, *60% will remain in Algeria and with no staff left here, who is going to spend it?*

Much more importantly, now that he had been given the 'bums' rush', who was going to pay him and how was *he* going to get *his* dinars exchanged or transferred into another currency?

It was only now that the full impact of Hubert's disposal of the top-secret paper struck home. Not only, had it cost the old Wali his job, but Zander's had gone with it and now he had no time to get his money out of the country.

*

When Zander finally received what should have been his golden handshake letter, an item in it, highlighted with an asterisk, 'reduced final severance' caught his eye.

*This variation is applied because your lack of language skills left you unable to fulfil your duties, as described in your contract. Consequently, to recompense the Company for the additional salary and expenses involved in providing you with an interpreter, the amount shown has been deducted.

S***, he thought, *Burning that bloody letter was Hubert's idea, not mine, but I am the one who has to suffer.*

44

Honours List   Constantine

Just over a year later, an invitation to re-visit Algeria dropped through Zander's letterbox. What he did not know was that, his former boss the Principal Vice-President had originally been its recipient. For the past two weeks it been passed like a relay baton, along a team of buck-passers until eventually it was routed through the British Foreign Office, to him. Inside the gold trimmed envelope was an official invitation to attend a grand celebration to mark the opening of the Boulevard de l'Est in Constantine, one of the City bypasses that Zander was involved in before his contract had so unceremoniously ended.

The Principal Vice-President and his Head Office underlings, knowing the true nature of the invitation, wanted nothing to do with a client who had dispensed with their services so abruptly.

In the Principal Vice-President's reply, he had offered his 'sincere personal regrets' to the Algerian Government and intimated that, as he and all of his other Vice- Presidents were committed to a meeting in the U.S.A on that particular date, they were therefore unfortunately unavailable. However, he was delighted to delegate Mr Duff, his former representative in Constantine, to attend in his place. That was how, unexpectedly and without knowing how it had come about, Zander went back to Algeria!

His arrival at the Airport was just like the good old days. An official met him and whisked him through the formalities, and even better, a big flashy limousine sped him along new modern roads to his hotel. There, a note from Robert told him that he would pick him up at 11am the next day.

*

Zander slept late that day in a beautifully decorated room and with the press of a bell, room service brought him a superb breakfast. He showered and shaved in a luxuriously appointed en suite bathroom and at 10.55am went downstairs to find Robert sitting waiting for him.

Things have certainly improved since my last visit to the Cirta Hotel. Moreover, wonder of wonders, Robert now spoke excellent English.

Their reunion was a meeting of old friends, with the usual embracing and air kissing. Robert took him outside where an official limousine, complete with liveried driver, was waiting to convey them to the grand opening ceremony.

Joining the throng of guests, Zander could not help but be impressed by the changes that had taken place since his last visit. Stretching into the distance, occasionally crossed by a slender bridge, was a brand new modern dual carriageway and on either side of it stood modern buildings and other architecturally designed structures.

A large crowd had already gathered around a raised platform and on it, the dignitaries were just taking their seats. Taking pride of place in the centre of the unoccupied front row was a large ornate chair. In front of which, just below the platform, a green and white ribbon stretched across the new road and to one side a military band was playing background music. This was where the opening ceremony would take place. Robert took Zander over to join a handful of people gathered near the podium from where the President would perform the ceremony.

Earlier Robert had told Zander that a German contractor had eventually completed his work. Apparently, the Germans had seamlessly slotted into the gap left by Zander's former employers. An uncharitable thought crossed Zander's mind; '*Had that all been arranged before or after Algeria's change of Government?*'

This train of thought was broken when, part way through a piece of soft music, the band broke into a rousing march, announcing the arrival of the President and his principal guests, who filed on to the platform and took their seats.

To rapturous applause, the president rose to his feet and made a speech; at the end of which, he nodded to a uniformed man holding a large pair of scissors, standing beside a green and white ribbon stretched across the new road. At this signal, the man bowed respectfully and with a flourish, cut the ribbon. The cheering reached a new crescendo, and when it did eventually die down, the people around Zander began to form a line.

An elderly official came over and gently nudged Zander towards the bottom of the platform steps. Above him, he could see the President whose full dress uniform, just like Robert's, was almost lost under a heavily ornamented green sash and a chest full of medals. His senior staff seated alongside him, were also sporting heavily bejewelled green and white sashes – the national colours of Algeria.

Zander, who was first in line and with still no idea of what was going on, felt a gentle tap on his shoulder and on looking round saw the elderly official was indicating that he should now climb the steps.

Arriving at platform level, the President beckoned him to come forward to stand in front of him. When a President says come, it is only common courtesy to do so. The smiling President shook his hand then turned to one of the officials, who took a gigantic medallion on a green and white sash out of a plush velvet case and passed it to him. The President put the sash over Zander's head, kissed him on both cheeks, still smiling as he did so, and unobtrusively indicated that Zander should now go back to his place. By this time, number two in line was already on his way to receive his decoration, a scenario that continued until everyone in that line had received their award. Now everyone rose and stood in silence while the military band played what Zander took to be the Algerian National Anthem, the final note of which was met with thunderous applause. The principal guests then left to attend the Grand Opening celebratory dinner.

At dinner, Zander was seated beside Robert, who told him that his decoration made him a member of a very special order. Usually it is only presented to lower levels of foreign royalty, foreign captains of industry or middle order members of overseas governments who had provided some special service to Algeria.

When Zander heard this, he immediately thought of the fine impression he would make at future formal occasions back home. *When I wear this green and white sash with its big gold medallion, across the shoulder of my dinner jacket, people will see just how important I am. Hmmm, it might look even better with my dress kilt outfit.*

Robert then blew away Zander's dream of grandeur by telling him that as only twenty of that particular decoration existed, they were used and used again and he would have to hand it back at the end of the day, which was in about three hours' time. In its place, Zander would get a beautiful illuminated Arabic scroll showing him to be a member of that august Algerian Order.

Later, still sitting beside Robert, his decoration in place and feeling the 'bee's knees', the man sitting on the side away from Robert, leant towards him and whispered in perfectly modulated English,

"I hear you have some Algerian Dinars that I may be able help you with."

Thinking that although this surreptitious approach could be just what he was looking for, without turning his head, he hedged.

"I might be interested. What rate of exchange can you get me?" Knowing that anything above 40% of the official rate is a good deal.

"I can't make any firm promises but I'm processing a large package of cash for a company working on the Northern Sahara gas fields and I believe I can get you somewhere between 30% and 50%."

Zander turned to look at the man who could well be his saviour, then, trying not to appear too keen, took his time before answering,

"That might be interesting."

His potential patron pressed on.

"If you can make up your mind now," he said, taking an official-looking document from his pocket, "I've taken the liberty of preparing release papers for your bank's local account and if you transfer the funds to me, your converted currency will be in your UK bank account within ten working days. All you have to do is sign this paper and Robert can act as a witness."

Zander's mind was racing. Here was an opportunity to get the cash that he had almost given up hope of ever seeing again. Taking the document from his 'benefactor', he passed it to Robert.

"What do you think of this?" Zander enquired, eyebrows raised,

"Standard form of transfer," responded Robert nodding his head vigorously.

Zander looked at him closely, his eyes flitting towards his possible saviour, "Do you know this man?"

More emphatic nodding came from Robert. "Sure, he's my sister's husband's cousin's son, who is in the currency transfer business. I asked him to come along tonight to see if he could help you."

Zander, somewhat humbled by this considerate act, thanked Robert with enthusiasm he did not quite feel. He then signed over all his Algerian assets to Robert's relative, received a duplicate copy in return, and a handshake sealed the deal.

After dinner, as everyone was preparing to leave, a uniformed official approached Zander and relieved him of his green and white sash. In return, he was given a beautiful gold worked silken tube, containing his illuminated scroll.

All very nice, but I would rather have the sash and medallion, thought Zander.

In company with Robert and his young relative, Zander stepped out into the brightly lit street where he and Robert got into the official car and Robert's distant relative, waved them off until they were out of sight.

On the way to the airport, the car stopped at Zander's hotel to collect his travel-bag. When they got to the airport, Robert escorted him through the formalities and into the Departure lounge, where he said his kissy-kissy goodbyes.

Zander attempted to find the French words to express his gratitude, failed miserably and ended up by just saying, "Au Revoir, mon ami."

*

Ten days after he got home, Zander checked his bank account, anticipating that it would show a significant increase in the balance, but nothing had happened. After a further three weeks, a letter arrived with Algerian stamps on it and on the back was the name of the sender, Robert Le Minestral.

Anxiously, Zander slit open the envelope; inside was a single page with a few typewritten lines in English;

I am sorry to be the bearer of bad news, but my sister's husband's cousin's son was arrested for the embezzlement of government funds. All his assets and papers were confiscated and are now in forfeit to the Government. Unfortunately, your signed currency release form was part of that Government seizure.

At the bottom was Robert's signature

Zander numbed, flopped down in his chair. With that one little note, his dream of affluence had gone up in smoke. Certainly, someone had benefitted from his Algerian nest egg, but not him. Then as he mulled over the enormity of what had happened, he could not help but think,

Although Algeria was now in a much better state than I remembered, my precious pension fund, which I had always hoped to recover someday, had evaporated without trace. Despite these years of working hard in difficult conditions and flying back and forth, the state of my finances has not changed one jot. I wonder if the Hon So and Bloody So will be as quick to take over a percentage of my losses.

EAST COAST DAYS

The Birds

45

For Want of a Nail   Granton

No wealthier now than he had been before he left for Algeria, Zander was back in the ranks of the idle retired. On the other hand, he had learned an expensive lesson; so overseas' postings no longer featured in his plans for the future. Moreover, this time he really meant it. After what had been a taxing period, he was finished with all that palaver of commuting between Edinburgh, London, Paris and Constantine and all he wanted to do now was slip back into his former reasonably comfortable lifestyle. Nevertheless, one essential part of that was missing; he had no boat. Although he looked at a number of possible candidates to replace his old Emerald, none had come up to his expectations. The asking price was always excessively high for what was on offer. Invariably Zander's values, never matched the expectations of others.

*

One day at the yacht club, Zander and Gilbert were tucking into a fry-up lunch – which they occasionally treated themselves to, provided their wives were not there – when the Club Commodore strode in dressed in a dark suit, black tie and armband. As there was no one else in the restaurant, he felt duty bound to join them.

"I see you've got your mourning gear on?" observed Zander, between mouthfuls of chips.

"Yes, old Dougie was cremated this morning. I went along to the service," the Commodore replied, his voice solemn and respectful.

All three then sat silently reflecting that one of the Club's characters, a free spirit and a marine engineer with an unrivalled knowledge of small boats, had passed on. He had been due to retire at the end of the month. Dougie was the man who was always available to help anyone whose boat had developed a problem. Sometimes he would even get his sleeves rolled up to help fix it. It was so unfair. His death would be a great loss to the Club and its members.

It was common knowledge that over the last few years Dougie had spent countless hours building himself a new boat. Only a month ago, he had announced that he had almost finished fitting her out and, had done so with the best equipment that money could buy. Soon he would retire and be off to realise his dream – to sail her round the world.

Sadly, Dougie did not get to live long enough to enjoy either his retirement or his boat. A few days ago, while cycling home from working on his boat he had stopped on a park bench for a wee rest, and passed away.

A local Samaritan who lived opposite the park, used to seeing Dougie sitting resting for a few minutes before moving on, became concerned when she noticed that he had not moved for about half hour. Thinking that he may have fallen asleep, the Samaritan went to see if he was all right, shook him gently and all Dougie did was topple over sideways. He was stone cold dead.

The Commodore continued with his tale.

"By all reports, Dougie had almost finished fitting out his boat. All that effort wasted, all that wonderful skill lost. Sad. Very sad. Very, very sad.

Zander and Gilbert, looking down solemnly into what remained of their fry up, had adopted a posture they thought fitted the situation and conveyed respect.

While the Commodore was speaking, Zander's mind had been racing ahead at breakneck speed. All he had heard was the voice of his own 'god of greed' telling him that; *here was a situation he could exploit to his own advantage.*

After what he considered a respectable pause, Zander slipped into attack mode and enquired 'innocently',

"Which boat is Dougie's, Commodore?"

With genuine innocence, the Commodore showed them.

"There she is," he said pointing, "The green trimmed job, out in the middle there."

Zander's heart leapt and he let out an involuntarily gasp.

"By Jove, she is a fine looking vessel."

With that, conversation dried up for a while as Zander, his glazed eyes fixed on the boat, enacted his dream.

The Commodore brought Zander back to earth by asking if either he or Gilbert knew anything about Dougie. Apparently, the Commodore was having difficulty in contacting the next of kin.

Ignoring the Commodore's enquiry, Zander slipped his brain into overdrive. Recently he had seen Dougie talking to the local bank manager and in passing, had heard the banker say something about an outstanding loan. Unfortunately, that was all he heard. *Is it possible there is a loan on the boat?*

Bit by bit, Jane's brother had paid back the loan that she – without asking her husband – had given him, so Zander did have some ready cash. With this knowledge, his supercharger kicked in. *If the repayments on Dougie's loan had fallen behind and the loan was for his boat, then the bank would have repossession rights. If that is the case then I might get this beautiful boat at a good price. Yes, there are distinct possibilities here!*

Vaguely cutting into his mental deliberations, Zander heard the Commodore expanding on his subject.

"You know, Dougie's been getting his pride and joy ready for some time now. It is only a couple of weeks since he put her into the water and from what I've heard; he has spared neither time nor money in fitting her out. If he's built her to go round the world, you can bet your bottom dollar everything about her will be in ship shape and Bristol fashion."

Zander nodding absent-mindedly had come to that same conclusion ages ago, but the most important thing now was to see if he could pull off a deal to make that superb vessel his own. If that happened, he might be sailing again sooner than he had thought.

As he gobbled down the rest of his lunch, he considered his next move.

Had Dougie's boat been repossessed? Will the money I have stowed away from the sale of the old Emerald, be enough to buy her? If I am going to get anywhere with my plan, I have to steal a march on anyone else interested in buying her. I'll go and see the bank manager now, and if things are as I think they are, I'll put in an expression of interest before anyone else has the time to think about it.

Zander knew that the man he saw talking to Dougie was the branch manager of the bank just along the road in Newhaven, so, with neither a word nor a sign to anyone present, he went off to see him, leaving Gilbert to finish his lunch alone.

Within twenty minutes of getting his brainwave, Zander was outside the bank. To say he had rushed there would be a relative term – remembering his build and his general lack of fitness – but he had moved with uncommon haste so that by the time he got there he was sweating like the proverbial pig. Striding in through the bank's front door and walking purposefully over to the counter, he asked to see the manager.

The minute Zander entered the manager's office he got straight down to business. On the way to the bank his racing mind – not body – had reasoned that a stealthy, measured approach was the best way to plant this own ideas into the manager's head. So he began with a diversion,

"I would like a loan to buy a new boat"

On the other side of the desk, the manager who recognised Zander as one of the local 'boat people' and rightly assumed that his unexpected caller was up to something and soon, he would find out what. Consequently, Zander's transparent ploy was already dead in the water. The manager knew that the late Dougie was way behind with his payments, and that he too might be in a difficult position, so he played Zander along,

"Have you got one in mind?"

Zander deciding to tackle this question head on with a white lie, replied in the negative. The bank manager knew that the money recovered from repossession of Dougie's boat – in its current unfinished state – was insufficient to pay off the loan. However, he also knew that if he played his cards right, the man sitting in front of him might just give him the opportunity to manage a deal to the bank's advantage.

Why not?

Consequently, with that in mind, he told Zander that, if he was in the market for a boat, this might just be his lucky day. A boat was about to be repossessed and would be auctioned off in the near future. The reserve price had still to be determined but it would probably be set at a reasonable level. Was Zander interested?

Zander, with the object of his desire plonked in his lap, could hardly believe his ears! Blurted out "Yes."

The manager getting up from his chair said, "Excuse me for a minute."

Leaving the room, he asked one of his assistants to calculate the settlement figure for the boat, write it down on a piece of paper and bring it to him as soon as he could.

It was only last week, while chasing Dougie to pay off the loan, that the manager had been on the boat, and for his own records, had written a brief report on its state of completion. It followed therefore that he had a good idea of its general condition and although he knew that there was much still to be done in one particular area, all he needed was the precise outstanding balance figure to complete his assessment.

The manager engaged Zander in small talk until his assistant came in and handed him a folded piece of paper.

"Would you like a coffee?" the manager offered, but Zander, with no time for such trivia, promptly declined.

"One cup only then, please," the manager told his assistant, who then left the room.

Making a rough mental calculation, heavily weighted in the bank's favour, the manager quoted Zander a price that the 'bank might be prepared to accept'.

The prospective buyer could hardly believe his ears! As an avid reader of the 'Boats for sale' section of the yachting magazines, he had a good idea of the current price for a boat of that type. So, pausing for what he thought was a suitable time before answering, Zander indicated that he might be interested and asked for access to the boat to inspect it. The manager opened his desk drawer, took out details of the boat and a bunch of keys and passed them over to Zander.

Zander struggling to keep a straight face until he was outside the bank, then leering like a pantomime villain he scuttled along the road back to the harbour, moving even faster now than he had done on the way out. In his mind's eye, he imagined 'his' new boat at anchor, fully rigged and sitting on a mirror-like sea – and provided you ignored the background of the gasworks, a scrap metal yard and other decrepit buildings, she was the epitome of a chocolate box image.

Going on board for the first time, Zander's heart leapt; she looked so beautiful! Her 'bright works', her snappy rigging and the other bits of kit neatly stowed on, or built into her deck, were all gleaming and pristine.

On venturing below, his new love revealed to him, her beautifully furnished cabins with a lot of ingeniously built in locker space. Her sails were brand new and in her cockpit was an unimaginable array of the finest of gadgets, befitting a potential round-the-world yacht.

He deliberated for a moment; should he get a full marine survey done before committing himself, or at least have the hull checked? No, it was obvious that this was all new kit and in taking account of the skills of her late owner, Zander reckoned that the price the bank manager had quoted was too good a bargain to miss.

Almost before the bank manager had finished his coffee Zander was back sitting in front of him and this time he lost no time in stating his business.

"That price you quoted for the boat, it may be that I don't need a loan." The manager raised his eyebrows in mock surprise and when Zander played his 'I have cash available immediately if the price could be negotiated' gambit, they jerked up even higher.

Over his cup of coffee, the manager had used the time to 'get his act together',

"Sorry, but that's the price and I have to tell you that in the short time you have been away, I've had another prospective buyer on the phone. That said, you made the first enquiry and if you meet the price quoted I am prepared to close the deal now. However, the sale must be concluded on an 'as seen' basis".

With an impetuous rush of blood to the head that may have clouded his reasoning, Zander, rather than miss a bargain, made a knee jerk decision by agreeing to both the price and the conditions. The long and short of it was that the deal was done there and then

The formalities took a further week to complete, during which time Zander spent his daylight hours in the clubroom looking longingly at his new boat, sitting there proudly on her mooring.

*

During the waiting period, Zander invited the Emeraldeers and all of his other friends – he does have other friends – to come to The Boat Club to see his acquisition.

With his world once more complete, Zander was now eagerly looking forward to taking possession of his beautiful vessel and making an early return to the sea. This time it would be at a level of comfort and technical excellence that he had never even dreamt about, let alone experienced.

46

A Kingdom is Lost   Leith

As soon as he got the keys from the bank, the boat's new owner rushed along to the harbour to find Gilbert waiting for him. Together, they launched the dingy, rowed out at what seemed like a hundred strokes per minute and clambered aboard.

Zander, standing proudly on *his* deck, master and commander of this fine vessel noticed that a few of the club's regulars were watching him from the panoramic window of the clubroom lounge. *Boy did he feel good*! So good, in fact that he favoured them with what he believed to be a regal wave, which to them though, looked more like someone drying lettuce, without the lettuce.

Zander was in raptures with his new boat's form and fittings, everything above the waterline was a joy to behold; going below he was overcome with emotion at the sight of the array of lovely gleaming gadgets with switches to twitch, screens and dials to look at and knobs to twiddle. *But, what were they all for and how did they work?* The fish finder, the satellite navigation kit and the sonar depth gauge were easy to identify but the function of some of the others was not quite so obvious. Just what did all this gadgetry do and how much information did he have at his fingertips? *Wow!*

Have I or have I not got a bargain? I am now the owner of the finest vessel in the Yacht Club's fleet.

Rubbing his hands together with miser-like appreciation, Zander took stock of his nautical asset. From what he could see, everything was in shipshape order, so all he had to do now was find the instruction books and fitting manuals to understand what all this gadgetry was about and how it worked. On thinking back to their first quick look around the boat, neither he nor Gilbert could remember seeing anything that looked anything like an instruction book, but then, they had not been looking for that sort of thing.

All will be revealed when I find the manuals, thought Zander; *they have got to be here somewhere, probably in a locker or chart table or safely stowed away somewhere.*

With increasing anxiety, he and Gilbert rummaged around, but they did not find any makers' instruction books or fitting manuals, certainly not in the places they would expect them to be.

Another longer, more thorough search into every nook and cranny and they were still no further forward.

So where could they be? Wherever they were, they were certainly not on board the boat!

During their search, they discovered that the interior lights did not work and it soon became clear that the electrical installation was not finished.

There and then, they decided, to look more thoroughly behind panels and bulkheads just to see the full extent of this problem. To their horror, this exercise only exposed tangles of unidentified cabling with loose ends sticking out from everywhere.

Anxiety brought an empty feeling to the pit of Zander's stomach and his mouth dried up. *Horror of horrors, none of these fancy gadgets arrayed around him and that looked ready to use, had not been wired up?*

As his worry-devils broke loose, Zander's hairline scrunched down towards his eyebrows and his bottom lip quivered; he was in the grip of the panic-stricken realisation that it was now imperative that he find these vital documents.

Slowly panic turned into dismay as Zander began to think the unthinkable. *I may have to do a complete rehash of the electrics, not to mention the near impossible task of finalising the installation of the gadgets, without fitting manuals.*

If he did not find these documents, the additional demands on his time – not to mention the extra expenditure involved – just did not bear thinking about.

Trying to think his way out of this dilemma, Zander's mind locked onto the hope that someone in the club would know where Dougie kept his work manuals.

With Zander leading, the two friends climbed into the dinghy and the instant the last buttock touched the thwarts, they took off for the shore. In transit, they set new standards for stroke rate and speed of movement.

Scrambling ashore, and barging into the clubrooms they put the crucial question to some of the regulars, who had pretended not to have noticed their frantic antics, but were all agog to know just what had brought about the speedy exit from his new vessel.

Among them, the club's ferryman and club gossip was obviously the first person to ask.

Yes, he knew where they were. Dougie kept his manuals at home. They were all in a black leather brief case with a crown on it.

Encouraged by this news, relief spread through Zander's being and with it, a distant chink of light appeared at the end of his long dark tunnel of despair.

Did the ferryman know where Dougie had lived? Yes, he did and he gave Zander the address. Zander's distant chink of light came right up to him and opened out into a blaze of brilliant light. Nevertheless, if he was to retrieve these valuable documents from the late Dougie's home, he had no time to lose.

After asking a pedestrian or two for directions, they found Dougie's house. It looked deserted. Nothing daunted Zander rang the doorbell. Nobody answered. He rang and rang and rang it again, still no response. The longer he rang, the fainter his glimmer of hope became. Eventually Zander's determined assault on the doorbell brought the man next-door out to see what was going on. He told Zander that house was empty so there was no point in ringing the bell. The owner had died more than a week ago and the sheriff's officers were at the house the day before yesterday to dispose of his things; the last of which was cleared out yesterday. This starkly delivered information snuffed out Zander's little spark of hope and sent it right back into the tunnel of dark despair.

47

Bonfire Night   Leith

With increasing disquiet, Zander wondered what he should do now. It came down to a single choice; he had to telephone the Sheriff's Office to see if he knew where Dougie's stuff had gone.

When he did phone, it transpired that the man he spoke to had been the officer in charge of the house clearance.

"Did you see a black briefcase with a crown on it?" Zander asked, his heartbeat pounding in his ears, as he waited for the reply.

"Yes, I did see a briefcase like that," the officer confirmed, "but it only had books and old papers in it, nothing of any value. I just left it to go out with the rubbish. If it's anything important, you could try asking the contractor who took it all away. I'll give you their contact details." After a few moments, he was back on the line and gave Zander a name and an address. "It's a scrap yard stuck away behind buildings in the middle of an industrial estate. You'll know you're getting near it, when you see the smoke of their bonfire. Good luck!"

After a short walk, Zander and Gilbert saw a column of smoke rising above a group of buildings. Quickening their pace, they homed in on the address they hoped would mark an end to their search.

A large metal storage container stood just inside the yard gates with a lopsided ENQUIRIES sign fixed to its door. Zander knocked and went in. A large man in overalls with greasy hair and dirty fingernails, sitting behind what was left of an old office desk, looked up inquiringly. Zander's eyes had immediately locked onto a bulging black brief case with a crown on it lying on top of the desk and with a sharp intake of breath he thought, *is that the one? It had to be.*

Zander's nervous spluttering enquiry about Dougie's house rubbish received an affirmative response. Yes, the contractor had cleared that house and yes, that briefcase had come from there.

Oh joy, oh rapture, please let it be stuffed full of the manuals, was the desperate thought galloping through Zander's brain. He stretched out and grabbed it, tipping its contents onto the desk. His jaw dropping in disbelief and he stepped back; all that had fallen out was some well thumbed holiday brochures and a squashed sandwich wrapped in wrinkled cellophane.

"What the hell do you think you're doing?" The man behind the desk demanded. Zander, ignored the question and holding out the briefcase, posed his own question,

"Was there anything else in here?"

The indignant answer was,

"Yes, and it's all over there," pointing through the door at the bonfire.

Without as much as a thank you, Zander rushed over to the bonfire, but when he got to it any fading hope he may have nurtured, died. What little remained of any paper, was now well and truly carbonised. Zander's world collapsed from under him; he had come so close but he had failed.

Close to tears, Zander trudged back to Gilbert, knowing that he now faced an unknown amount of work and an indeterminate drain on his finances. Regrettably, as the sale had been '*as seen*' he could claim nothing back from the bank.

Although Zander's enthusiasm was temporarily dampened, his inbred optimism soon came back and in time, he grudgingly accepted that the bank manager had put one over on him. At least he still had a great looking boat, appropriately named 'Free Spirit'. It was not the end of the world and when she was ready to put to sea, he would have her renamed Emerald; so as far as he was concerned, she would still be the best boat in the world.

By necessity, he postponed the pleasure of sailing her; the sooner he got on with sorting out her problems, the sooner that would happen. Right now, his pressing need was to put a plan of action in place.

The most important item on his agenda was to contact the makers of the various gadgets and get copies of their manuals. This in itself was easy, but before he could place any orders, he would have to creep and crawl around inside nooks and crannies to find makers' names and model numbers. Whether it would be better to try to unravel the wiring and try to make sense of it or strip everything out and start again, was a decision he still had to make.

In the meantime, before Zander and Gilbert got on with what they could do themselves, they ran a further check on the boat, just to make sure there were no further snags. Zander would then hire a professional to do the jobs that he and Gilbert could not do themselves. Eventually Zander got a man in to sort the electrics out which cost him an arm and a leg.

But, knowing that when Grunt and Murdo were back in the fold, it would not be long before he would embark on fresh adventures in his new 'Emerald', Zander paid up.

48

Gilbert Takes the Plunge   Granton

Grunt and Murdo had gone home. Emerald, moored on a pontoon inside Granton Harbour, was almost ready to go to sea. The pontoon was made of a number of heavy timber units bolted together and linked by short lengths of chain, all sitting on top of empty oil drums. A rusty old vertical ladder bolted to its masonry wall provided access from the main pier down to the pontoon. While the upper bolts were sound, those within the normal tidal range had almost rusted through.

At low tide, Granton harbour dries out to a muddy bottom. A significant number of the boats moored there are bilge keeled – as the tide recedes, they settle down gently on to the muddy bottom and when the tide comes back in, they refloat.

Over the period of low tide, Zander and Gilbert were working on the final bits and bobs needed to complete Emerald's fitting out. Sitting below decks taking a break, chatting and putting the world to rights, the movement of the boat refloating prompted Gilbert to look at his watch,

"Hells bells," he erupted, "Look at the time! I'm going to be late for the theatre and I've still got to get changed."

As he scrambled up the companionway, he called down,

"Cheerio. See you tomorrow."

Zander hardly lifted his head from the little nut and bolt gismo he was absentmindedly twiddling.

"Fine," he replied distantly.

Splash!

Zander stuck his head above the hatch, there was no sign of Gilbert neither could he see anything amiss. Thinking, *wonder what that was all about*, he went back below deck. With Gilbert gone and no longer needing to share, he decided to get himself a beer from his secret store. However, even before he could do that, he heard more sounds.

"Splutter! Arrrgh! Help!"

This time he went up on deck and heard a louder,

"Splutter! Help! Splutter! Help! Splutter! Splutter!"

Looking over the side, he saw a face peering up at him from the narrow gap of water between the pontoon and the jetty and through the slimy mask of seaweed covering it, he recognised Gilbert.

"Get me out of here," implored a terrified Gilbert, perilously close to being crushed between the jetty and the pontoon.

Zander, for once acting as quickly as he thought, found a rope, threw it to Gilbert and hauled him back onto the pontoon.

A sorry-looking Gilbert, with water streaming off him, stood shaking and dripping into the growing pool of water that was oozing out of his shoes. His timbers were well and truly shivered.

"Phew, you don't half pong! What happened?" was Zander's unsympathetic query.

"I don't know. One minute I was stepping on to the ladder, the next thing I was in the water."

It took only one look at the access ladder, to see what had happened. Deep new score marks had appeared on the edge of the floating pontoon and the bottom of the ladder had come away from the jetty. At low tide, the edge of the pontoon must have slipped under the foot of the ladder where, trapped by the rising tide; it only needed the addition of Gilbert's weight to free it. When the pontoon sprang free, the sudden release of its pent up energy had thrown Gilbert off and into the harbour.

Had he not been in such a hurry, Gilbert might have noticed that the rusty, fragile ladder was an accident waiting to happen but unfortunately, he did not.

Gilbert now gingerly tested what remained of the ladder before trusting his weight to it again, said, "I'd better get home." Then satisfied that everything was all right, he climbed up it as quickly as his soggy-trousers would let him.

To avoid any drips, Zander waited until Gilbert was well clear of the top before following him up. On their way to Gilbert's car, Zander picked up a piece of polythene and spread it over the driver's seat before Gilbert got in. When Gilbert's car was out of sight, Zander let out a long suppressed smirk.

Gilbert, conscious of how little time he now had left to get ready for the theatre, parked his car, sloshed and squelched his way through the common entry door leading to his first floor flat then dripping his way up the stairs, got to the door of his flat.

Home at last, looking forward to a little sympathy and comfort, he pressed the doorbell. When his wife opened the door she took one look at him, held up a forbidding palm and in a voice that brooked no argument, said, "Wait there! Don't move an inch."

Soon, she was back with a towel and a large plastic laundry bag and with gestures of hand, head and finger, instructed the forlorn figure to remove his wet clothes and put them in the bag.

Stripped down to his socks and Y-fronts, Gilbert moved to go inside. His wife's wry expression and twirling fingers intimated that she wanted him to do a 'Full Monty'. If that was the price he had to pay to get into his house, then so be it.

With Gilbert's last undergarment deposited in the laundry bag he bent down to retrieve the towel lying at his feet and heard the entry door open and voices of people starting up the stair. At that same point, his white haired next-door neighbour opened her door to take her wee dog out for its daily walk. The dog, rushing out ahead of her, saw the towel.

The dog loved to play tug of war with its mistress and knew exactly what this loose bit of cloth meant. With synchronisation that would normally take years to perfect, the dog snatched up one end of the towel just as Gilbert picked up the other. A ferocious struggle ensued.

The neighbour, in the act of following her beloved dog through the door, saw her wee darling fighting with a naked apparition over a towel. She stopped, eyes bulging and mouth agape. By this time, the people on the stairs had joined her and were just in time to witness the conflict.

Only Gilbert's superior strength allowed him to drag the straining dog into his house and close the door. Then, a moment or two later, the door re-opened but only wide enough to allow a small yelping dog to fly through it, land on its backside and with paws in the air, slide and skitter over the landing to end up in a whimpering, crumpled heap against its far wall. Gilbert slammed his door shut and leaning back on it, heard the distressed screams of his neighbour and the roar of laughter coming from his audience.

It was a long time before Gilbert could face any of these witnesses to his shaggy dog story again.

49

Trials and Tribulations   Firth of Forth

After a few false starts, Emerald was at last going to sea. Zander and Gilbert chose a date that suited them before contacting Grunt and Murdo, hoping that they too would be able to join them for the new Emerald's maiden voyage.

Unfortunately, this turned out to be not the best of times to recall the Emeraldeers to arms. Grunt and his wife Lucy were in New Zealand visiting relatives, and would still be there at the time of Emerald's first cruise. It also turned out that Murdo would be staying with 'relatives' in Oban that week – a cousin no doubt!

Naturally Zander was disappointed that neither of these formerly trusty crewmembers were available, *Why is it that when I need them, they do not come rushing to be with me? Why are they not always on standby, so that when I call, they are ready at a moment's notice to sail with me again?* Gilbert whose recent immersion had done nothing to dampen his enthusiasm was the only one that Zander could depend on.

Accordingly, on the appointed weekend, to carry out what they pretentiously called 'sea trials', the pair of excited born-again sailors sallied forth into the Firth of Forth on the new Emerald. Her rigging would be tested and fine tuned, the sails given a blow and following the electrical engineer's work on the various instruments and gadgets (that had cost Zander a small fortune) they would find out if, and how, they all worked.

Under a partly cloudy blue sky, the smell of clear salty air gave a sense of anticipation and set the mood for Emerald's crew as they went through the formalities of their sea trials. The light morning breeze promised a fine day for sailing so, for the adventurers the world in general has dawned brightly on them.

All they needed for the short trip was already on board so Emerald's skipper and mate motored out of Granton harbour and into the Firth of Forth. As soon as Emerald got clear of the breakwaters, Zander turned her to starboard leaving a wide spreading arc following in her wake.

The Forth Estuary has well-defined shipping lanes for oil tankers, cruise liners and big ferries, but there is still plenty of sea room left for smaller boats.

"Let's get the mainsail up and see how she goes," was Zander's first command.

The sail was on a roller, so when the up-haul was reeled in, the sail set easily and without mishap. Things were going to plan and the new Emeraldeers were feeling well pleased with themselves.

"Let go the Genoa," was the proud skipper next command.

Gilbert released this sail in increments until it was fully set and was driving the boat along beautifully over a slightly lumpy, blue-grey sea.

A short while later Gilbert took the helm and in no time at all, he was enjoying himself immensely. As far as he was concerned, the world was a beautiful place.

Below decks, Zander was sitting in front of the control panel, pushing buttons and switching switches. He was still trying to identify which switches operated the GPS, the fish-finder and the sonar and trying to fathom out exactly how these things worked. Sorting this lot out might take him a little time, but he was confident that soon he would get the hang of things. If not, he could ask around the Club for advice, a thought that sent another one into his head,

It's a pity Dougie's not here to help me. It would have been so much easier if I could have asked him. Instead I have to refer to owner's manuals and instruction books, written by people whose first language is not English.

A third thought brought him back to reality,

This fine boat would not be mine if Dougie were here!

Later, with Emerald going through her paces, her crew took lunch on the hoof. Minute by minute Zander became more and more convinced that Emerald was a great bargain, even accepting the trauma he had experienced looking for the lost manuals, the extra cost he had incurred in replacing them, not to mention hiring the services of an electrical engineer.

*

The sun had chased the clouds away and a blue sky looking as if it was here for the day saw Emerald turning for home, her crew well satisfied with what they had so far accomplished. However, as any sailor knows, the weather is not always to be trusted. Almost as though someone above had shut a big door, the light breezes disappeared and Emerald 'lost way'. *This is not good,* Zander thought. Now he would have to motor sail the rest of the way back to Granton. Calling to Gilbert to take down the mainsail, he pushed the button and started the engine. They would now just putter back, and finish off what remained of their liquid supplies on the way.

Emerald's limp foresail was proving to be more of a hindrance than a benefit, so they furled it in. Still thoroughly enjoying themselves and continuing to bask in the satisfaction of a good day's work well done, they continued to motor in the general direction of Granton, confident that all their problems were behind them. After all, it was summer and there was plenty of daylight left, they had a good supply of fuel and if the wind did come back, they could put up the sails again. All they had to do now was idle their way back to Granton.

Zander began to feel concerned when for no obvious reason he heard the engine revving up spasmodically. However, still not unduly worried, he surmised, *maybe it is something to do with the swell.*

These unaccountable accelerations became more frequent and the engine vibrations more marked; yet he had done nothing to change things and the sea was now even calmer than before. Unease stepped up through concern all the way to panic when he realised that he was no longer in control of the engine.

Matters came to a head when the engine flew into another of its tantrums but this time showed no sign of settling down. Nothing that Zander did had any effect on the racing engine. Faster and faster it ran, until it was screaming like a banshee. What Zander could not understand was, that it was a newly reconditioned Post Office van diesel engine, a type renowned for its reliability. This should not be happening – but for some unknown reason it was.

Trawling the depths of his memory and with a speed that surprised even him, Zander, found a little grey cell from his 'degree' days – he had studied heat engines – that recognised the possible source of the problem and remembered that he was experiencing something inherent in diesel engines when the fuel-return pipe is blocked. This almost forgotten memory cell then told him that when this happens, the engine takes up fuel from the sump, until eventually; it is running on sump fuel alone and out of control.

For Emerald and her skipper, this was not good, not good at all. Her motor was not responding to the throttle, neither could it be switched off. What could he do?

Zander brain cell then remembered that the answer was to either hit the decompression lever (not normally recommended) or starve the engine of air. That was it; he would remove the air filter, close off the air supply and shut down the engine. However if he did that, he might not get it started again and he did not like the idea of being stuck out at sea.

Looking towards the shore, Zander saw that they were just off Anstruther in Fife, so while moving her from side to side, trying to lose way, he turned Emerald's bow in that direction. On the approach into Anstruther harbour, with Emerald still going at a fair rate of knots, Zander had little time to do what he knew he had to do.

Passing the helm to Gilbert, he went below, exposed the engine, removed the air filter housing and closed off the intake. With what sounded like a disappointed splutter, the engine died. The silence that followed was overwhelming. He had carried the day but only just, because Gilbert, on the helm, was becoming uncomfortable with their approach speed and getting ready to sheer off to regain the safety of the open sea.

Clambering back on deck, Zander took back the helm, called out mooring instructions to Gilbert and with just enough residual way managed to steer Emerald in and alongside the harbour wall. Meanwhile Gilbert, appreciating that everything was now down to him – and that there would be no second chance – had one of his better days. Leaping ashore, he threw a loop over a bollard and with all the aplomb he could muster, stopped Emerald's drift and made her fast.

For the benefit of the bystanders and any real sailors watching, Zander composed his features into a look of calm competence – not an easy task when your heart is pumping and you are puffing like an old train – and waved a hello to Anstruther.

50

Gilbert's Overnighter   Anstruther

With Emerald tied up, two hot and sweaty sailors went below, out of the public gaze and breathed sighs of relief. Then, to gather their thoughts and decide what to do next, a can of beer sounded like a good starting point.

Zander's main concern was how to get Emerald home to Granton on the opposite shore of the Firth of Forth. Under sail with little or no wind, that trip would take ages.

With feelings of apprehension, he suggested to Gilbert – who still had no idea what was going on – "Let's see if we can restart the engine."

Having made sure, that Emerald was secure, and that the air filter was still lying where he had put it, Zander tried to fire up the engine, but without success.

"Well that's that, the engine's knackered, moving is out of the question today, so we can't get her home tonight," Zander said with depressing finality.

"Can't you fix it?"

"No!"

"What are we going to do then?" a worried Gilbert asked.

"We'll just have to leave her here and get the bus back. Unfortunately when we got on board, I left my wallet in the car, so you'll have to lend me the fare."

"Sorry, I left mine at home as well and I've only got some small change in my pocket," was Gilbert's disappointing response.

Emptying pockets, fumbling under bench seating, feeling in chart table drawers etc, they gathered in a meagre collection of cash, which when totalled up, was just enough for one single bus fare back to Edinburgh.

"I repeat, what do we do now?" Gilbert asked again, this time even more plaintively.

Zander, chin on chest and twiddling with his nut and bolt gismo, replied, "Don't know." Then, a moment or two later, with a sly gleam in his eye, looked up and asked Gilbert, "What are you doing tonight?"

"Nothing really," Gilbert admitted, missing the expression on Zander's face.

This was the just the answer that Zander had been hoping to hear.

"You'll have to stay here and look after Emerald then."

"Why me?" demanded the flabbergasted Gilbert.

Zander came back at him, "Because it's absolutely essential that I get back tonight."

Zander whose nut-turning ploy, had given him enough time to put together what he thought was a foolproof reply to the question he knew Gilbert would ask, went on, "All I know is I must be back for a dinner party tonight. One of Jane's sisters and her husband are here from Australia and tonight I'm meeting them for the first time at their hotel. They are only in Edinburgh for one night so Jane will be furious if I don't turn up. I've just got to be there, and anyway you must agree that someone has to stay with the boat." This hastily contrived 'porky', put over with a hangdog expression and despair-laden slouched shoulders, had left Gilbert cornered and with no option but to agree.

Mumbling his thanks, Zander gathered his bits and pieces into a plastic bag, hopped ashore and hurried off to catch a bus to Edinburgh. His parting words were,

"I'll be back early tomorrow and we'll sort everything out then."

Thus, it came about that Gilbert, with the bedding not yet on board, was facing the dismal prospect of an uncomfortable, cold and miserable night. On top of which, he did not even have the price of bag of chips from Anstruther's famous sea front fish and chip shop, so would have to make do with whatever leftovers he could scavenge from the day's provisions.

*

The following morning had come and gone with no sign of Zander. It was late afternoon before he finally appeared, sailing into harbour on the 'Puffer Twins' boat. He had persuaded them to bring him over, either to shepherd Emerald back to Granton, if the winds permitted, or as a last resort, to tow her back.

Gilbert, after asking Zander 'where the devil he had been' and got no answer, tried another tack,

"What was the family-do like last night then?" There was a pause before the hesitant,'

"Er, all right," came the reply, confirming for Gilbert what he had already suspected, *Family-do my foot!* Zander had been home, had a good meal and been tucked up in bed all night. *I've been conned again!*

*

For once, luck favoured the Emeraldeers. A light to fresh wind sprung up, which, escorted by the Twins, allowed them to sail Emerald back to Granton harbour and drop the anchor, near high water, where, at low tide, Emerald would settle down and beach.

51

Emerald Forgets to Float   Granton

Next day, Zander was down at the harbour watching Emerald settling down on the receding tide. He intended to have a look at her engine while she was sitting on the bottom and if he could, fix it himself. Anxious to get on board, he jumped into the dinghy, rowed over to his precious boat and climbed aboard to see what he could do.

Firstly, he tried to start her engine hoping that the trouble would have cleared itself. It fired, but did not catch. After a few attempts, it did kick in but screamed straight up to the top of its rev. range. Clearly, the problem was still there, so again he resorted to cutting off the air to the engine and the engine coughed to a stop. Afraid that it might overheat, Zander opened the seacock to cool it down. There was only one thing for it, he would have to expose the end of the fuel return pipe, clear it and while he was at it, he may as well clean out the sump as well.

Still hoping against hope that the problem was what he thought it was, it did not take him long to discover that his diagnosis had been correct; the fuel pipe was clogged up. Now that the root of the problem was established, it did not take him long to clear the blockage, clean out the sump and put everything back to what it was.

Here we go, fingers crossed, he thought, starting up the engine. It fired first time, purred away nicely and responded smoothly to his touch on the throttle. Zander was again a happy little sailor boy.

He had just completed his mental 'finished with engine' routine, when his mobile phone rang. It was Jane and she sounded upset. She had come back from shopping to find the kitchen floor under water; a pipe behind the sink had burst, she had called a plumber but he had not yet turned up and she was getting desperate.

With one success under his belt already today, Zander collected his tools and, just like Tarzan, took off to fly to Jane's rescue. If he got there before the plumber and did the job himself, he would only have to pay the call out charge. However, by the time Zander got there, the plumber had already saved the day. As luck would have it when the plumber got Jane's emergency call, he had only been a few streets away and had responded, fairly quickly.

Zander's dash only got him home in time to negotiate a cash discount; so even though he had had to hurry away from his boat, so far, he was reasonably well satisfied with his day. Never the less, he should have remembered that fate has a habit of not playing fair with him.

Before going back to the boat, Zander decided to take a wee rest. Sitting in his favourite chair, enjoying a well-deserved cup of coffee, he gave Jane an account of how well he had done down at the boat. For a while, she listened, but in time wandered off to do something else, leaving Zander relaxed in his chair and thinking that a little nap might be a good idea. Then, in the flicker of a drooping eyelid, he was fast asleep.

His nap lasted for well over an hour. When he woke up, he looked at the time and knew that the tide would now be high enough for him to get Emerald off the beach and back on to her mooring. He phoned Gilbert and arranged to meet him at the clubhouse in fifteen minutes time.

Gilbert was already standing waiting for him when Zander got to the clubhouse. The look on Gilbert's face told him that there was something wrong. Gilbert, too overcome to speak, took him round the clubhouse and on to the harbour wall, from where, he pointed to a wheelhouse and mast sticking out of the water exactly where Emerald had been sitting.

What Zander saw was a yacht with most of its hull underwater. Frantically he searched for Emerald, hoping against hope that he would see her floating somewhere, but there was no sign of her afloat anywhere in the harbour. His heart, like Emerald had done, sank like a stone.

Surely, that is not my beautiful Emerald!

A closer look at what remained above water, confirmed his worst fears. It was Emerald. His shoulders slumped and his chin dropped onto his grimy Aran sweater.

Fate had just dumped on his day! Zander's personal view of this disaster was expresses by a short sharp "S***".

How the blazes had that happened?

Then mentally cataloguing his morning's actions, he tried to answer his own question. Then, in an instant of unbelievable realisation, it came to him and he screamed, "No o o o o!" And, with bile rising in his throat, he gave a despairing sigh and hissed, "The seacock. I forgot to close the bloody thing off before I went home!"

His precious Emerald had taken on water and sunk – and it was nobody's fault but his own.

While he and Gilbert were trying to decide what to do, they noticed the club's tender heading out towards Emerald. Within the space of a few minutes, the ferryman had tied a line on Emerald, taken it ashore to a winch and hauled her into shallower water; now at least, she would not sink any further.

Zander thanked the ferryman for his prompt action and 'salvage money' moved from his pocket into the ferryman's inadvertently open hand. At least one sailor had known what to do.

Two disheartened Emeraldeers knew that until her hull had drained, it would be pointless to go back on board Emerald, they would have to wait until low tide and the harbour had dried out before boarding her.

Their first glance told them that all of Zander's new gadgets and equipment would need sorting out, as would the newly upholstered seats – not to mention the engine. However, it was also clear that before anyone could start to repair the damage, Emerald would have to come out of the water therefore, a salvage operation was their first priority.

In the space of a few hours, both Zander's house and boat had been flooded. It had not been the good day he had thought earlier, and it had all happened just as he believed he had cracked it and had at last got things right.

Zander, already shattered by what had happened to his precious Emerald, then remembered that he had left his mobile phone and laptop on board; suffering was now piling up on suffering and all because he had forgotten to check a silly little seacock.

For want of a nail, a shoe was lost, etc... Zander's kingdom was not exactly lost, but his confidence and self-esteem had suffered badly.

For the time being anyway!

52

All Together Now   Granton

It was a month before Emerald was ready to go to sea
again. All of her visible parts were back in shipshape
condition and the other bits returned to full working order.
Now that he had 'fixed' her, and knowing that the work
had not come cheaply, Zander was keen to be out on the
water to see how his reconditioned boat would perform.

Under his command, the reunited full crew of Emeraldeers
took the boat out into the Firth of Forth for supplementary
'sea trials'. By the end of the day, Zander was satisfied that
his crew and boat – and that included the engine – were
all working well.

With the confidence brought on by a period without
incident, Zander was now ready to up the ante by entering
Emerald for a race and, the sooner the better.

In the clubrooms, a race calendar showed that entry forms
were currently available for a weekend race to Dundee, on
the Firth of Tay. Unfortunately as Gilbert was not available
that weekend Emerald would only have a crew of three.

Almost purring with pleasure at the prospect of
subjecting his pride and joy to a longer voyage, Zander
was eagerly looking forward to testing her against other
yachts.

Thinking, *if Emerald is going to be involved in a real race, it might be a good idea to get my crew into racing trim before the big day*, Zander entered her in one of the club's regular, shorter evening races – weather and tide permitting. Because he would not be involved in the big race, Gilbert did not take part in the 'practice'.

Even though Gilbert was the only crewmember with a competent crew certificate, his absence did not particularly worry Zander. He knew that he would still have the services of his faithful workhorse Murdo and the 'gorilla' Grunt. Anyway, he reasoned, *the boat would be that much lighter and go that bit faster with only three onboard.*

*

The BBC's weather forecast for the evening of their 'practice' race out of Granton predicted light winds and the possibility of a sea fog.

True to form, Zander took no heed of the forecast; and thinking *nothing ventured, nothing gained*, cheerfully sailed Emerald off its moorings and out to join the muster at the start of the race.

The race was over the course of a single closed circuit; a leg eastwards in the Forth Estuary, a rounding of the island of Inchkeith and another leg westwards to the finishing line.

Zander felt happier now that Grunt was back in harness. Allied to his physical strength, which coupled with Murdo's and his own combined nautical skills they would have a fair chance of finishing the course – they might even beat someone. Stranger things have happened.

*

In the muster area, an eclectic fleet of yachts was milling around the start line. Each skipper manoeuvring his boat into what he believed to be the best position to take advantage of a slack tide and a very light wind.

Emerald's crew had just decided that the sails needed changing when they heard the starting gun. Zander was caught with his sails down. The fact that they were facing away from the start was just another little handicap he had to take on board.

Eventually Emerald got off to a flying start, all-be-it in last place and a fair way behind the boat in second last position. Once again, everything in their favour had gone against them.

By mid evening, the wind was only occasionally blowing and then only in light zephyrs that hardly ruffled the surface of the sea, let alone rippled their sails. Emerald's progress slowed down to almost nothing, until they were making no perceptible movement at all. At that stage, a drizzly mist came down and enveloped the fleet and shortly after that, darkness chased away the last vestiges of daylight.

For some time now, Emerald's disheartened crew had heard their unseen fellow competitors start up their engines to abandon the race and motor back to harbour. In spite of their determination to hang on and try to finish, they heard through a blanket of gloom, the moaning of the recall siren; there was nothing for it, they too would have to give up and motor back. This, the formerly enthusiastic Emeraldeers believed, was not how racing should be. Now cold, miserable and thoroughly fed up, all they wanted to do was get ashore, go into the warm clubrooms, have a meal, a drink and get home.

As Zander pressed the starter, everyone on board held their breath, but thankfully the engine fired first time and while they were motoring back, a discussion ensued as to whose round it was. The skipper lost the democratic vote by a majority of two to one; after all, he was the one who had dragged them into this fiasco.

Later, sitting in the clubrooms, comfortably warm and well fed, they convinced themselves, that tonight's event had only been a club race and that their main test was still to come.

That, would be a different matter altogether!

53

The Main Event   The North Sea

Dawn on the morning of the Dundee race saw the clubrooms at Granton abuzz with crews and officials preparing for the big race. Among them Zander and his crew with their pre-race preparations completed, were as ready as they would ever be. Because they would be away for three nights, each of them had bid their half-asleep loved one, a barely acknowledged early morning farewell.

Zander checked that Emerald's name was on the start list pinned to the notice board and confirmed to the officials that he would muster at the start.

In fine fettle and excited at the prospect of the race, the three Emeraldeers boarded their yacht and sailed out to join the fleet of yachts milling around the committee boat at the start line, each skipper vying with his rivals to be in the best position to get away when the starting gun was fired.

Inexperienced and terrified of being left behind, Emerald's crew were copying their opponents pre-start sail tweaking and rudder adjustments before making a positive move towards the start line.

Carried along by the euphoria of what he was involved in, Zander's approach to the start was spot on. By making a clever, but in fact accidental, tacking and gibing manoeuvre and with Emerald under full sail and heeling well over, Emerald got away to flying start. Wow! They were one of a small, detached group sailing some way ahead of the bulk of the fleet.

For the first half hour, Emerald held her place among the leaders. Her crew constantly trimmed sails and adjusted their physical ballast to get the best out of the fine vessel they were racing. Zander just could not believe how easy this race sailing was proving to be.

"This is the life, eh lads! Aren't we doing well?" Emerald's self-satisfied skipper shouted above the slap of the sea on the hull, the thrum of the stretched sail and the roar of the wind rushing past his ears.

Their trip along Easy Street did not last long however and as the race developed, Emerald's crew were being continuously tested, and found comprehensively wanting. As their confidence ebbed away, with sickening regularity, boat after boat hauled them in and sailed past them.

Zander looked around and was stunned to see that Emerald was now alone and a long way behind the fleet. 'Tail end Charlie' had found his rightful place at last.

Recently Grunt had been on a bigger, even better boat, one equipped with powerful motorised winches for everything and had been able to do what he did best, just laze around. Now he was doing all the heavy work and forever under the cosh of his moody captain. This trip was not what he had expected so he made his feelings known to the skipper. Firstly he pointed out Emerald's lack of labour-saving devices and equipment, then muttered a few aspersions about Zander's racing skills before finally dropping a bombshell by telling his skipper that because he had not sailed much recently, he was not up to the task.

Naturally, Zander, not used to this sort of abuse from his 'underling', leapt into attack mode. After informing his mutinous friend that, not only was Emerald a fine, well-equipped vessel, built for the specific purpose of sailing round the world, but that it was *he who* was the problem because since the last time they had sailed together, Grunt had become far too soft.

An awkward silence descended on the little craft heading out towards the wide mouth of the Firth of Forth and the open sea beyond.

After an hour or so, the wind dropped and a swirling sea mist came up, engulfing them, making all of the familiar landmarks difficult to spot, let alone identify. By the time Emerald reached the open sea, she had fallen so far behind the other boats that, with nothing to race for, it no longer mattered. Knowing this, Zander dared Grunt to take the helm and show him how Emerald should be sailed.

Grunt retains a ferociously competitive attitude and hates being put down or put upon, so when the challenge came, he promptly accepted it and took over the helm, albeit with a lot less confidence than he showed.

By this time, the mist had thickened considerably. With Grunt in charge and his shipmates assured that Emerald had plenty of sea room, they left him to it and feigning a lack of interest, sat down beside him, all the while keeping a weather eye on what he was doing.

It was not so long ago that Zander and his gallant crew had believed that they would soon be across the finishing line on the River Tay and that the race would be over, but here they were, hardly out of the Forth and floundering around in the doldrums. With no wind at all Emerald had virtually stopped moving. Everything was so different now.

Zander and Murdo with nothing to do were bored and the longer they sat, the more lethargic they became.

After a short period of uncomfortable silence Zander gave Grunt a compass bearing, told him to stay on that heading, formally passed over command and went below for a nap. Not long after that, Murdo followed him.

Last night while finalising their race details in the club, both Zander and Murdo had taken in a fair bit of liquid refreshment. Now battened down in the warmth of the cabin their earlier indulgence caught up with them. Their eyelids became heavy, their eyes flickered and closed and, with their breathing rate slowing down they finally dropped off to sleep.

Meanwhile Grunt, alone on deck, was sticking doggedly to his task, although not at all sure of his own capabilities, particularly in these conditions. He had become oblivious to everything except a compass that would not stay on the required heading and although the boat was hardly moving, he was continuously making small rudder adjustments, just to keep the needle on course.

*

With the first traces of dawn breaking in the East, a light slapping of a sail and a zephyr of wind brushing across his face brought Grunt out of a fitful dose. Then, when he felt some resistance in the rudder as the boat gathered way, his spirits rose. Almost immediately, he spotted, through the thinning, patchy 'haar' something appearing out of the mist, a little way up ahead. Squinting a little, he recognised it as a signpost. Picking up binoculars, he took a closer look but still could not read what it said.

Thinking, *this might be a problem,* he let the boat drift in closer until the indistinct lettering came into sharp focus and he read:

NO CYCLING

Alarm bells jangled in Grunt's head and a surge of adrenalin shot through him as he put the helm hard over to gain 'sea-room' from the sign and away from the land that it was obviously planted on. Good fortune rather than good seaman-ship, favoured his action and he neither hit anything nor ran aground.

This near disaster shattered Grunt's confidence and grimly holding course he was relieved to see the hazy light of the rising sun filtering through the mist. Bit by bit the light improved, the breeze got up and the mist thinned out. As the wind strengthened even more, the main sail filled and the rudder became more responsive; the reluctant helmsman was again in control. At last, he had time to look around and was reassured to see that the vague darker grey shape of the land mass was now a comfortable distance behind him.

Grunt, who counted map reading as one of his skills, had sufficient general knowledge of this shoreline to know that if he kept Emerald running parallel to the land on the port side he would eventually come round into the Tay Estuary and then on up to Dundee.

Although tired, Grunt stuck to his task resolutely and when the mist finally cleared, he saw that he was in what could only be the Tay Estuary. In the distance up ahead, was the grey smudge of Dundee, its railway bridge and on its waterfront, a group of boats marking what might be the finishing line? Evidently, Emerald was back on course. *Funny though*, he mused, *there are no sails between us and the finish, or anywhere around us for that matter*. All the sails he saw were way behind him. *I'll just head for the finish*.

To the thud and bang of a gun firing across the water Grunt singlehandedly and with no need for a final tack, took Emerald across the finishing line.

At the sound of the gun, Grunt's fellow Emeraldeers below, who had slept soundly through the violent course changes when he had almost crashed into the mainland, woke up. Stretching, rubbing their eyes and yawning they came up on deck to find out what was going on. Zander looking round recognised the Dundee shoreline and the anchorage. Then seeing that the committee boat defining the finishing line was behind them, thought *Emerald is over the line!* He could see no other boats from the fleet ahead of them. Could *Grunt have achieved the impossible?*

Already Grunt saw from Zander's face which way the cookie was crumbling. He may have been the hero of the hour, but Zander was going to be the one who accepted the plaudits. So, thinking, *To hell with him,* Grunt said nothing.

Emerald moved on to a mooring just off the quay to wait for the rest of the fleet, still some way behind and still racing.

As the other competitors finished and took up moorings around Emerald, many a ruffled owner asked Zander how the blazes he had brought his boat home so quickly. Zander, a world champion at the art of basking in someone else's glory, was full of praise for his boat's achievement and naturally gave no credit to Grunt. Proudly he proclaimed that by smelling the sea, he had found a pocket of wind on the edges of the mist, which had carried him on a much tighter line than the rest of the fleet, consequently, he had made a very fast middle leg of the race.

That evening, at the après-race celebratory dinner and prize giving, the crew of Emerald had just taken their seats, when Francey – Zander's protagonist from way back – sidled over and with a smile that did not reach his eyes, congratulated Zander on his win. Astounded, Zander found it difficult to believe what he had just heard; *imagine that, congratulations from Fancy Boy!* For once, everything was going well for Zander and his Emeraldeers.

A 'silent' Grunt, maintained a low profile and when spoken to just emitted one of his 'grunts'.

What Zander did not know was that the last two boats coming in, well behind the others, were flying 'objection' flags. The skippers of these boats were Francey and one of his pals. Having started late and only going along for the social event, they had not been racing. That was until some way adrift of the fleet while peering through the gloom, they had watched a boat meandering up the coast and cut well inside the outer marker buoy. When he recognised the registration number of the miscreant Francey could hardly believe his luck and then could not get in fast enough to report the incident to the judges.

Traditionally, race results are announced and prizes handed out immediately after the dinner, so throughout the meal Zander, thinking about the prize he had won, was having great difficulty in containing himself. Every time he caught Fancy Boy's eye he would give him a self-satisfied smile, but then could not understand why he got a faint smirk in return. Oblivious to the 'funny looks' he was getting from the other skippers and crews; Zander was already silently rehearsing his acceptance speech.

(Anyone familiar with Zander's 'successes' will know that – not for the first time – he has a shock coming!)

After dinner, the Commodore got to his feet and made a short opening speech before getting down to the business of the award ceremony. He started by saying he would announce the result in reverse order, and then as each prize was handed over, Zander nodded condescendingly and with an overdone show of enthusiasm, applauded its recipient. (All sounds familiar.)

At last, the Commodore was ready to announce the winner.

"First place in our grand race this year, winning a prize of £100 and this superb trophy are------------"

Throughout this statement, Zander already half out of his seat and looking around to see who was watching him, heard names he had not anticipated hearing. They were Not Emerald and Not Him! From being half way to his feet, he slumped back into his chair, eyebrows up, mouth agape and wondering *what was happening?*

His thoughts went back to Eigg Highland Games – another occasion when the sweet cup of success was dashed from his lips, and how Grunt had played a significant part in the matter. (See, *A Storm in Any Port*)

Allowing the cheers and applause to go on for what he felt was an appropriate length of time the Commodore held up his hand for silence and invited the winning skipper to propose the customary vote of thanks.

The winning skipper got to his feet, paid tribute to the organisers, said all the usual right things about everything and everyone associated with the race. Then in conclusion, he offered his sympathy to the owner of the first boat across the line, which, following a late protest lodged by the last boat to arrive, had been disqualified. As a second skipper had corroborated the objection, the organisers had no option but to uphold the objection and disqualify the offending boat.

He then went on to say the organisers and the rest of the competitors were grateful to Mr Francey and his colleague for bringing Emerald's unfortunate oversight to their attention. A disclosure that made Zander look over at Francey and then had to watch Fancy Boys self-righteous expression turn to one of unrestrained glee. Clearly, he was thoroughly enjoying Zander's discomfort.

In spite of having to suffer in silence, Zander now knew whose fault it was. He glared at Grunt who over the rim of his pint glass, mildly looked back at him and muttered, "It serves you right! If you'd given me half a chance I'd have told you."

Sorely disappointed and highly embarrassed, the skipper of Emerald waited for what he thought was a respectable interval before bundling the Emeraldeers out, back to their mooring and back on board for the night.

*

The humiliated Zander was now worrying about how the other competitors would react to his 'cheating', no matter how innocently done, and found it difficult to sleep. Lying wide-awake in his bunk mulling over the situation and searching for a way to avoid the ribbing and ridicule he was bound to be subjected to in the morning, the answer flashed into his head. It was so simple; *if I am not here, no one can say anything*. For that to happen though, he would have to be up and away before any of the other crews were stirring.

Although in the future, he knew he would still have to take some stick at the club, however, that lay in the future. What concerned him now was the present so, with that in mind, and when he shook them awake in the early hours of the morning Murdo and Grunt got their first inkling of what Zander had in mind,

"Quiet!" Zander whispered. "C'mon, get up, we're going now."

With the usual grumbling of those unceremoniously wakened from a deep sleep, Emerald's crew got up and got dressed.

"What are we doing?" a sleepy voiced Murdo enquired.

Grunt offered no contribution to the conversation, he was busy scratching in places that only he would touch, stood alongside his bunk and judging by his facial expression, had also discovered a bad smell under his nose.

"I've had enough of this racing lark," confided Zander. "We're leaving now but we don't want to wake anyone up, do we? So we'll cast off as quietly as possible and go."

Now that they knew the reason for their early call, the crew agreed to go along with Zander's suggestion, realising that once again they were victims forced to suffer an inconvenience just to save Zander's face.

"With the minimum of sail, we'll free the moorings and slip quietly downstream," whispered Zander as they prepared to go up on deck.

Zander went to the tiller and signalled for his men to cast off. Immediately the fast ebbing tide took Emerald off the mooring. *There's something wrong. What was happening?* Emerald was not responding as she should and Zander had no control over her. Emerald now picking up speed at a disturbing rate, was running stern first between a long line of moorings and getting alarmingly close to other boats

Emerald, caught in the grip of a fast receding tide, which, augmented by a turbulent river current flowing out to sea was held fast in this combination of supercharged forces and, out of control.

Any chance of a discreet retreat had gone and Zander, with increasing concern about damaging Emerald, tried valiantly to steer her clear of the inevitable collisions; to no avail.

Thump! Clatter! Scrape! Screech! These were the terrifying sounds that broke the morning silence and announced that Zander had lost his one sided battle with nature.

On top of which, he could not get Emerald's motor to start.

The impact of Emerald hitting the first boat had set her off on a bagatelle table like run. Bouncing off the first boat, she took a glancing hit on the port side, only to clatter into one on the starboard side, and so on down the line. Emerald had become a water-borne pinball!

To the accompaniment of frequent coughs of Zander's failed attempts to start her motor, Emerald passed through the lines of moored yachts. The bang, thump and thud of her sideswiping yacht after yacht, brought angry shouts from the rudely awakened crews, which in turn, brought other half-dressed, half-awake crews further down the moorings, on deck to find out what was happening. In the grey, early morning light what they saw, sent them scurrying around like headless chickens in frantic attempts to move fenders to places of potential impact and to pick up boathooks or anything else to fend off the boat careering wildly towards them.

Emerald's arrival in Dundee had been a triumph, but her departure had been potentially threatening and spectacularly embarrassing. It is understandable therefore, that her send-off contained not a word of fare-thee-well in fact, the sentiments expressed were quite the opposite!

Consequently, it was a boat full of relieved Emeraldeers – shattered from the exhausting and frantic attempts efforts to fend off disaster – who emerged into the sanctuary of the open water of the estuary. Behind them, the Emeraldeers could still hear the faint hubbub of angry sailors sorting out the mayhem they had created.

Back there in that channel between the two lines of moored boats, had been a nightmare. And, as if to prove that Sod had something to do with it, as soon they were out of danger and Zander pressed the starter button, the engine burst into life.

54

The Birds   Inchkeith

On the way back from Dundee, just short of the well-known island bird sanctuary of Inchkeith, Murdo broke a lengthy silence with a suggestion,

"Why don't we go ashore for a look around? We've got time kill and it'll be a bit more interesting than hanging around waiting for the tide to let us get back home."

Inchkeith is an uninhabited little island off Edinburgh, lying in the middle of the Firth of Forth. It boasts a number of interesting features such as, an old lighthouse, some wartime gun emplacements and the rusting wreck of a long grounded Fisheries vessel. To the Emeraldeers the island was just part of the local scenery, which, until now, had not registered on their wish list. Zander, glancing at his watch, took a quick look at Grunt, who nodded his agreement, then made the decision to land.

Under a clear sky filled with clouds of screeching, whirling seagulls, they dropped the sails and glided in to nudge gently against the small stone jetty. Then, almost deafened by the shrill screeching of the gulls and the overpowering smell hanging in the air, they tied up and the three not too nimble explorers clambered ashore. Zander's first act was to give Emerald a once-over to see if she had sustained any damage during their hurried departure from Dundee but was relieved to see no visible signs of any real problems.

Satisfied that his boat had escaped relatively unscathed, he looked up towards the top of the island, raised his voice to make it heard above the shrill cries of the seagulls and said,

"It looks like this path goes straight up to the lighthouse!"

"It's a bit steep." Murdo added," and there's a hell of a lot of seagulls around."

"Let's get on with it," countered Zander half shouting over his shoulder as he set off up the steep path.

In line, they scrambled up over the rough stony ground, making the odd stop to look at the remains of some of the old gun emplacements dotted around the wild, feather-littered terrain. Half way up the path, they stopped to take in the spectacular panoramic view of Leith and Edinburgh just across the sea. Just beyond that to the south were the magnificent, rolling Pentland Hills.

All around their feet gulls were either nestling down or waddling around making little or no noise and only moving out of the way as they closed up to them. Overhead the airborne residents were wheeling gracefully and calling noisily to each other, as seabirds do.

Unperturbed, even though close up, these birds were a lot bigger than they at first appeared, Emerald's crew continued on their quest onward and upwards towards the lighthouse.

The trio had gone a fair way up the track and an appreciable distance away from the boat, when they became conscious that the birds on the ground were now less willing to move out of their way. More worrying though, were the shadows on the ground of those in the air, swooping, flitting and screeching all around them. They too looked much bigger than they had done a few minutes ago. The concerted noise of their shrieking got louder and angrier; the once serenely beautiful gliding birds were now flying much lower and frequently darting in bringing them even closer and more menacing.

Each of the 'invaders' could feel the hairs on the back of his neck rising. In a short space of time, a feeling of increasing apprehension had supplanted their feel-good factor.

"What's going on?" Zander shouted above the shrill screeching and the rush of near-miss wings.

Grunt, waving his arms over his head and flinching involuntarily at every passing shadow answered, his voice demonstrating his concern.

"Looks like we're not welcome here!"

Murdo had already turned round and was heading for the boat.

The whirling gulls seemed to sense the Emeraldeers' discomfort and upped the ante. Individual shadows had become a mass of feathered Kamikaze pilots that took turns to swoop in on them from all angles – still not quite striking them – but releasing streaky stink bombs, which did.

Meanwhile, the mob on the ground flapping their enormous wings, were now lunging and vehemently spitting gobs of oily regurgitated gunge at the visitors, as they passed by.

Zander was next to desert the macho code by scampering towards the boat after Murdo, shouting as he retreated,

"To hell with the lighthouse! I've had enough of this!"

Grunt his pride intact, was the last to capitulate but soon he too chased after the others. On his way down, Murdo had picked up a discarded broom handle and was waving it over his head and round his legs, trying to keep the determined attackers at bay. As he ran past a bush, Zander found a piece of plywood about half a metre square and used it in his defence, as best he could. Grunt just kept going and in racing past both of them, left them to the less than tender mercy of the flying squad.

The Emeraldeers' puny defensive efforts incited the gulls to even more ferocious attacks during which they brought into play precise flicks from beak and webbed feet, aimed at injuring unprotected heads and shoulders. This game was no longer a non-contact sport and to make matters worse, the ground troops – apparently so docile on the uphill walk – were now just as aggressive as their airborne colleagues.

Completely out of their environment and in serious threat of injury, the three explorers were in a terrifying world of cacophonous noise that was battering their eardrums and making every stride of their downhill retreat more urgent than the last.

Their initial capitulation, which began as a trot, eased into a shuffling stride, and in no time at all, became a hell-for-leather sprint down to the boat. With their heart rates also going faster, gasping for breath and trembling uncontrollably – as much in fear as from exertion – the Emeraldeers clambered on board Emerald and promptly cast off.

It was with a tremendous and heartfelt feeling of relief that they heard the engine fire first time and allowed them to beat a hasty – if undignified – retreat.

Moving steadily out to sea, Zander looked back at a scene, which a few moments ago had contained all the elements of a Hitchcock movie, only to see that normality had returned.

High overhead, clouds of gulls were wheeling gracefully, caw cawing to each other in tones that sounded – to the three on board anyway – like jeers of triumph.

Grunt stopped scraping the daubs of guano off his clothes to point to the board Zander had used as a shield, now lying face up on deck.

> THIS IS THE NESTING SEASON
> THE BIRDS CAN BE A LITTLE
> TEMPERAMENTAL.
> SHORE TRIPS ARE <u>NOT</u> ADVISED.

"Do you see that?" He said, "They're not temperamental! They're downright bloody vicious!"

*

One trip and two little notices had made an almighty difference to what should have been a great few days.

'Sod' was still flying around somewhere nearby, but which one was he?

55

Goodbye Emerald   Firth of Forth

For a good few days after getting home, Zander lived in dread of a letter arriving from his precious yacht club, demanding that he remove his boat from the harbour and return his membership card and clubhouse key forthwith.

Fortunately, the dreaded letter never arrived and no one ever referred to the incident again. Understandably, the only exception to this was Francey, who given half a chance, would offhandedly ask Zander,

"Have you done any racing lately?"

However, as far as Zander was concerned, 'Fancy Boy' was a 'nobody' so anything he said was of no consequence.

That aside, Inchkeith was the last straw for Zander and convinced him that Emerald was an unlucky boat. From day one, she had been a continual source of problems and not for a moment did he consider that this had anything to do with either himself or his crew. Murdo though, with his deep rooted, sailor's superstitious streak, put her misfortunes down to Zander having changed her name.

Zander would have none of this. All that superstitious nonsense had nothing to do with it – she was only a boat. Yet, it was apparent even to him, that he had to do something. Thus, to clear the slate, Zander decided to sell her.

*

Emerald's record of bad luck was as nothing compared to the misfortunes that befell the K boats near Inchkeith.

On 31ˢᵗ January 1918 during a naval exercise, this tiny island was the pivotal scene of a naval fiasco during which they suffered their worst of all bad days.

The K boats were steam-powered submarines that, before submerging, had to withdraw their upstanding funnels into their hulls and then close watertight doors across the funnel apertures. Occasionally the seals on these doors failed; a design flaw that caused a number of catastrophic accidents and sadly many fatalities.

Not far from the island, K22 collided with K14, which, later that day sank following an incident with the battleship H.M.S. Inflexible. Sadly, there were no survivors from her crew of more than 300 men. Ironically, K22 was the resurrected K13 which, in 1917, had foundered when the watertight door seal failed while undergoing trials in the Gareloch, and sank, again with the loss of the full ship's complement. She had subsequently been salvaged, refitted and renumbered K22.

To compound that disaster, during that same exercise, after colliding with H.M.S. Fearless, K17 sank not far from May Island, in the mouth of the Forth Estuary

Remembering that K13 was renamed, K22, perhaps Murdo was right.

*

On this particular occasion, Sod must have taken pity on Zander and, was for once playing on his side, because within three weeks of deciding to sell her, Emerald was sold.

The sale had been so easy too. On the Club's hard standing Zander had struck up a conversation with a man, looking at the boats. The man turned out to be an enthusiastic sailor just back from overseas who was looking for a new boat.

Zander invited the man on board Emerald and following a tour of inspection, the man made Zander an offer he could not refuse. It is possible that the buyer knew something about boats that Zander did not, or maybe he had more money than sense. Anyway, buy it he did.

All of Zander's associates know about his deeply rooted belief that, *anything he sells is of great value while anything he wants to buy, is not*. (This philosophy becomes incongruous because when he sells that same 'anything' and remarkably, its value has gone up).

If Zander had so readily accepted the offer, we can assume that the price paid was a *very* good one indeed.

TRANSIT OF THE GREAT GLEN

The Bikers

56

Wonderful Windfall   Edinburgh

Almost four months to the day after the sale of the second Emerald, Zander received a letter that brightened up his currently depressed view on life. Recently he had financially bitten off a little more than he could chew and his perpetually rising and falling financial affairs saw him struggling to get through a rough patch. He had invested the vast majority of his assets, including that from the sale of Emerald, in the stock market. Unfortunately, he had put his faith in what turned out to be volatile shares at inflated prices that, since he bought them, had all suffered a disastrous fall in value. Zander being Zander, determined that he was not going to suffer a loss, was resolved to hang on to them and wait for the stock market to recover. Consequently, this pig-headedness had tied up all of his money

The letter that changed his fortunes arrived in a plain brown envelope, bore no identification mark and because of this, he ignored it. As far as Zander was concerned, envelopes like these contained; begging letters, wonderful prizes that he had no chance of winning, bad news, unexpected bills or even worse, final demands. Experience had convinced him into accepting the philosophy of *what you do not see; you do not have to worry about.* As a result, along with the other junk mail, he consigned the letter to the waste paper basket.

Luckily, for our hero, Jane does not have her husband's head-in-the-sand attitude so – even if only to keep a record of the state of their joint finances – she always went through his discarded mail.

At dinner that evening, with scorn written all over her face, an exasperated Jane, planted the letter on the table in front of Zander. Initially referring to his carelessness, she went on to give him a telling off for his pathetic attempts to shun responsibility. As usual, Jane's scathing look went ignored, and her salvo of angry comments did not penetrate Zander's cloth-eared insensitivity. Offhandedly however, he picked up the letter and with a surly sigh began to read it.

He had only read a few lines before that sigh became a whoop of joy, as Zander started to appreciate what the letter meant. Another sigh then breathing out the words, he said, "I'm saved. Good old Uncle Jim and good old Auntie what's-her-name."

Auntie what's-her-name, widow of his boyhood hero, the late Uncle Jim, had died. Never having had a family of her own, she had been touched when Zander named his boat after her husband's old wartime ship H.M.S, Emerald. So much so, that she had named Zander, as the sole beneficiary in her will. The amount of cash shown in the letter had Zander counting the noughts and the sum he arrived at confirmed the magnitude of the cash now under his control. Zander who had heard the expression, 'money is like manure and is only useful when it is spread around to help things to grow,' thought, *I am not that old, am I? I want to grow, do I not? So I'll spread it around by spending it on myself and buy a new boat for the coming season.*

Running on a parallel track in his brain, was the further thought that, after settling up his financial burdens he could also take a little holiday, possibly to the south of England, where purely by coincidence, the Boat Show is held.

It should come as no surprise then, to hear that Zander took Jane for a few days' holiday in London and since they just happened to be in its vicinity, he just had to go to the Boat Show.

At the sight of all these wonderful boats, Zander's appetite for sailing grew and as a result he spent a few happy hours walking amongst them, thinking, *I've died and gone to heaven.*

As it turned out, as far as finance is concerned, heaven was not quite ready for Zander. All the boats there although highly desirable, were far too expensive for him, or more precisely, did not provide the level of value for money he demanded. On the other hand he did not come away empty-handed because, at no cost, he collected the means which was to prove crucial to his future as a boat owner. So, as he walked around the stands, he picked up complementary copies of the current and back-issues of yachting magazines, and it was from these pages, that the information emerged which led him to his next Emerald.

*

On his return to Edinburgh, Zander spent hours poring over the 'For Sale' advertisements in these magazines and by repetition, the focus of his search kept coming back to one particular boat advertised for sale at Nairn, in the North of Scotland. For its type and price, it looked to be just what he was looking for. The advertisement showed her to be bigger than any of his previous boats, the price was within his budget and Zander detected a sense of desperation in the wording of the latest entry of the advert.

Zander's next move was to go to the yacht club and by looking through back numbers of yachting magazines, establish exactly how long 'his next boat' had been on sale. Sure enough, he discovered that 'his new boat' had been for sale for a good few months and, since the first advert, the asking price had followed a steady downward path.

The stage was now set for Zander to acquire his new Emerald. Obviously, that was not her name yet, but in spite of Murdo's warnings, he would deal with that minor detail when the time came.

A telephone call to the boat's owner confirmed that the boat was still for sale. Then following his pre-planned script, Zander asked where the boat was berthed, details of its accommodation, age etc., and ending up, by asking the owner if he was open to offers. When he heard that the unsuspecting owner would consider any reasonable offer, his face took on the look of Dracula looming over the throat of his warm-blooded victim. Well pleased with the progress he had made so far, he arranged a viewing the following Saturday.

On the Saturday, Zander arrived at Nairn harbour to view his new yacht and, it was love at first sight. She was definitely the boat for him and the fact that the owner had already paid for months of berthing and advertising, gave him a sound platform from which to get her as cheaply as possible.

Zander's wearing-down process is the opposite of that of a doorstep sales representative; he did not rush things, he allowed them to fester.

In three other 'I was just passing' journeys to Nairn, each one in bad weather he insisted that the owner go to the boat with him. Once there, Zander kept the poor chap out in the rain, waving aside any suggestion that these discussions should move to a more amenable place, or even be wound up for the time being. Zander was not going anywhere.

A further period of softening up ensued with Zander engaging the owner in lengthy telephone calls, seeking further clarification of the boat's fitting out and condition: all of them at an unsociable hour of the day and a chipping away of the asking price, a ploy that left the owner in fear of answering the telephone

Thus, it came to pass that, to retain some semblance of sanity and peace of mind, the shell-shocked owner eventually gave in and agreed to sell his boat to that persistent, pestilential, pain in the posterior, Zander.

A marine inspection was organised and the boat was certified as being in excellent seaworthy condition. Even at this late stage, Zander was still half hoping that some minor flaw would come to light to give him the grounds to renegotiate a further price reduction; but there was none.

The way was now clear for Zander to take charge of his new toy. With the financial matters agreed, the handover date and final formalities would take place when Zander picked up the boat at Nairn. Furthermore in keeping with Zander's time-honoured sentiment the boat was to be named Emerald.

Judging by Zander's day-to-day mood swings, his Emeraldeers had known for some time that there was something afoot. Consequently, it came as no surprise when an excited Zander made contact to tell them that he was now the proud owner of the finest yacht in the whole of Scotland and if they were available, they should travel north with him, to witness the handover of his beautiful new vessel and take part in her subsequent sea trials.

57

Murdo Mortified   Nairn

Zander's ever-faithful wife Jane drove him, Grunt and Murdo up North to pick up the new boat. For some time now, she had promised to visit an old friend in Beauly, so a side trip to Nairn would not take her too far out of her way. And, because Gilbert had something else to do that day, his wife would drive him to the rendezvous tomorrow.

Following the take-over, Zander planned to take Emerald out on a 'shake-down' cruise, then sail her south through the Caledonian Canal to a new home, somewhere in his old hunting grounds on the West Coast of Scotland.

Jane had been only too happy to trade off the drudgery of a long car journey against a few days of peace, tranquillity and some girl chat in her old friend's cottage.

It was well into the afternoon before Jane dropped the excited Emeraldeers off at the harbour. Zander's new yacht, was there, tied up against the harbour wall and displaying her freshly painted new name, Emerald. Jane, after a brief look at her husband's latest toy, said, "Very nice dear" then drove off.

Climbing on to the well-scrubbed deck, Zander and crew went on a tour of the yacht, which, they were sure, would bring them many happy hours of pleasure.

"Ahoy there", Zander shouted in his best seafaring voice, but there was no answer.

Murdo in a louder voice, added, "Hello-o-o-o," echoed by Grunt's finite question, "Is there anyone on board?"

Emerald stayed silent and the hatch to the below-decks area was padlocked. A disturbing thought loomed over what until a moment ago, was a bright horizon; *was there a mix up about the date or some other misunderstanding?* Zander looked at his calendar watch. The date was right, *had he said he would come up the day before? Yes he was sure he had. Had he mentioned that he would like to sleep on board? No, he had not.*

On the assumption that the owner would be waiting for him on board, Zander had thought that all he had to do was turn up and then he and his crew would spend the night on board, ready for the hand-over next day. The simple, smooth take-over Zander had so looked forward to, was now at risk, as was the intended early sail away – as soon as Gilbert turned up. Instead, they were on a locked up boat with no sign of the seller.

Perhaps the seller was not too far away and would be back soon?

The Skipper-to-be convened a confab on deck with the crew-to-be, and they all agreed to try to find out where the owner was.

Looking around, the only person they could see was a man some distance away on the hard standing, working on a boat. Almost sprinting over to see if he could get help, Zander, a bit short of breath, enquired,

"Do you know the owner of Emerald?"

"No, I don't." the man replied. But I've heard that he's a miserable, stuck-up, swanky Edinburgh man, who hasn't arrived yet." Then adding almost as an afterthought, "I believe the hand over is tomorrow."

"No, it's the former owner we are looking for." Zander explained.

"Oh," replied the man, "He was here a wee while ago, but he's gone out fishing with one of his pals, they could be out 'till the early hours."

That was when the leaden- penny dropped; there would be no free accommodation tonight.

Disgruntled and more than a little disappointed, the Emeraldeers would have to find somewhere else to sleep tonight; a guesthouse, a bed and breakfast or even worse – from the point of view of cost – a hotel. This left them with a problem. It was the start of the holiday season and already early evening. By now, hotels and other accommodation would already be full of transient travellers who around 4.30pm, descend on them like locusts. Up until then, everywhere you look there are 'Vacancy' signs in abundance. Magically, at 4.31pm, the signs all have a 'No' prefix. Frustratingly, today this maxim proved to be the case.

Eventually, after walking around for what seemed like hours, they found a large hotel with two available rooms, one a single the other a twin, both with en suite facilities. Zander commandeered the single, leaving Grunt and Murdo to bunk up together in the twin. They agreed that after dumping their kit they would meet in the hotel bar. Conscious of the long day they had ahead of them tomorrow, the reluctant paying guests decided to have a drink, followed by a meal before going off to bed.

They had their drink in the busy street-level bar. About ten minutes later Murdo, put his empty glass on the table, stood up, said "See you later and left. Puzzled, the others waited for him to come back, until driven by hunger they gave up on their 'show' of good manners and went into the dining room. A short while later Murdo came in to say he had met up with a cousin and that she was waiting for him outside.

His mates thought about this; *is there no limit to his supply of cousins? But then again Murdo came from these parts, so maybe this time she really was a cousin.*

Murdo went on to say that as he was having dinner with her he might be a bit late; so they should not wait up for him. With that, he left for his assignation, leaving Zander and Grunt to share each other's company at dinner.

By the time they finished their meal Murdo had still not come back, so as he had suggested, they went up to bed and exhausted from their long journey north, both quickly fell asleep.

Someone shaking his shoulder dragged a soundly sleeping Grunt out of a pleasant dream. He opened one eye, looked at the bedside clock to see it was 2.30am. He swivelled that eye up and saw that standing over him was a swaying Murdo, wide-awake and obviously more than a little the worse for wear.

At this time of the morning, Grunt was long past the point of being reasonable and opening his other eye, he hissed grumpily

"Leave me alone, go to bed."

Murdo in a garrulous mood was not to be denied, he wanted to tell Grunt all about his adventures with his cousin. Sharply this time, Grunt told him to go to bed and sleep, or he would throw him out.

In Murdo's present state, this warning carried no fear for him. Grunt repeated his threat, which again, was ignored. Grunt threw back his bedcovers, rolled out of bed, grabbed Murdo by the scruff of the neck and the seat of his trousers, frogmarched him over to the door, opened it wide and, throwing him into the corridor, slammed the door shut. The bundle of tipsy flesh and bones that was Murdo, skidded uncontrollably along the polished floor, ending up beside a fire extinguisher with his head resting on a red bucket marked, sand. Somewhat confused, he just lay where he had landed. He heard Grunt locking the door, then silence.

A few minutes later, an already exasperated Grunt heard a timorous knock on the bedroom door and a pleading voice saying,

"Please let me in, I've nowhere to sleep."

Grunt ignored it.

Murdo repeated his hopeful appeal.

Grunt by this time, with neither patience nor sympathy left for his crewmate, got up again, pulled the single mattress off the other bed, dragged it over to the door and threw it, the bed covers and pillow out into the corridor.

"There, you have somewhere to sleep now. Don't bother me again or you'll be in even more trouble than you are now." The slamming of the bedroom door and the noisy turning of the key in the lock added finality to his action.

For a while, Murdo continued to knock feebly on the door, offering Grunt all sorts of inducements if he would just let him in. The appeals bounced back off a wall of silence. Eventually the pleading and whinging stopped and Grunt got back to sleep.

About half an hour later, Grunt's sleep was again disturbed, this time by a more persistent knocking, accompanied by the sound of a sharper voice. Pulling the bedcovers over his head he paid no heed.

Still awake, Grunt's bedside telephone rang. Angrily he picked it up, and being Grunt, grunted. "What!"

"Excuse me sir, this is the night porter. Is there anyone missing from your room? I found someone sleeping in the corridor and I can't wake him up to find out which room he's in."

"Sorry, can't help you. Goodnight," Grunt replied abruptly and for what he hoped would be the last time.

With the hotel full, the night porter had nowhere to put the sleeping beauty so he left Murdo where he was.

Around four o'clock, Murdo, blithely unaware of the trouble he had caused, woke up in desperate need of spending a penny, possibly more. Convinced that Grunt would not let him in to use the facilities in their room, he wondered what to do.

Then a thought occurred to him *Zander's room is on the floor above. I'll go up there and use his.*

Wrapped in a sheet, he staggered up the stairs, found what he was sure was Zander's room and tried the door; it was unlocked, so he went in. By the light of a bedside radio alarm clock, he could just make out a still figure lying on the single bed, with his back towards him. Beyond the bed, in the far corner of the room, he saw the door to the en-suite. *Funny,* Murdo thought to himself, *the red light of the bedside clock makes Zander's hair look ginger.*

Pleased with the knowledge that he was using one of the comfort stations he had partly paid for, he went about disposing of what he had to.

With his business completed and with no further need to be there, Murdo let himself out; went back to his impromptu bed in the corridor, fell into it and promptly fell asleep.

Next morning Murdo woke up to find that people on their way to breakfast were stepping over and around him, all of them taking a puzzled glance at the pathetic, half-dressed figure lying curled up on the mattress in the middle of the corridor.

Murdo, more unsettled than embarrassed by all these strangers going back and forth, gave up any thought of a long lie and got dressed. It now struck him that disturbing Grunt was not a good idea. The answer therefore, was to go back up to Zander's room, perform his morning ablutions and become semi-respectable again. So again using his bedding as a dressing gown, he did just that.

Borrowing the towels and toiletries from the *en suite*, he shaved and showered.

Now feeling much better, so as he bundled up his sheet to leave, thought he should wake Zander up or he would miss breakfast, shouted a breezy, "Good morning" and left the room

In the downstairs corridor, all signs of his overnight stay had gone and when he went into his room, he found that Grunt was not there, so throwing his well-travelled bundle of bedding onto what should have been his bed, he headed for the dining room.

Surprisingly, Zander was already sitting at a table with Grunt and they were well through their breakfast. Murdo was perplexed. How could Zander be up, dressed and halfway through his breakfast when, only a few minutes ago, he was fast asleep in bed?

Zander greeted him with a hearty good morning and a smile. Grunt sullenly acknowledged his presence with a growl.

"How did you get down here so quickly?" he asked Zander. "I left you in bed just a minute ago." Then went on to explain, "You've probably heard by now that Grunt threw me out last night and I had to use your bog in the middle of the night and again a wee while ago, for a shower and shave."

"Been down here nearly half an hour," Zander replied, showing little interest.

"You can't have been! You were lying in your bed not two minutes ago."

"Nonsense, I've been here for ages. Get on with your breakfast and let's get going," Zander said dismissively, popping a piece of toast into his mouth.

Puzzled, Murdo sat at the table and ordered breakfast, determined not to say any more about his early morning activities. At least, not until he had things sorted out in his own mind.

From his table companion's near empty plates, it was clear that they had been here for some time. *What's going on? Am I suffering memory loss, or even worse, hallucinating after last night's drinking?*

With no inkling of Murdo's confused state of mind and doing their utmost to ignore him, Zander and Grunt finished off their breakfasts.

Murdo was well into his tea and toast, when a highly agitated man almost falling over his feet, burst into the dining room, scurried over to the adjoining table and breathlessly blurted out,

"Ginger's dead!"

"What? How?"

"Heart failure, I've been up to his room and he's lying on his bed, dead. The manager told me a doctor had told him, that he has been dead for some time. He believes that Ginger went to bed last night and passed away in his sleep. What they don't understand is that there's still warm water in the basin and, as if he'd just had a wash and shave, his towels are damp."

Murdo stopped eating. *Ginger, lying there, warm water, shave......* These words brought a shocking thought into his already baffled mind.

Gulp! Surely, that was not Ginger's room I was in? Was that the late Ginger lying dead in his bed?

Even the possibility that it had been a corpse made the hairs on the back of his neck stand on end. Now, Murdo was in an awkward dilemma,

Should he own up and help to solve the mystery of the warm water and shave?

However, it did not take him long to come up with the answer. No, he had been in enough trouble last night, so he would keep his mouth shut.

Coming out of his deliberations, Murdo saw his table companions looking at him strangely.

"What room <u>did</u> you go into?" enquired Zander eyebrows raised, and now showing interest.

"First on the right at the top of the stairs directly above ours."

A smug smile spread over Zander's face and he whispered, "That's not my room. My room is the first on the left."

With his underlying fears confirmed, a tingling sensation of panic flooded through Murdo's being.

Still whispering and like a terrier with a bone, Zander persisted,

"Murdoooo, what have you been up to now?"

"Nothing!" the pale faced Murdo said, standing up and putting on a show of composure he did not feel. "See you down at the harbour", he said and slunk out of the dining room, leaving his breakfast uneaten.

Sitting mulling over Murdo's faux pas and eyeing up his untouched breakfast, Grunt and Zander could not help but overhear what the people at the next table were saying. It turned out that Ginger was a member of a fishing party from England that had come north to try their luck in the Highland lochs and rivers. It also transpired that Ginger was not only their star angler but that he tied his own flies and would not let anyone see them, let alone use them. From what Grunt and Zander gathered, these flies were worth their weight in gold.

Even though Zander and Grunt thought it a bit tasteless, the group were more concerned about who had the best claim to Ginger's fly box, rather than mourn his passing.

Apparently, they had already decided among themselves to carry on fishing- "It's what Ginger would have wanted." In addition, collectively and unanimously they had already agreed to send his rods and stuff back to his family and draw lots for his flies.

Having heard the callous attitude of Ginger's friends, Grunt and Zander felt less inclined to disclose their suspicions about Murdo's part in last night's events so, with that resolved, they nodded to each other, divided up and polished off Murdo's breakfast.

When he got to his room, Grunt found the cleaner tidying up. Murdo's bag had gone and as he picked up his own bag, the cleaner handed him a small tin box about the size of a tobacco tin and told him that it had fallen out of the bundled up sheets on one of the beds. When he looked inside, he found row upon row of fishing hooks, each one decorated with brightly coloured feathers. What he was holding, was a work of art in a tin box.

If any confirmation was needed, Grunt had it in his hands. Murdo had visited Ginger's room; twice! So, picking up a piece of hotel stationary he wrote,

> *This tin case was the property of your recently deceased guest. Please put it in a sealed, registered envelope and send it on to his next of kin.*

Then popping the note into an envelope, he sealed it and carefully wrote on the front,

> *For the personal attention of the Manager.*

On his way out Grunt handed the little package to the receptionist, stressing that under no circumstances was she to give it to anyone other than the manager, thinking as he did, *and let that be a lesson to them.*

Safely out of the hotel before anyone had twigged their involvement in last night's activity (or non-activity on Ginger's part), Zander and Grunt went straight down to the harbour to see if the boat's owner had turned up.

What they did find waiting for them, was an edgy Murdo sitting on his kit bag. Grunt told him about the fly-box turning up, which made Murdo even more nervous. It was bad enough waiting for the strong arm of the law to arrest him on a murder charge but now he knew that evidence of his involvement existed, in the shape of the fly-box found amongst his bedding. Murdo stood up and dragging his kit bag behind him sloped off and hid behind a pile of fish boxes.

Almost as soon as Murdo had disappeared, Gilbert's wife, who had driven through half the night, to get him here, dropped her husband off. Emerald's full crew was fully mustered, even if one of them – tucked up in his little hidey-hole – was conspicuous by his self-imposed absence.

As it panned out, they did not have to wait long before the boat's owner turned up and completed the transfer; with no further incident, the deal was concluded.

It was only after the seller had gone that Murdo emerged from his hidey-hole and furtively scurried aboard, imploring his shipmates to get underway as quickly as possible. Zander and Grunt, keen to avoid any further problems, agreed.

What this now meant was that the future shake down sail, came forward into the immediate present.

They were well out to sea before Murdo felt comfortable enough to let out a heartfelt sigh of relief.

58

Clunk Click   Moray Firth

It was a beautiful sunny day and Emerald was making good progress. Under a scrap of sail, Zander had her gliding along at a steady rate of knots on the flat sea of the Moray Firth. Everyone on board was getting a taste of the weather that this area of Scotland regularly benefits from.

As was his way, Zander's personal agenda took precedence over that of his crew and saw him steering Emerald towards a specific place west of Nairn, intent only on showing his captive audience another of his engineering triumphs – while at the same time give them a fright.

Murdo was first to notice the danger, "We're on the wrong side of that buoy skipper; shear away, starboard!"

Zander played him along, "What? Where?"

The others chorused Murdo's frenetic alarm call.

"Come about! Turn out! Quick, shear away" as well as the more expressive, "S***!"

Zander knew that by sailing Emerald just landward of the buoy marking the seaward end of an underwater pipe – not something any sensible sailor would do – his crew would be anxious. However, Zander knew something they did not.

Sitting on his own island of tranquillity surrounded by an ocean of his shipmates turmoil, Zander watching the faces of his wide-eyed uneasy crew, burst out laughing and said,

"Gotcha! It's ok. I designed this outfall pipe and I know we've got at least a metre of water under the keel." Just then, a thump, followed by shudder that ran the full length of Emerald, nullified his reassuring statement and made everyone on board freeze. They had hit something!

In his calculations, Zander had not taken into account the fact that Emerald was sailing in an area of high pressure pushing the sea level down by a significant amount, which in this case, it had. It was an irresponsible prank to play and had the sea level been a fraction lower, they would have been setting off flares, bailing out Emerald and calling out the Life Boat Service.

Red-faced and frantically trying to cover up his mistake, Zander made a pathetic attempt to reassure his crew by declaring,

"There are a lot of dolphins around here. That must have been a really big one that hit us just now."

Everyone, including Zander, knew perfectly well that there had been no dolphin but something a lot more substantial. What Emerald had just bumped over was the top of 'his' sewage outfall pipe; fortunately encased in a thick concrete surround, but Zander's confidence had been dealt a shattering blow.

A short while later, while sailing under the Kessock Bridge, Zander sub-consciously revealed just how mortified he was. Everyone knew – because he had told them often enough – he had worked on this fine bridge, yet, he said not a word.

For the rest of the way, his messmates heard nothing from him until they were tying up for the night in Clachnaharry, (the northern entrance basin to the Caledonian Canal.). There he found his voice again, even though commands were short and to the point. Afterwards, with Emerald finally tied up for the night, he disappeared below and retired to his bunk, without so much as a Goodnight.

59

Bunfeast Bounty   Clachnaharry

By next morning, Zander was back to his usual ebullient self. Later, when he and his crew went ashore – everyone to do his own thing – they agreed to meet up on board about six o'clock, to go out for their evening meal.

As the day wore on, the weather deteriorated. By the time everyone was on his way back to Emerald, the temperature had dropped, the wind had risen, and the heavens had opened up, sending the rain plummeting down in stair-rods.

To the cold, miserable Grunt, walking back to the boat it looked as though the bad weather was set in for the night. He did not fancy the idea of going out again and when he saw the sign of a popular Scottish-named but American-based fast food outlet not far from the boat, he had an idea.

It would be good to batten down for the night, eat on board, get to bed early and be ready to make an early start in the morning.

The more he thought about this the more he liked it. Not only was it a good idea, but it would kill two birds with one stone. Firstly, he knew that the others would be only too happy to accept a meal that someone else had paid for; secondly and more importantly, it would be inexpensive and push back the time when he would have to 'stand his hand' again.

Grunt, sure that his shipmates would appreciate his foresight and generosity, headed back to Emerald carrying a bulky parcel containing two hamburgers and chips, a jumbo drink and an apple pie for each of them.

Grunt was the first man back to Emerald. Clambering on board, he paused at the top of the companionway to watch the sheets of rainwater, driven by a brisk wind, flushing across the adjoining paved jetty and spotted Gilbert not too far away. Gilbert had his thin summer jacket pulled up over his head that gave him no protection from the appalling weather which, when coupled with his sandaled feet splashing through puddles, made him a sorry looking sight. Grunt turned and went below to wait for him.

In a minute or to, Gilbert was on board and before shaking the loose drops of rain off his sodden jacket, he passed a bulky plastic bag down to Grunt. Grunt thought it looked familiar and on putting it on the mess table beside his own, he knew why. They were the same! They had bought identical twin suppers.

"What's this?" he shouted up to Gilbert who was taking off his sopping wet socks and sandals before coming below decks.

"With the weather being what it is, I thought we'd eat in tonight. We need to be away early in the morning, so I stopped at a place just up the road and bought us some burgers and stuff. Good idea, no?"

When Gilbert got below, he saw Grunt hands on hips, nodding in the direction of the mess table and following the line indicated, saw that his package had somehow replicated itself. He shook his head, rubbed his eyes and looked again; yes, he was right, it had.

From above a voice bellowed, "Hello, there," Murdo had come on board, and as he passed a heavy plastic bag down through the hatchway, demanded of no one in particular, "Here take this,". "I've just got to say cheerio to my cousin. I'll be back in a minute."

Grunt, standing on the bottom step of the companion way took the package. It was now his turn to do a 'double take'. *Surely not another of the same?*

With a shrug and a look of "*I do not believe this*", he passed the third plastic bag to Gilbert who, with an equally bewildered expression, put it beside the others on the table and said, "Now we've got triplets!"

After a few minutes, Murdo, his goodbyes over, came below and when he did not get the welcome he had expected, his face fell. Instead, he was told that his contribution had just increased the number of burger and chips with gherkins, chillies, tomato and bits of lettuce to 24, not to mention the 12 jumbo drinks and the 12 chunky portions of apple pie, smothered with lashings of fresh cream; there was enough here to feed a regiment! Moreover, there was still no sign of Zander.

Pretty sure that there was no chance of getting their money back from the fast food outlet, the thought uppermost in everyone's mind was, *how are we going to eat this lot?*

The enormity of the gastronomic task ahead of them was still unresolved, when they heard Zander calling from the shore,

"Is everyone on board?"

His crew chorused an affirmative.

There then followed the sounds of Zander climbing aboard, and saying,

"Phew, what a lousy night to be out in and I don't think it's going to get any better. Never mind lads, we are in for the night and do I or do I not have a big surprise for you! When I get below, we'll batten down for the night and eat."

How could he know we are going to eat on board?

Right now, with the amount of food that all but covered the top of the mess table, they could eat on board for the rest of the voyage and still have plenty left over for Murdo to feed to the seagulls. *(See A Storm in Any Port)*

Three perplexed Emeraldeers heard the companionway hatch close then watched their skipper's backside coming down the ladder with him hiding something from them.

Zander's gallant band, standing between him and the heaped mess table, were waiting to find out what his 'big surprise' was.

Their skipper, so wrapped up in thinking about how clever he was, had failed to see either the packages on the table, or the baleful looks of his crew. At the bottom of the ladder, he turned and with a smug smile on his face, shouted "Tarraaa, supper!" and produced another pea from the fast food outlet's grub pod.

Still unaware of the significance of the baleful faces looking at him, he went on,

"We don't have to go out tonight. We can eat in, get an early night and be off first thing in the morning."

Grunt, who had seen his first bundle become a twin, then a triplet and now one of quads, could not keep the exasperation out of his voice when he said disconsolately,

"Just put it with the others."

Then after doing a bit of mental arithmetic, added with a touch of sarcasm,

"Thank you, Skipper! We now have: *32* burgers with dips, chips, gherkins and chillies etc, plus *16* chunky portions of apple pie with a bucket load of fresh cream. Not to mention the *16* Jumbo soft drinks to wash it all down. We are never going to be able to eat all that! What do you suggest we do with it?"

Aghast at what he now saw piled up on the table Zander's next thought was not about his crew having too much food, but that had he known, he could have saved his money.

Fatalistically, the four men sitting below decks on that lousy night came to accept that there was nothing for it but to eat as much as they could now and dispose of the rest later; if and when, they could.

It was not long before the sight of so much food curbed their appetites and the thought of eating any more, 'scunnered' them. Consequently, the Emeraldeers went to bed nursing bloated bellies and trying not to think about what they would be eating for the next few days. Wrapped in their sleeping bags, they were soon lulled to sleep by the combined effects of the boat rocking on the choppy water, the splatter of rain scouring across the deck and the wind singing through the rigging. Occasionally though, below decks the night's peace was disturbed by other 'windy' noises coming from over-full stomachs.

Four minds had had but a single thought, but they had had it at the wrong time and in the wrong place.

60

Water Walk   Loch Dochfour

Unsurprisingly, their planned early morning start did not materialise. Zander had made the executive decision to stay in the canal basin and to breakfast on last night's leftovers before tackling the locks leading to Loch Ness and all points south. As a result, it was shortly after noon before they actually got underway.

Leaving the basin and heading for Loch Ness, they were now travelling in Murdo's home patch. It was here he had served as a volunteer unpaid local councillor – and well paid poacher – so, when the Tomnahurich cemetery came in view, he was the one with the local knowledge and was determined to let his shipmates know it.

Clearing his throat noisily and pointing to port, he pompously announced,

"Do you see that hill over there? That is Tomnahurich, the Hill of the Fairies, in the Gaelic. It is the scene of one of the Brahan Seer's prophesies."

Gilbert cut across Murdo's verbal flow by saying,

"Who or what is the Brahan Seer."

Murdo enjoying his shipmate's admission of ignorance, smiled, resumed his orator's pose and continued.

"He's the famous Scottish prophet who said, "Ships with unfurled sails shall pass and re-pass Tomnahurich.'"

"So what's so wonderful about that?" Gilbert pressed, his voice emphasising the last word of his question.

"D'y'no see man? He said it in the 17th century, a hundred and fifty years before they built this Canal and when Tomnahurich was more than two miles from the sea."

Murdo paused for effect, "So you see, The Brahan Seer foretold the building of the Caledonian Canal. Now is that not something?"

Emerald's crew were now open-mouthed in amazement. Murdo had strung together more words in the last few seconds than he usually did on a whole voyage. Zander had begun to think, *why is Murdo doing a running commentary? I'm the skipper and I should be doing that.* Deep down in Zander's brain, his earlier *faux pas* forgotten, his natural optimism re-emerged. So that by the time Emerald reached Dochfour Weir, where the River Ness begins, he was more than ready to re-establish his authority.

One of the main reasons for Emerald's trip through the Caledonian Canal was to let Zander visit Dochfour Control Works, a structure he had designed some time ago and had not seen fully built.

As Emerald motored out of the end of the man-made section of the canal and into Loch Dochfour, Zander began to mimic Murdo by dramatically stretching out his left arm to port and saying,

"See that concrete structure at the far end of that long masonry weir? That is Dochfour Control Works. I designed that."

"Oh God no!" groaned Grunt. Gilbert's eyes tilted heaven ward, showing he was of a like mind.

Zander though, was now well into his stride and determined to continue.

"That's an essential part of the Foyers Pumped Storage Hydro Electric Scheme. When water is pumped up out of Loch Ness into the Loch Mhor storage reservoir up there," he said – waving his hand vaguely at the hilltop on the left – "the water level in Loch Ness drops and the flow over that weir can get very low. A couple of big sluice gates in that building pass enough water through them, to stop the river below from drying out. As soon as I finished the design, I left to go to another job. This the first time I have seen it completed."

Then, pointing to the rusty remains of a weed covered, flat-bottomed boat lying on a beach a little way upstream, said without a pause, "And that's what's left of the old ferry boat. It was still operating when I did the original site survey."

Oblivious to the fact that no one was listening, Zander pressed on,

"We'll go on a wee bit further and drop anchor. I'm going ashore. Anyone want to come with me?"

Murdo, loyal to a fault and the only one to take up the offer answered with, "Aye, why not?"

They dropped anchor just south of the weir and a little way off shore. Zander and Murdo got into the dinghy and headed for a small rickety timber jetty, not far from the old ferryboat's final resting place.

As the dinghy approached the jetty, its passengers saw two large slobbering Rottweilers crouching, Sphinx-like, at its shore end and noted that they were taking a keen interest in the dinghy's progress.

Zander nudged the small boat against an old rubber tyre fender, took the painter and stepped on to the jetty to tie up.

Murdo who only wanted to go ashore to stretch his legs was not the least bit interested in visiting Zander's masterworks; to him all of his creations were boringly dull and each one even less interesting than the one before. However when he caught sight of the dogs and saw how big and mean they looked, he gave up on any thought he had of going ashore.

Oblivious to the fact that he was on his own, Zander strode confidently along the jetty, his mind set on seeing the result of his brainchild. Reaching the jetty's landward end Zander passed the silent, unblinking dogs and strode out along a rough path cut in the long grass towards his goal. He had walked about ten metres when he heard the dogs' menacing growl.

From the safety of the dinghy, Murdo was watching the dogs and it looked to him as if up until then, they had only been monitoring Zander's progress; but now, they had taken up station in the middle of the path behind him; effectively cutting him off from the dinghy. Their growling grew louder and more threatening and when Zander heard the change in tone, he turned round and in that moment, felt the first prickles of fear. Standing stock still, menace glinting in their eyes, slobbering lips pulled back to show him rows of yellow teeth, proved that these old dogs knew a trick or two, when it came to dealing with intruders.

Number one dog barked aggressively and moved towards Zander; dog number two turned round, and in great lolloping strides that shook the flimsy jetty's to its core pounded towards Murdo. When Murdo saw the way the cookie was crumbling he threw loyalty to the wind, loosed the painter and rowed away.

Zander now cut off from the jetty and feeling vulnerable, thought, *to heck with this – I am getting out of here, but where can I go?*

With both of the brutes now sitting at his end of the jetty, growling as though daring him to pass, he looked around for an escape route. His eyes lit on the wreck of old ferry not too far away and it occurred to him that, *if I get to that, Murdo could pick me up*

With his situation becoming more desperate by the second, Zander burst into action. Pointing to the old ferry he screamed, "Over there!" climbed over the chest-high wire fence between him and the ferry, and through long thick nettle-filled grass, made a mad dash towards it.

For once, Murdo was quick on the uptake and paddled as hard as he could towards the old ferry. For Zander, it was now a race between him on one side of the fence and the dogs on the other.

The dogs howling like banshees and their tongues hanging out, saw what he was doing and were loping along the fence to cut him off where it ended on the shoreline; a few paces short of where Zander would meet the dinghy

As soon as the dinghy grounded, Murdo screamed "Hurry! Get in – jump!" For Zander already in a perilous situation and at his wits end, things got decidedly worse. Out of the corner of his eye, he saw that the blood lusting dogs had already reached the end of the fence and, like the hunters they were, homing in for a 'kill'. By now trembling uncontrollably and gasping for breath, Zander grabbed the engine mounting to push off to safety, and that was when things went terribly wrong.

Instinctively Zander had looked down to check the depth of the water and saw that the bottom was only a few inches below the surface. Assured that all he had to do was take one-step in the water, push off, jump into the dingy and he would be safe. He took the step, expecting it to land on firm ground, found no bottom and before he knew what had happened, he was floundering and spluttering, up to his waist, in icy cold water. As ever, the resourceful Murdo came to his rescue. Leaning over the back of the dinghy, he grabbed a fistful of Zander's clothing and dragged him aboard, where from face down in the bottom of the dinghy, he was muttering curses to the universe at large. Meanwhile Murdo had paddled to a safe distance and was directing his own curses at the smugly silent dogs.

The dogs began to bark again, this time however with what sounded like a fanfare of triumph. When Zander had struggled into a sitting position, he plucked a gob of yellowy mud from his trousers; looked at it closely, sniffed it, rubbed it between finger and thumb and declared knowingly.

"Sand saturated with sawdust and wood shavings!"

"I should have known," he whinged, "Nettles grow where old buildings have stood. I also remember seeing there was a sawmill shown on the old ordnance survey plans and that the last time I was here, its ruin was still standing. Now it's gone and over time, the mass of waste wood shavings has consolidated and become a foot or so of mush. "Then, glaring at his rescuer said, "That's the only bit of soggy bottom for miles around, and you found it!"

Looking back at the scene Zander saw the dogs were again lying down like Egyptian tomb sentinels guarding their territory and staring challengingly after them. As he watched, the dogs stood up well satisfied with their part in the downfall of the day's intruders, turned round and with tails wagging happily, strutted off

Back on board Emerald, Zander stripped off his sodden clothes, pulled on dry ones, took the helm and gave his grinning crew – who had not missed a second of the action – an overloud order to get Emerald moving.

Then with a pathetic display of defiance, Zander took Emerald, motor running flat out, through the narrows at the south end of Loch Dochfour and on into the deep, dark monster-infested waters of Loch Ness, disappointed that he had still not seen his masterpiece, close up.

All Zander wanted to do now was stop somewhere, put his ordeal behind him and take time to recover.

It was not to be.

61

Mooring Mishap   Urquhart Bay

Zander decided that he had done enough sailing for the day so they would stop overnight in Urquhart Castle Bay on the west side of Loch Ness. His crew, ever sensitive to his mood, offered no objection. If Zander wanted to go there, that is where they were going.

In what was left of a beautiful summer evening, Emerald goose-winged south, her deck littered with Zander's clothes, still drying out. All around them, reflections on the mirror-like surface of that world famous Loch made it look as if they were travelling on top of an upside down panorama of blue sky and heather covered hills. Occasionally a fish jumped, glimpsed by the peripheral vision of half-shut eyes but never quite seen, its re-entry splash leaving expanding circles rippling over the smooth surface of the Loch. Everyone on board had a glass of wine in their hand, taking in the overpowering beauty, atmosphere and silence of The Great Glen. All of it a reminder of why they went sailing.

As they drifted down the loch, discussing the world at large, it is only natural that the subject of the 'Monster' came up. Three of the crew who were scornful of the idea of Nessie's existence, did, never the less, keep a wary eye on the loch just in case she graced them with a 'sighting'. Murdo, a true believer was the exception. After all, his long career as the best poacher of his generation around here, had endowed him with an unparalleled fund of knowledge of the loch and everything in it. Looking around mysteriously, he assured his messmates that, conditions on the loch were perfect for Nessie-spotting.

Alas, if Nessie was there they did not see her. She must have been away visiting relatives in some other part of the twenty-mile long loch! Maybe even a cousin!

Sailing in to Urquhart Bay, Emerald's sails came down, her motor switched on and with the sound of it echoing back across the water; she puttered her way in towards the anchorage.

As usual, the Emeraldeers adopted their standard anchoring routine, i.e. keep away from official berths or moorings – which cost money – and find a place close to them and drop the hook, free of charge.

In the fading twilight, the crew saw up ahead red and the green painted oil drums that marked either side of the channel leading into the landing place directly below Urquhart Castle. Tucked away on the opposite side of the bay were a number of mooring buoys, some already occupied. Zander, in spite of Murdo's reservations, decided to anchor a little way outside these moorings.

The reason given was, as Loch Ness is deep – nearly 1000 feet in places – and even though it shelves steeply, if they were just outside the marker, the water would only be slightly deeper there than that within the line of official buoys.

Zander manoeuvred Emerald into his chosen spot, dropped anchor, made fast and her crew settled in for the night. An evening meal, was cobbled together from last night's re-heated burgers etc. The more they saw of the stuff the less palatable it became. However, this slight irritation was more than made up for by the sound night's sleep they all enjoyed afterwards. Meanwhile, Emerald continued to float on this beautiful loch in a silence broken only by ripples lapping on the hull or a breeze rattling her rigging against the mast.

Next morning as the sky began to lighten, the harsh cry of a big bird penetrated the quiet below decks and the Emeraldeers stirred. On deck, they saw that the early morning surface of the water was still flat calm and again, faithfully reflecting the details of the heather-covered hills. It was just idyllic.

After eating a proper Scottish breakfast, the Emeraldeers agreed to dump what was left of the fast food from Inverness, over the side.

Zander's plan this morning's was to run down the loch to Murdo's home village of Foyers, to allow him to fulfil a promise he had made to a relative. Grunt was to give him a hand. Zander and Gilbert would then carry on down the loch to Fort Augustus where, before entering the locks at the start of the next section of the Caledonian Canal, they would all meet up.

Skipper Zander was in the cockpit getting Emerald ready to move off; Gilbert was tidying up below, daydreaming about what was his first visit to this delightful highland loch, while on deck Murdo was washing it down and the gorilla Grunt getting ready to haul up and stow the anchor.

Emerald motored out of Urquhart Bay and heading for the middle of the loch, swung to starboard, on what should have been a gentle curve. Almost immediately, her crew heard soft scraping noises coming from below. A loud crunching sound followed and Emerald came to juddering stop, throwing everyone on board off balance – and broke up the perfect curve of her wake.

Zander first to recover, banged the engine into reverse. It had no effect. Emerald was stuck fast. An expletive from Murdo shattered the idyllic splendour of Loch Ness. * * * * "We're aground!"

At this point, with the Emeraldeers running around like headless chickens, each man offering his idea of a way out of their predicament, Zander called them to order and told them they needed a council of war and not a fishwives' chattering spat.

After due deliberation, it was agreed to put out a kedge anchor, in the hope that the combined effort of winching from it and running the engine in reverse, would pull her off. This they did, but Emerald stayed where she was.

Eventually, by a process of elimination, they decided that their best chance of success was to attach a line to the top of the mast, take it ashore in the dinghy, tie it round a rock or tree and then try to tilt the masthead over far enough to free the keel. Grunt, the obvious man to do the pulling, rightly pointed out, that the more people doing the pulling the easier the mast would be tilted over; so Murdo was press-ganged into helping him.

The pair took off in the dinghy, Murdo rowing and Grunt holding a rope, the other end of which was attached to the top of the mast. The human mules scrambled ashore where, under Gilbert's superfluous directions from on board, their Herculean efforts to pull the masthead began. Meanwhile Zander in the cockpit, with the motor idling in neutral, felt a slight tremor under his feet and saw that Emerald was slowly heeling over to starboard. At which point, his little gismo comforter, laid down to free both hands, slipped off the bench, rolled across the deck and was heading overboard.

Desperate to save his valuable little artefact – his constant companion in moments of stress or indecision – he lunged for it. And, in bending, his none too slim rear-end pushed the gear lever into reverse.

In that same instant – just when Grunt and Murdo were standing at the water's edge and had managed to tip the masthead over a few degrees – a seiche* passed under Emerald's hull, lifting her a couple of inches. The extra lift, delivered by the natural phenomenon, was enough to release Emerald's keel and with a loud sucking noise, she suddenly righted herself, and took off backwards..

Grunt and Murdo who had no time to let go their end of the rope were dragged forward a few tottering steps then, like synchronised divers, executed perfect head-first entries into the cold waters of Loch Ness and aquaplaned out towards Emerald.

Zander, bundled into a corner of the cockpit by the sudden movement, managed to stand up and disengage the gears, slowing Emerald down. When reason resurfaced in the minds of the two mini Loch Ness monsters, they let go of the rope and freed themselves from their involuntary, water-sport activity.

The free end of the rope slithered under water towards Emerald like a snake, and slid under her keel just before Zander cut off the power.

With the engine silent, the others heard Gilbert's cry for help. Thrown overboard when Emerald righted itself he was now up to his neck treading water near where Emerald had been aground.

Zander, who was the only one still dry, quickly recovered his little gismo and under his breath – loud enough for all to hear – muttered his views about his crew's stupidity, ignoring the fact that his reluctance to pay mooring fees was what had got them into the mess in the first place.

As he climbed back on board Grunt noticed that part of the rope he had recently been attached to was floating alongside the hull with its free end somewhere below the water line. Leaning out over the stern, he could see that the end had wrapped itself round the propeller.

"Hey Skipper, come and see this!"

Zander came, and looking down to where Grunt was pointing, said,

"What is it?"

"It looks like the end of that rope has wrapped itself round the prop."

Zander, hoping that what he was seeing was a water-distorted image said, "Oh no!" and reaching out over the stern, caught hold of the rope and gave it a tug.

"****! It's stuck!" (He too remembers the language of the Clyde.)

"What are we going to do?"

With that, the soaking wet figure of Murdo, who had swum back to recover the dinghy, slipped into Zander's line of vision.

"Murdo, that rope you let go of is twisted round the prop. See if you can do something about it."

"Why me?" he queried.

"Because you were the last one to touch it, you're responsible." Zander told him aggressively.

Murdo came straight back with,

"But Grunt was there as well."

"He's already on board, drying off and getting changed."

Murdo, normally a man of easy disposition and of non-confrontational nature, took some time to absorb

Zander's reasoning, *Yes, I can see some justification in what Zander is saying and yes, I am already wet and yes, I was partly to blame, so maybe I should make amends.*

"Okay, pass me the boathook."

Gilbert who was also still wet, went down to steady the dinghy. Murdo, prepared for the worst – a bad tangle and another swim – prodded around the rope, hooked into a loop and to his relief the rope came away easily. A glint of metal caught his eye, it was coming from an object lying on the gravelly bed of the loch and it looked familiar.

Half buried on the bottom lay an anchor just like Zander's spare one. The last time Murdo had seen it, after the unsuccessful attempt to use it as a kedge; it was lying unshackled on Emerald's deck. He pointed it out to Gilbert, who after taking a look himself, climbed back on board to see if Zander's precious new anchor was still there. It was not.

When Zander heard about their discovery, he suggested that, because Murdo was still wet, he should dive in to recover it. Even for Murdo, helpful chap that he usually was, this was a step too far.

"Forget it! Go get it yourself."

So emphatic was his refusal that Zander knew from experience, that when Murdo really made up his mind, no one could change it.

---

* **A seiche** (saysh) is the large, regular oscillation in a long lake, caused by wind driven water reverting to its natural level after reaching one end of the lake. In Loch Ness, this process occurs every 30 minutes approximately.

62

Diver Direct   Urquhart Bay

Zander had been let down; none of his mutinous crew would recover his precious anchor. *What can I do?* With yesterday's episode at Dochfour still fresh in his mind, he certainly did not fancy another stomach-clenching immersion in cold water.

Still mulling over his problem, he noticed a group of people in wetsuits carrying a rigid inflatable over a small beach towards the water. All except one climbed aboard, the outboard started and the inflatable took off. The one left behind started back up the shore, obviously not involved in the day's activity. A flash of inspiration lit up the inside of Zander's head,

There is just the man to recover my anchor.

"Yo, there," Zander shouted across the water.

"What do you want?" the reply came back.

"My anchor's lying on the bottom. Could you get it for me?"

"Where is it?"

"Right under my boat."

"Sure I can do that, but it'll cost you £20."

Zander had to think about this – it was going to cost him money. He gave his gismo a few more turns. *A replacement anchor will cost a lot more than that*, so grudgingly, he agreed to the recovery charge.

The diver went back up the beach and a minute or so later, re-appeared kitted out in flippers, snorkel and goggles. Wading backwards until the water was up to his knees he sat down, rolled over and with powerful strokes swam over to Emerald. Hooking one arm over the transom, he took a line from Zander and with a flick of his flippers – giving Zander a glimpse of his wet-suited rear end – dived under the boat.

With growing interest, Zander's crew sat quietly watching this development. They had been listening in to the ship to shore exchanges and knowing how painful this situation was for Zander, were amazed that he had agreed to pay someone to recover his anchor.

This just goes to show that, even with a dyed in the wool skinflint like Zander, you cannot be right all the time!

In no time at all, Zander felt a tug on his end of the line, hauled it in and when the anchor surfaced, the diver appearing with it, said, "Permission to come aboard?"

"Please do," replied Zander, the picture of charm.

The diver pulled himself out of the water, climbed aboard and was invited below for a wee dram, before he went back to the shore. Removing his flippers, the diver accepted.

As Zander and his newfound guest were disappearing below decks, he indicated to his crew that he was not to be disturbed.

Almost immediately, those not invited to Zander's party could hear, filtering up from below, the unmistakable sounds of people laughing and having fun. Now they understood what Zander was up to, he was plying the diver with whisky in the hope that he would either, forget to collect his fee or waive it.

Half an hour later, the companionway door burst open and two giggling figures staggered out. Exchanging a solemn handshake, the giggling diver struggled into his flippers, slipped overboard and swam away. A broad, satisfied smile lit up Zander's face, even though what had been left of his bottle of whisky had gone, he still had his twenty pounds; it had been a good trade-off.

After the swimmer had gone about twenty strokes, he stopped, turned back, looked up at Zander, and said

"Oh, I almost forgot. Can I have my £20 please?

63

Fishermen's Foibles   Whitebridge

Murdo had promised his Aunt in Foyers to find someone to help him to move a motorcycle for her. It was his cousin's bike, this time a male cousin, who had immigrated to Canada and sold the bike to someone in Fort Augustus. Murdo had no motorcycle license but Grunt did and although he had not used it for some time, it was still valid. Murdo needed a license, Grunt had one and wherever the license went, Grunt had to go as well.

To encourage Grunt to help him, he told him that the road on the east side of Loch Ness, from Foyers to Fort Augustus is lightly trafficked and a fantastic road to drive a motorbike on. It would be just like riding in an Isle of Man T.T. race. Then he put the icing on the cake by saying, "The bike is a shaft-drive BMW and on top of that, we'll get a free dinner in a hotel."

All of this sounded good to Grunt, so he agreed.

The pair got leave of absence from Emerald to move the bike and they would meet up with Zander and Gilbert later that evening, in Fort Augustus.

*

Gilbert grounded the dinghy on the beach just south of where the River Foyers runs into Loch Ness. Murdo and Grunt stepped ashore. Then turning the dinghy round and waving them goodbye, he headed back out to Emerald.

Although Murdo had not said anything, as well as moving the motorbike, he planned to catch up with his family and friends who still live in the village.

Grunt only found out about Murdo's social intentions when at the first house they came to Murdo knocked on the door, where, although Murdo's welcome was warm and sincere, his visit was plainly unexpected.

A couple of houses later with still no signs of either the Aunt or the motorbike, Grunt put the obvious question to his companion,

"I thought we were here to pick up a motorbike?"

"We will, we will, don't worry. We've plenty time."

Their round robin of visits just went on and on and in each one; Murdo was 'persuaded' to accept some highland hospitality. Grunt however, who was driving, was forced to abstain.

It was only when Murdo realised that it was getting near lunchtime – and they still had four miles to go to the Whitebridge Hotel for their free lunch – that he finally knocked on the Auntie's door.

Grunt was over the moon, when he saw the beautiful, gleaming beast he was to drive to Fort Augustus. Although he had not ridden a motorbike for at least ten years, and that was a little 150cc job which would hardly pull the skin off a rice pudding, here was a magnificent, 1000cc animal that looked capable of pulling a steam train, its carriages plus a full load of passengers up a steep hill. Impressed and eager to have a go Grunt climbed on, pressed the starter and heard a gurgling murmur, his only proof that the bike's powerful engine was running, and set off on a test run around the village.

Automatic gearbox, beautifully balanced, goes like a dream, almost drives itself, I can live with this. Fort Augustus here I come!

In spite of his preoccupation with the powerful machine, he did remember to go back for the not too sober Murdo, who climbing on behind him and holding on as though his life depended on it, took his leave of Auntie and set off for Whitebridge – and a free lunch.

Grunt drove past the famous Falls of Foyers through Upper Foyers, along a quiet, winding road that nestles in the sun-dappled valley of the River Foyers before joining the B 862.

The Whitebridge Hotel stands a little way north of a collection of houses that constitute the tiny highland village, of Whitebridge. Behind it is one of General Wade's old stone-arch bridges. Half close your eyes and Whitebridge could be Brigadoon.

Walking into the hotel Grunt felt he had taken a step back in time, but came back into the present when he entered a dining room full of people in smart, casual dress, and not as he had almost expected, in old kilts with hairy sporrans, woollen bonnets and tartan plaids.

*

After enjoying a first class meal the 'bikers' retired to the lounge where a waiter brought them coffee, mints and a large Drambuie each.

Murdo had a mouthful of coffee then went to reception and asked to see the old fishing catch records. The receptionist told him that they were in a cupboard down the hall and that she would bring them to him in a few minutes, which she did.

As soon as they arrived, Murdo passed one of the dusty old ledgers to Grunt who, in flipping through its pre-ruled, well-thumbed pages, found that each page was full of copperplate hand-written entries, itemising the daily catches from the nearby lochs.

In his hands, Grunt held a detailed history of the principal recreational pursuit of the visitors to this area of the highlands, in times long gone by, and what interesting reading they made. It was noticeable, that the majority of the entries were those of English fishing parties.

Typical examples from the late 19th century read,

> The Rev. Mainwairing of Preston and party fished Loch Knockie, 12 rods, weather fine, catch 135 fish, total weight of catch 38lbs3 oz, largest fish 12oz. Comments; it was a delightful day. <u>The Lord be praised for his wonderful bounty.</u>

> Mr Fotheringale of London and his party fished Loch Faraline, rods 4, weather cloudy, occasional sun, light rain, catch 8 fish, total weight of catch 14lbs, largest fish 2lb 5oz. Comments; many undersized fish caught were put back unrecorded. <u>An excellent and productive day's fishing.</u>

Grunt spent some time thumbing through the books but soon found the entries, although interesting, were all much the same, so laying the book down on the table he stood up and said, "Time to go."

While his tongue was still searching the bottoms of the tiny glasses for the last dregs of the Drambuie, Grunt felt a presence behind him and a voice saying,

"Those were the days. Eh!"

Turning round, he saw the manager pointing at the fish books.

"They certainly were." Grunt agreed with a hint of a sigh, "I'd liked to have lived when the world was like that."

The manager added a qualification,

"Aye, but only if I had pots of money."

Then pausing for a second to reflect, he went on,

"How was your meal?"

Murdo, piped up, "Magic!" after all, it was his show."
Grunt, who correctly assumed the question was aimed at him, answered,

"Excellent. Most enjoyable."

"Thank you." said the owner, paused then added. "Would I be right in thinking that you're the driver?"

"Yes."

"Then you'll know that the deal was a free meal for the driver taking my son's bike down to him in Fort Augustus." Then turning to Murdo, handed him a piece of paper.

"Your bill, Murdo."

In the blink of an eye Murdo sobered up and his face became a mask of tragedy and he blurted out, "Bill? It's all paid for."

"Sorry, the arrangement was dinner for the driver. You can pay at reception on your way out."

64

Crow's Contribution   Whitebridge

On their high-speed run over what used to be General Wade's Military Road between Inverness and Fort Augustus, Grunt was revelling in being in control of this wonderful motorcycle. For a lot of the way, the road was virtually straight and when he opened up the beast's throttle, the wild and rugged scenery slipped by in a blur. Behind him, Murdo, hanging on like grim death, kept his eyes tightly shut for most of the way. Alternatively, maybe he was recovering from the shock of paying for his dinner.

Grunt with the terrified 'monkey' on his back, roared past Loch Knockie then rattling over a few deer grids, rode up to the high point of the road that looks way, way down on Loch nan Uan. He then negotiated the gently winding road down to Loch Tarff, where they stopped for a few minutes to take in the view. Grunt, who had never travelled this side of the Great Glen before, found it far more interesting and infinitely more spectacular than the road he usually took on the west side of the Loch.

On the final downhill stretch into Fort Augustus, Grunt took pity on his passenger and eased back on the throttle. Rounding a bend on the fenced, tree lined road with the bike making hardly a sound, Grunt – who was still cornering like a TT driver – startled a big black crow resting on a fence post.

The bird, catching sight of a silent predator coming from nowhere, moved – twice. Firstly, a panic-stricken flight across the road right in front of the predator, the second left a terror-induced ribbon of pongy bird poo streaming in its wake. Grunt who caught a glimpse of the bird flying away wondered, *what's that smeared across my visor? It smells funny too.* Stamping down hard on the brake, he brought the speeding bike to a shuddering stop then putting it up on its stand, had a look.

Something had done a whitewash job all over his jacket, helmet and goggles. Murdo sitting behind him, although protected from the worst of the effusion, had not escaped. "Bloody crows!"

What they needed now was somewhere to clean up, and the sooner the better. From memory, Murdo knew there was a public convenience just along the road, so wiping off as much of the gunge off as they could, they remounted and headed for it.

When they got there, its door was shut and locked. Murdo walked round to the back of the building and in a few moments, came back, waved to Grunt to follow him who, on turning the corner, saw Murdo standing with one hand on a water tap and in the other a short length of hose.

Grunts immediate thought was, *It s better than nothing and it will do for the time being.* Then, after lightly hosing each other down, the slightly cleaner bikers got back on the bike and drove on to complete their mission.

By some miracle, not a single drop of the effusion had touched the bike and ten minutes later, in almost the same pristine condition as it had been when they started out, they delivered it to its grateful new owner.

Understandably, the stinky pair declined his offer of a cup of coffee.

A whisky on the other hand would have been a different matter, but that was not on offer.

65

Poachers Plunge   Fort Augustus

It was from the grounds of the Fort Augustus Monastery in the 6th century, that Saint Columbus reputedly had the first sighting of the 'Loch Ness Monster'.

The Emeraldeers' rendezvous was the little harbour behind the Monastery's building. When Grunt and Murdo got there, sure enough, Emerald lay at anchor a short way off a small stone pier jutting into the Loch.

Murdo called over to her, "Ahoy, Emerald." his voice booming out over the loch." There was no response. They then noticed Emerald's dinghy tied up to an iron ring beside a little slipway, made from two parallel steel piles.

"The boys must be ashore," Grunt observed, somewhat unnecessarily.

At that, there was a shout from behind them as Zander and Gilbert, carrying bulging plastic message bags, appeared out of a clump of trees a short distance away.

Murdo was bringing the dinghy alongside the pier for a quick getaway, when his poacher's eye caught a flash of silver under the water and he thought; *there's a decent sized fish down there!* His instincts now took over and in a flash of his own, he was lying face down on the slipway, his face a picture of concentration. Gradually he inched his way down one of the piled channel sections, and gently reaching under the steel he began to feel for his supper. His fingers touched something, so he began 'guddling'. His fish moved a fraction away from his hand. Murdo, intent only on maintaining contact with his semi-mesmerised prey, began inching forward, totally unaware that his frictional contact with the highly polished surface was, inch by inch, getting less and less until, with a sinking feeling he realised he was very slowly sliding down towards the water.

"No-o-o- o-o-o," he screamed in alarm.

His cry focussed his messmate's attention on his predicament and with plenty of time to enjoy it, they watched his almost imperceptible creeping descent become a frantic hand clutching, toe scraping downward slide towards the dark, cold waters of Loch Ness.

The moment Murdo's head touched the water, his whole day flashed in front of him,

...dragged underwater at Urquhart Bay, stuck with an unexpected bill at Whitebridge, hanging on for dear life on an interminable, hell-for-leather motor bike ride, crapped on by a crow, hosed down by Grunt and now this, at which point he gave up all efforts to save himself and gracefully slid in and under the surface of the water.

Amidst a round of applause, Murdo spluttering and gasping, surfaced just in time to hear Zander solemn declaration,

"I name this idiot Murdo Grant and may God help all who sail with him!"

*

It is worth reporting here that the fish was not hurt in any way and lived to swim another day.

66

Canal Capers   Fort Augustus

During the summer months, the towpath alongside the Caledonian Canal at Fort Augustus is a popular attraction for locals and visitors. Today was no exception and a good crowd of 'gongoozlers' (people with an interest in canals and canal life) had gathered there.

In preparation for Emerald's transit through the locks, Zander had dressed to impress. Standing with one hand on the wheel, he was wearing a white Aran sweater, plush mustard-coloured cords, white boat shoes and a bargee's hat with 'scrambled egg' on the brim,' and doing his best to convince any observers that he was the man in charge. With a pair of large binoculars slung round his neck and a determined look on his face, he certainly looked the part – provided one did not have access to his long history of misdemeanours.

Emerald's transit began smoothly enough until a lock keeper stopped her from going into the first lock when it was obvious to Zander that there was still plenty of room for her to get in; they would now have to wait for the next lock-cycle. Convinced that the canal official had deliberately picked on him, this did not go down at all well with her skipper, who took the rejection personally.

In due course Emerald did get into the lock and being the first boat in, finished close up to the forward gate. Zander, still festering at what he saw as a bureaucratic misuse of power, had begun to climb the ladder up to the towpath.

Wrapped up in the justification of *his* case and more than ready to discuss it with the official, Zander had not noticed the lock starting to fill up. Whether by accident or by the lockkeeper's design, the incoming water was nudging Emerald's bow towards the lock gate. The lockkeeper, who wanted nothing to do with his awkward customer, was looking past Zander, which made Zander wonder. *What is he looking at?*

Following the lock keeper's gaze, Zander saw that Emerald's pulpit rail was touching the lock gate and more alarmingly, it had snagged under one of the gate's cross-members that was slowly pushing her nose down.

Straight away Zander abandoned any thought of argument and shouting a warning to his crew, scuttled down to get back on board.

On deck, Gilbert and Murdo, still oblivious to the pickle they were in, heard Zander's shout, looked around, saw the problem and rushed forward to free Emerald's bow. Meanwhile, in Zander's panic driven rush to re-board he had got down as far as deck-level and his brain had already told his legs that Emerald's pulpit was still stuck under the lock gate and it was safe to board. What his brain did not know was that by the time his legs obeyed, Emerald had lurched free. She reacted in two planes, one backwards the other pushing her bow up. Neither of these sudden movements had come into Zander's calculations, so by the time a new instruction, *'don't go!'* screamed into his brain, he had already gone.

At the back of his throat, Zander sensed the acidic smell of old car batteries, and using another instinctive sense, self-preservation, he panicked. Now tottering over the gap where Emerald had been, he was canal bound!

Grunt, who had let the others cope with the first emergency and now seeing that Zander was in no position to help himself, leapt to the rescue. Grunt's firm hold on the seat of mustard coloured velvet cords, gave Zander just enough time to grab and hang onto a rope dangling over the edge of the lock. With one end of the line attached to the shore and the backside of his trousers clutched in Grunt's hand Zander had become a human mooring line.

When the rest of Zander's crew saw his predicament, they stumbled over the still wallowing deck to help him. However as a result of Grunt's prompt intervention, Murdo's skilful prompt manoeuvring and Gilbert's words of encouragement, Zander was able to slide along the rope and get back on board Emerald.

The gongoozlers already watching the action were joined by Passers-by, who drawn by the commotion, were looking down on the sorry sight of a heavily breathing Zander, valiantly doing his best to give the impression that nothing untoward was happening. After a minute or two, Zander flexed his muscles, moved his arms and legs around to make sure there was nothing broken and was relieved to find that, apart from rope burns on his slime-covered hands, he was still in one piece.

His posh clothes however were a different matter.

The sole of one of his white boat shoes had come away from the upper, the white Aran sweater was badly soiled with a green brown slime and his mustard coloured velvet cords were mud smeared and torn at the knees. There was no sign of his hat but thankfully, his binoculars were safe and apparently unscathed.

A loud cheer went up and when Zander looked, he saw the lock keeper pushing a long boathook out towards Emerald; hanging from the end of it was a dripping wet, piece of dark blue cloth. It took Zander a moment of two to recognise the lock keeper's offering. *Not my beautiful hat, it can't be*, he thought despairingly; but it was and the scrambled egg on its brim had become a lump of slimy green moss and it was an even sorrier sight than Zander.

With little grace, Zander took his hat, wrung it out as best he could, swung it round to remove as much water as possible and, to a titter from his audience, clapped its shapeless mess on his head.

With what little dignity remained, this sorry slime-scarred figure, with a clown-like flapping shoe sole, turned, strutted over to the hatchway and disappeared below. The last thing Zander saw as he dropped down the companionway was the lock keeper's face beaming down at him.

Understandably, Zander did not appear on deck again until that section of the canal was well behind them.

*

During the course of the morning, the Emeraldeers discovered that their toilet was not working properly and by midday, it had stopped functioning altogether. By the time they reached Laggan in the afternoon, the situation on board was desperate. Whenever possible anyone feeling the need, had taken *over-the-side* relief, but more often than not, there was either a lady walking her dog along the towpath, picnickers in the adjoining fields or another vessel close by. *Where did all these people come from?* Consequently, the Emeraldeers did not often get to do what comes naturally.

Eventually, in the late evening arriving at a quiet spot, Emerald's crew took the opportunity to ease the pressures that had built up inside them all day. Proving that what has to be got rid of is much easier to dispose of in the dark!

In the fading twilight of what had not been a good day for her skipper, Emerald arrived at the head of Loch Lochy.

67

Emerald's Entertainers   Corpach

Next morning Emerald motored down Loch Lochy, passed through the southern section of the canal and dropping down an impressive series of locks – the Devil's Staircase, came out into Loch Linnhe near Corpach. In spite of the 'ups and downs' of their passage, the Emeraldeers were a well-satisfied crew. By completing the transit of the Caledonian Canal, they had achieved what they had set out to do.

Sorting out 'the heads' though, was something that could wait until the morning, as right now the Emeraldeers had a far more important item on their agenda, to go to the Corpach Hotel, have a beer or two and then enjoy a good meal. Which, they did.

At closing time, in inky black darkness, Emerald's happy crew left the hotel and before going back to Emerald with its' 'broken bog', they stopped in the car park to do what had been denied them all day.

Facing the hotel, lined up like a firing squad and ready for action, the skipper gave the command to fire. Just then, the hotel doors burst open and a crowd of customers streamed out. Under the comforting cover of pitch-darkness, this posed no problem to the 'toileteers', who just carried on with their own relief of Corpach.

What they had not noticed was that, earlier a number of people had come out of the hotel and were already in their cars. This timing is important!

With the Emeraldeers at full stream ahead, these early leavers switched on their engines and headlights. The driver of an open sports car also turned on his radio at full volume, filling the car park with triumphant, symphonic music.

The car park had become an arena, the headlights providing the lighting, a car radio the music and the 'toileteers' the dancing waters.

Corpach's first *'Son et Lumiere'* was happening right in front of a large, uninvited audience!

To raucous cheers and applause, the performers fled the arena. Later on board Emerald, large damp patches on the crew's trouser fronts exposed their frantic failure to zip up their flies, on the run.

68

Feeling Flush   Corpach

Although a few minor snags found during the voyage still needed his attention, Zander felt comfortable enough to leave sorting them out until Emerald was back on her home mooring. What Emerald did need though, was a thorough clean up.

In his delegating mode Zander was playing with his nut and bolt. Gilbert was on deck inspecting the rigging and checking the sails. Grunt too was on deck pretending to polish the bright-works, while Murdo, in the water, was standing on the dinghy scrubbing his way around the hull.

With the hull cleaned to his satisfaction, Murdo decided to clear the blockage in the soil pipe, by rodding back through the hull. Every time he pushed the rod in, he pushed himself away from Emerald. Shouting up to Grunt, he asked him to come down and steady the dinghy for him.

Meanwhile Zander, his self-allotted (non-existent) tasks completed, decided to carry out his Captain's inspection. His first port of call was 'the heads', to see if they were still blocked. It so happened that Zander did his system test just as Murdo was removing the rod from that unit's exit pipe.

The occupants of the dinghy heard the self-sealing toilet lid drop and the flushing lever cranking. In the nanosecond between realising what the noises meant and taking the necessary action, it was already too late!

In a torrent, the gunge-laden contents behind the blocked pipe gushed out of the discharge pipe and splattered all over Murdo and Grunt. Clearly, the obstruction was now clear, but the 'clearer' had not had time to get himself and his helper clear.

Murdo managed to stay on the dinghy but Grunt was now swimming in a sea of disgusting yuck, surrounded by bits of goodness knows what. Clearly, someone had disposed of some of the excess food from their Inverness bun-feast by breaking it up and stuffing it down the toilet. No wonder their bog had not worked – it had been well and truly, bogged up!

The commotion brought Zander up on deck and when he looked down on the unfortunates, he averted his gaze, pinched his nose between two fingers and enquired,

"What's going on?"

Then taking in the evidence of his own eyes, observed unfeelingly,

"Phew, that water's a bit manky for swimming, I suggest you both go ashore and get cleaned up because you're certainly not getting on my boat in that state." Then, adding insult to injury declared, "And, while you're there, clean up that dinghy.

69

Grunt's Gaffe   Fort William

Zander dropped anchor in Loch Linnhe a little way west of Fort William and with Grunt in tow went ashore to have a look around the town. Dragging the dinghy up onto a little beach not far from the centre of town, they wandered up an alleyway and mingled with the throng of visitors window-shopping along the main thoroughfare.

They had hardly gone any distance when they heard a shriek of, "Stop thief!" coming from behind them.

Turning as one, the Emeraldeers saw a distraught woman pointing a shaking finger at a running man and screaming hysterically,

"He's stolen my handbag!"

The dynamic duo, brought up in the days of chivalry when it was the 'done thing' to help a lady in distress, sprang into action. Zander taking charge, jerked a finger at the fleeing man and told Grunt,

"Get after him! I'll find a policeman!"

Grunt who had already taken off in pursuit of the bag snatcher, hardly heard his skipper's superfluous instruction. In the short chase that ensued Grunt caught up with the fugitive, jumped on his back and forced him, face down on to the ground. No match for Grunt, the thief with a great lump of flesh and muscle sitting on his back, was quickly immobilised.

Grunt looked around but could see no sign of the snatched bag and although he asked his captive what he had done with it, he could hardly breathe let alone respond.

For once Zander was in luck; even as he turned to look for a police officer, two, alerted by the woman's screams, appeared on either side of him. "Over there!" Zander said, pointing at Grunt sitting on his floored captive, a short distance away. "My man has already caught the villain!"

And, turning to address the sobbing woman, added,

"Don't worry, madam, we've got him. Everything's all right now."

Taking the woman's arm and glowing with pride, Zander walked after the police officers to join the tableau of police, pursuer and captive.

By this time a number of nearby pedestrians were already giving Grunt, still restraining the footpad face down on the footpath, a round of applause for his heroic act of civil duty. Zander now full of himself, began to force a way through the crowd shouted,

"Make way. Please let the police through to help my associate to take the despicable thief into custody."

One of the policemen, rolling his eyes up in their sockets, shouldered his way past Zander, tapped Grunt on the shoulder and said,

"All right then, sir. You can let him up now, we've got him," and with his partner's help, got Grunt off the almost senseless man.

Bloody, dishevelled, and still in no condition to speak, the thief was unceremoniously hauled to his feet, handcuffed and held fast between the two custodians of the law. When the victim saw the thief's face, she screamed even louder than before,

"That's not him, that's my husband – he was chasing the thief!"

Ignoring the police, the woman threw her arms round her husband and began to console him with sympathetic words and soothing endearments. In the trice that it took, for the police to absorb the truth of the situation, they turned their attention back to their 'helpers'. They were no longer there.

It was not too long after this that, the police officers, the victim, her husband and the assembled crowd, unaware of its significance, heard an outboard motor starting up.

Had they looked in the right direction, they would have seen a dinghy, stern down bow-up, accelerating out into the bay and making a beeline for Emerald. In it were two men with their waterproof hoods pulled well up over their heads.

For once Zander and Grunt had timed their exit well. They came, they saw, they had created mayhem and thanks to Grunt's brave intervention, the real thief got clean away.

70

Heading Home   Ardfern

It was with genuine regret that the Emeraldeers said goodbye to Emerald. She had been their home for the past week, but now they were heading back to their dry land homes. Lucy, Grunt's wife, drove her husband and Gilbert back down to Edinburgh. Murdo did not say where he was going; only that he was going to stay with a cousin. Enough said!

Jane, who had driven up with Lucy, would stay on board Emerald, now berthed at Ardfern. From here the new master and mistress would take her out, as and when they felt like it, and with Jane on board, it was unlikely that anything untoward would happen.

The disbanded crew had a lot to tell friends and family, particularly about the stupidity and thoughtlessness of their shipmates. Naturally, one never said anything about his own shortcomings and always 'generously' attributed things disreputable, to someone else.

One thing is certain; the Emeraldeers will always create mayhem, otherwise life for them would be dull. For the time being though, they were all going their separate ways, each of them reverting to his former uneventful, mundane life.

Still, with Emerald in Ardfern ready for the next adventure, her now fragmented crew were confident that they would all sail again but when, who knows?

TWO MEN ON A BIG BOAT

The 7th at Pebble Beach

71

On a Real Boat   Cruising

Much later in life, Zander and Grunt took their wives Jane and Lucy, on a cruise. At dinner on the first evening, their table companions were two Welsh couples, and an Italian and his wife – who the Welshmen had mentally designated, foreigners and subsequently ignored them.

Thereafter, every evening at dinner, in voices that overflowed into the listening space of the adjoining tables, the Welshmen held forth about their own and their compatriots' musical talents. Normal conversation for those within earshot was drowned out by overloud views and assertions, such as,

"Do you know, Boyo, I'm a leading tenor; baritones are ten a penny, but tenors, really good tenors, are a rare breed indeed. You know I can move up to my 'head' voice seamlessly and the tonal quality and purity of my voice makes wine glasses resonate to destruction." or, "The Welsh are not only the greatest singers in the world but the finest rugby players."

Dinner at that table and for those nearby, had become a hurried 'sit, order, eat, drink and get out as soon as politely possible' affair. Zander and Grunt could have asked for another table but they did not want to make a fuss.

It started innocently enough one evening when the one of the 'singers' smugly stated,

"Bet you wish you had sung in public like us. Marvellous it is, to give so much pleasure to so many people."

The non-Welsh at the table smiled tolerantly but by now, Zander had taken more than enough and slamming his way into the conversation and pointing to Grunt said,

"I will have you know that my good friend here was a leading soloist in a production at the first Edinburgh International Festival of Music and Drama. He just chooses not to sing in public anymore."

This revelation, apart from raised eyebrows, made no impression on these 'real singers', but it did draw nods of approval from the Italian couple.

Next morning, Grunt, lying on a lounger, quietly working on his tan, felt someone thump his sun bed and brought an abrupt end to what had been a contented snooze. Opening his eyes, there was a figure blocking him off from the sun and when it spoke, his heart sank,

"There's a talent contest on tonight, Bach. We are going in for it and I tell you, man, we'll be very hard to beat. We're off now to rehearse. You must come and hear us?"

For years now, Grunt had enjoyed life without singing, except to himself in the shower, pottering about in his workshop or in duets with his car radio. For him singing in public was a definite *no-no*. The rudely wakened sunbather, shading his eyes like a sailor saluting, said dismissively, "No thanks. I'll wait for the main event."

*

That evening, all the way through dinner, their Welsh table companions boasted about how easily they were going to win tonight's talent contest.

"You must come and see us, Bach, we'll be great."

Later on, misplaced politesse saw Zander, Grunt, their wives and the Italian couple sitting in the theatre.

The 'Welsh wonders' were the finale to a string of hopeful acts that successively failed to improve as the evening dragged on. Grunt had his own biased opinion about Welshmen and believed that whenever two of them sang together, one will always be the conductor and this pair of troubadours confirmed his view. While sharing the microphone, one waved his hands to generate the timing and the inflection for every phrase and note, while they both over-exaggerated the pronunciation of each word.

The fact that they had supplied their own music and had a long discussion with the band, about key and tempo, added little to their performance. The unfortunate pair did not have a true note between them; their breathing control was non-existent, any harmonies they attempted shrieked of discord and while one sang on beat, the other was somewhere near the backbeat. To top this off both of them strained their voices to excess, each one trying to sing louder than the other. They were terrible, and embarrassingly so! The bottom of the barrel was some way up from where they were. Now even some of the preceding acts were beginning to look good.

In the embarrassing silence that followed their act, the Host felt he must say something to cover up the fiasco.

Grabbing the microphone, he thanked the Welsh troubadours, put on a big cheesy grin and invited the audience to show their appreciation. Then, still grinning, tried to mask the desultory applause by asking if anyone else would like to perform. This appeal came just as Zander's group – their duty done – stood up to leave.

One of the Welshmen on his way off stage, turned back, grabbed the microphone and pointing at his dinner table companions already walking towards the exit suggested,

"Why not get them to do a turn; one of them has sung at the Edinburgh Festival."

A spotlight was trained on the group and the Host pounced, "Give them a big hand, folks," waving an invitation to Grunt's group, now standing trapped in a spotlight.

Grunt and Zander, frantically waving their rejection to the suggestion, felt a light touch on their elbows.

"Don't worry, we sing together. Yes?" the Italian said and winking reassuringly added, "Just follow me." Turning to Zander he said, "You will be the conductor."

The Italian made his arrangements with the Host and the accompanist, ignored the microphone, and began to sing in a beautiful and effortless tenor voice. All Grunt had to do was sing along in his quiet baritone, harmonizing appropriately either a third above or below. Zander, genuinely carried away by the sheer magnificence of what he was hearing, was waving his hands in the air in time with the music.

When their performance ended, there was a moment or two of silence, before thunderous applause interspersed with whistling and stamping, filled the theatre. As far as Grunt was concerned, the dumbstruck, faces of the Welshmen, standing in the wings, had made his return to singing in public, well worth doing.

Dinner the following evening was a pleasure; not only did everyone around not have to listen to the absent Welshmen, but also were free to enjoyed the pleasure of uninterrupted conversation.

It turned out that the quiet Italian was a member of the chorus of his countries' national opera company. His mother was an Italian, his father Welsh, and strangely enough, his name was Jones!

He also confided to his remaining table companions, "I do believe that the Welsh are good singers, particularly if like me, they are blessed with a little bit of Italian blood. However, that pair were the worst of what are usually a good crowd. I just could not resist the temptation to put them in their place. Please forgive me."

Although Grunt had thoroughly enjoyed singing with the Italian he also knew when to quit, so once again he did just that.

72

Reality is Virtually Unreal!   Cruising

On every cruise, there are passengers who treat the onboard activities as deadly serious competitions. There are bowlers, deck tennis hands, darts players, whist and bridge aficionados and golfers who are only there for what they can win. Each one a dedicated eyeball to eyeball pothunter.

Jane was having a facial; Grunt and Lucy were on a shore excursion which left Zander at a loose end. Sitting in the library reading a book, he was only vaguely aware of the ship's announcement.

Anyone intending to participate in the golf competition should assemble on deck 10 immediately."

At the same time a figure appeared between him and the large porthole window, cutting off his light. Looking up he saw that the culprit was a long-legged platinum blonde, entertainments team, crew member and his intended angry outburst died on his lips.

"C'mon sir, you look like a good golfer."

"No thanks," was all he could blurt out, staring at the vision in front of him.

"Why not join in?"

"I don't play golf."

Fluttering her long false eyelashes, she bent over him bringing her barely concealed bust down to his eye level and treated him to her impression of a 'Marilyn Monroe' pout. "That doesn't matter it's only a bit of fun." Embarrassed as much as anything, Zander relented. He was taken by the hand, escorted to the assembly point and introduced to the strapping young man in charge. 'Marilyn' meanwhile, her duty done, breezed off to round up some more punters.

When the strapping young man thought he had enough players, he announced that he would start by dividing the group into two lots, one to play crazy golf, the other to go inside the reality golf studio to take part in a near-est-the-pin competition. Then later, the two lots would swap over.

Zander went into the studio and took a seat against the back wall. The lights dimmed and on the wall opposite him, the picture of a golf green, as seen from the elevated tee, appeared on a screen. A tiny green, guarded by six bunkers, stuck out into the ocean at the far end of a narrow peninsula, with fearsome waves crashing onto its rocky shore margin. Lettering materialised across the top of the image reading, 110 yard Par Three 7th at Pebble Beach, There was a gasp of expectancy from the audience, they were about to take on one of the most famous, hazardous and daunting tee shots in golf.

The strapping young man explained,

"Each competitor will have three shots to get as close to the hole as he can." and pointing to some clubs leaning on the wall beside him. "When it's your turn grab a club and go to the mat." pointing again. And good luck!"

Where Zander was sitting meant he would be last to play. He sat and watched competitor after competitor, select a club, waggle it a few times, step onto the mat, place a ball on the tee, take a couple of practice swings then smash the ball at the screen. When the golf ball hit the screen, its screen image continued to fly towards the green, its direction and trajectory calculated by a hidden computer.

Most of the shots landed on the green and bounced to a stop; the computer then calculated how far it had stopped from the hole and that distance was shown at the bottom of the screen.

As each successive competitor 'demonstrated' his skill or more likely chanced his luck, Zander started to feel more and more uneasy because nearly everyone was landing at least one ball on the green. Stuck in a dark corner, with the door shut and nowhere to go, when his turn came, he had no option but to play.

Going over to the clubs, he searched through them and picked one up. A couple of his opponents sitting nearby murmured their surprise. The strapping young man came over and in a patronising voice said,

"Sorry sir, that shouldn't be there, it's a putter. Here try this one," handing him another club.

Blotted my copybook already and I've not played yet.

Then, imitating those who had gone before, Zander picked up a ball, placed it on the mat, waggled the club a few times and took a swipe. There was no sound of the club hitting the ball, no shock to his hands and no thump of the ball hitting the screen. He had just demonstrated a perfect fresh air shot.

To quell the sniggers rippling around the room the strapping young man held up his hands and said, "Try again, sir."

Zander sucked in a big breath, teed up for his second attempt and took a slower, more deliberate swipe at the ball. Contact, then relief, the ball thumped into the screen – its image taking an enormous slice – missed the green on the right, bounced about on rocks and plopped into the Pacific Ocean.

This brought an ironic round of applause

Well, it will all be over soon, Zander thought, and placed his third ball on the carpet.

Wiggle, wiggle, twitch, twitch, slash, click; Zander had hit the ball. There followed a thwack on the screen and after a brief pause, the ball was seen heading in the direction of the green.

In the squash court like vault of the small cinema, Zander, the strapping young man and the rest of the golfers watched in silence as the ball reached its zenith, began to drop, still in line with the flag, bounced three times, hit the flagstick and disappeared into the hole.

The room erupted to the sound of pre-recorded cheers, and then emblazoned across the screen in huge letters flashed the words,

CONGRATULATIONS!
A HOLE IN ONE

The lights came on to illuminate Zander's fellow golfers climbing over each other to be the first to congratulate him. Until now, they had jeered, but now they were cheering and crowding around patting him on the back, trying to shake his hand and saying things like,

"Great shot." and "Well done.".

Still unable to believe what was happening, and to the strains of a recording of #Congratulations#, the strapping young man presented Zander with a prize voucher.

Clutching his prize in one hand and fending off his enthusiastic admirers with the other, Zander told the strapping young man that he would give crazy golf a miss. After all, he had achieved something that every golfer dreams about doing but few ever do. He got a hole in one; anything else now would be an anticlimax.

After Zander had gone, the strapping young man went into the computer room.

"How on earth did that happen," he demanded, "that was a bloody awful shot."

The man who manipulated the gadgetry replied defensively. "Poor guy, I felt so sorry for him. That last shot of his was going nowhere near the green, but luckily it was so far off target I had time to flick the switch that superimposes the perfect shot onto the screen."

Later that evening when Zander entered the bar, his fellow golfers greeted him with more backslapping and hand shaking before reminding him that tradition demanded he buy drinks for everyone. One of the more sensible ones, pointed out that, in a crowded bar containing only a small percentage of his fellow competitors it would be better if he bought a bottle of whisky and placed it on the bar for golfers to help themselves. Which he did and so did they.

On the last day of a cruise, winners could redeem their vouchers in a special cabin. Zander, wondering what his prize would be, could hardly contain himself. He knew that professional golfers often won a car for a hole in one, so it stood to reason that his prize must be something special, maybe even a free cruise or a holiday.

Buoyed up with expectancy Zander found the special cabin, went in and handed his voucher to the crewmember sitting behind a desk.

"Mmmm, a gold voucher, not often I see one of those."

Wow! Zander though, *this should be good.*

The crewmember went on with what he was saying,

"That means you can have any prize on the top shelf: A blow up teddy dressed as a sailor with the ship's name printed on its shirt. A set of hardboard drinks coasters with a photo of the ship on them. A lovely plastic case for carrying your passport round your neck, emblazoned with the ship's name. Or what about a little gift for your lady, a woven canvas bag showing a lifebelt inscribed with the ship's name printed on it............"

What a load of old tat! And it's already cost me a bottle of whisky!

Turning away in disgust Zander grunted, "Bloody golf!"

73

They Saw Him Coming   Ukraine

In the Crimea, Zander went on a shore excursion leaving Jane onboard to visit the hairdresser and the beauty salon.

Before they started the tour, when he and the other passengers had settled down on the bus, their courier told them that the country's armed forces had not been paid for some time. And, because of this, they should not be surprised if, the minute they left the bus, soldiers or sailors would try to sell them cap badges, items of uniform, tin helmets and other bits of military paraphernalia.

Zander then went on to spend an enthralling three hours at the Rotunda, where a three-dimensional 360° painting of the Siege of Sevastapol is its principal feature. Before this, he had been to the harbour and seen the well-hidden high security tunnels formerly used by the old Cold War Black Sea Fleet submarines. In spite of the courier's advice, he had already succumbed to temptation and for a single US dollar, had bought a forage cap covered in colourful enamelled army badges. *What a fantastic bargain. I wonder what else I can get.*

The excursion leader had now met up with an English speaking Russian guide who had taken the party to the spot where Lord Cardigan and his entourage had watched the Charge of the Light Brigade. And, while everyone was looking out across the broad flat valley between rolling hills, to hear how this infamous episode had unfolded, Zander moved away from the main party to where he could photograph the Valley of Death, without the rest of the party appearing in the image.

A noisy 'Sssst' came from behind him. He turned 'Sssst!' There it was again and, from a few of yards away, a soldier emerged from the shrubbery signalling for Zander to follow him into the clump of light shrubbery behind him. Which Zander, after looking around, did.

Emerging into a small clearing, Zander was in what could well have been a front line battle position. Laid out on the ground was an array of automatic rifles, machine guns, side-arms, mortars and standing behind them, soldiers all looking in his direction, each man vigorously vying for his attention and clearly offering for sale, what was on display.

Furtively, a scruffy, waif like, girl soldier came into the clearing, holding a pair of trench periscope binoculars, something he had always fancied but back home, were far too expensive to buy. As he walked towards her, two bigger and older soldiers chased her away by slapped her and kicking her departing backside.

Zander had seen enough. He wanted no part of this. Smiling his best smile he held up both hands palm forwards, backed out of the clearing and rejoined the tour party.

About two-hundred metres down the track with the tour party slowly wending its way back towards the bus, Zander slightly detached from it, heard another 'Sssst' coming from the hedgerow bordering the track. This time the 'Sssst' trying to gain his attention was female rather than a male.

Looking through a gap in the bushes Zander saw the waif like girl soldier holding out the periscope binoculars with one hand, while with the other, was rubbing her forefinger and thumb together. "Fifty dollars." she said, holding up a hand with the five fingers extended. *That looks like a good deal,* Zander thought. However, Zander being Zander he wanted a better deal so, he pulled a twenty-dollar note from his pocket and offered that to her. In a flash, the girl was through the bushes, thrust the binoculars into his hand, snatched his twenty-dollar note, and in an instant, had vanished back into the woods.

Zander had just become the owner of a pair of pristine, prismatic trench binoculars which, when he held them up and looked through them, brought distant things right bang up close and with sharply focussed three-dimensional clarity. *What a piece of kit this is, and for only twenty dollars. Something like that would cost a small fortune back home.*

Zander then rejoined the group who were by now filing back on to the bus and once on board he sat down beside a window.

For a good five minutes, the bus did not move and there was no sight of the driver. Then, the local guide accompanied by a police officer came on board, made straight for Zander, held out a hand clearly demanding that he relinquish his recent purchase. What could he do but reluctantly hand them over.

The police officer then got off the bus, the driver got on, the visibly anxious tour guide, staring at Zander and daring him not to do anything, only relaxed when the doors closed and the bus had moved off.

With the police officer gone the tour guide came to Zander and told him that although the 'Powers that be' do tolerate the sale of some military goods, his trench binoculars did not come into that category.

As the bus was leaving, through the window, Zander noticed the police officer and beside him – holding his trench binoculars and a twenty-dollar bill – stood the scruffy waif like girl soldier.

74

Grunt Has a Ball On Board

Grunt had pre-booked a cabin on Deck 6, the promenade deck. When he got on board, however, he was delighted to find that he had an upgrade to a more luxurious cabin, one conveniently situated near the sun deck on deck 9.

The first couple of days saw Grunt falling into his usual on board activities – breakfast, sunbathe, lunch, after lunch snooze etc. etc. Then on the morning of the third day tied up in port, as he looked through the day's on-board activity list, the word 'basketball' jumped out at him, *Hmmm, he* thought, *It is a while since I tried that. I'll go and find out something about it.*

At reception, he was informed that the basketball court was on deck 10 then handed a basketball ball. *How good is that* he thought, *and it's only one deck up from our cabin?* Consequently, ball in hand, he found the court and went into his warm up routine – lay-ups, hook shots and set shots. Soon a group of passengers had gathered to watch. Passing the ball to one of them, he encouraged him to come and play. Others soon joined in. It was not long before the number of initiates was enough to make two teams so Grunt left them to it and went for a morning coffee.

Half an hour later he went to his cabin, lay down on the bed and fell asleep.

He was wakened up shortly afterwards by a thump, thump, thumping on the ceiling and it only took him a moment or two to realize that the floor of the basketball court was directly above his cabin roof.

Next day after suffering the same continuous thump, thump, thumping and knowing that he would not be able to sleep with all that noise going on, he went to reception to complain and ask for a change of cabins, even to go back to the level of his old smaller one. The receptionist apologetically said that every cabin on board was occupied adding that until he came on board, the basketball court had not been used for ages. She then sympathetically explained that by upgrading some passengers who had pre-booked, the cruise company could advertise a cheaper last minute holiday in the lower deck cabins and thus achieve the economic benefit of sailing with a full ship.

Every day after that there was always someone playing basketball so for the remainder of the cruise Grunt did not get his little 'naps' but, on reflection, he knew that he was the one who started the basketball craze so his predicament was of his own doing.

WHAT ALL GOOD THINGS COME TO

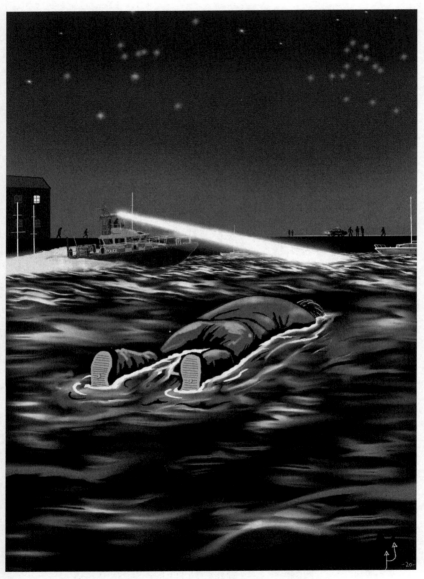

Christmas at Granton

75

They Should Have Known   Granton

It was just before Christmas and a clear sky suggested that the temperature was hovering around zero. From the East, one of the last incoming flights of the evening, with its headlights piercing the black of a star-filled sky, settled on its final descent into Edinburgh Airport. Its excited passengers, mostly Scots, were coming home for their seasonal holiday and looking forward to being with their families and friends. Those with portside window seats could see the myriad of light clusters of the City suburbs that ended abruptly at the south shore of the Firth of Forth, marking where the sea took over from the land.

Almost at the edge of that dense expanse of black, stood a building on the western breakwater of Granton harbour, its windows ablaze with light and its position giving the impression that it was floating on the inky surface of the sea. The locals on board knew it was the clubrooms of the Yacht Club.

Cocooned in the plane, these observers could not see that the inside of the building was alive and throbbing with the sounds of music and the raucous chatter of people enjoying themselves. Tonight was the club's Annual Dinner Dance.

In a corner of the main function rooms, four elderly men in dinner suits were sitting, huddled together like conspirators round a small table. This was the only place they could hear themselves speak above the noise created by the younger – and what they believed flashier – club members, all of whom were trying to convince everyone else that they were the ones who were having the most fun.

Apart from the occasional nod to a familiar face, the ruminative quartets' contribution to the evening so far, had been the occasional sip from their glasses of beer. In their sailing days, this little group had called themselves the Emeraldeers and had once been the most notorious and mischievous members of the club. Two of them even claimed to have sailed the South China Seas; in the days before life jackets. All of them had been mariners in the days long before gadgetry, such as satellite navigation, all-round sonar, mobile phones and other such fripperies existed – inventions that made a modern day sailor's life so much easier. In truth at one time, they did make a half-hearted attempt to embrace these new fangled gismos, but to no avail.

There was a time when these reprobates were the talk of the Club. A time when everyone knew who they were, what they got up to and all about their exploits and transgressions; but no longer. Since the heyday of the Emeraldeers, the character and interests of the club member had changed and now with most of their contemporaries dead, retired or just gone away, there was hardly anyone left who knew who these old farts were. These days everyone was more interested in enjoying their own life to the full.

Had these elegantly dressed, modern day yachtsmen taken the trouble to find out more about the Emeraldeers, they, their wives, families and guests might have felt uneasy to see them in their midst that evening. However, to them, unaware of the fire that had once burned in the old bellies, hearts and minds of these insignificant ex-mariners, they were just some old guys, quietly sipping their beer in a corner. Never the less, anyone who had known the Emeraldeers of old would have told them to keep a weather eye on these old codgers. Where there was trouble, they were either the cause of it, or in the thick of it.

The atmosphere in the present day clubroom was no longer anything like the one that the Emeraldeers had known. Gone were the days of the genuine "hail fellow well met" and the natural camaraderie they had enjoyed. It is strange how the memory retains the good things while discarding the unpleasant ones. Now people address each other in the loudest possible voice, with some inane comment or other, that leads to an insincere enquiry about their health and ends up in an exchange of personal trumpet blowing like, "I can go faster than you, have a bigger boat, a more expensive car or a better looking wife." – *Ad infinitum* (or perhaps that should be *ad nauseam*). Ageing being what it is, it was only natural that the Emeraldeers held today's younger members in contempt.

Recently, the Emeraldeers enjoyment of the Club had taken a downturn. Their archrival Fancy Boy had come back to the Club after working abroad.

The years had been kind to Francey who, from the top of his pomaded silver hair, down to his highly polished shoes was now the epitome of the elder statesman and a natural 'committee' man. It should therefore not have come as a surprise to these oldsters that right away Francey inveigled himself on to the committee and even more unbearably, been elected Commodore.

Life for the Emeraldeers could not get much worse! Zander, their leader, had always thought himself eminently more suited to that high office. His crew Grunt, Murdo and Gilbert, thought so to – at least to his face.

Throughout his life Fancy Boy had been more shrewd and more socially active than Zander, who, unlike his Nemesis, had either done the wrong thing, said something offensive or perhaps not been in the right place at the appropriate time to find favour with the 'powers that be.'

Sailing demands a level of fitness, agility and strength that the Emeraldeers could no longer call upon; muscles that once rippled now sagged, reactions that had once been instantaneous took a little longer to work and objects that used to be shifted with ease, now seemed immoveable. These long-gone attributes may not be required all of the time but when you're sailing they are needed now, if not sooner. Boats are no place for the unwary and the sea seldom offers a second chance – the only prisoners it takes are 'lifers'.

In spite of everything that had happened over the past few decades, this gallant if incongruously assorted crew still enjoyed each other's company. Sadly, the time had come to move on and accept, however reluctantly, that they were no longer capable of messing about on boats. On top of all of this, Zander and his crew had become uncomfortably aware that over the past few years, the club itself had been changing, and they did not like what they saw. This was no longer the place they wanted to be.

*

For some time now, Zander had been bereft of his beloved yacht Emerald and Murdo had run out of 'cousins', so in the days stretching ahead of them, the only sailing they could realistically look forward to, was the second hand enjoyment of watching other sailors sailing. There would be no more fair weather, fair winds, freedom, fun, and foraging in far-away fancy places that they had enjoyed together. Thinking back though, the majority of their misadventures had occurred on land rather than at sea, but without a boat, these events would never have happened.

For some time now, they had put their collective minds – which did not amount to much nowadays – to thinking about making a grand farewell gesture, some mischief that would be their final act of defiance; regrettably, though, it would mean some sacrifice.

Long before the function was due to finish, the Emeraldeers slipped out, ostensibly just four old men, leaving early to go home to their beds.

Poor old sods!

*

About an hour later, the sound of police sirens and the screeching of tyres drowned out the noise of the activities inside the clubroom. A loudspeaker amplified a voice that penetrated into the clubrooms demanding that everyone, "Stay exactly where you are. Police! The building is surrounded. No one is to leave!" Immediately after this, everyone heard a loud banging on the front door, accompanied by someone demanding "POLICE! Open up."

Commodore Francey took command and opened the door, only for a horde of police officers in full riot gear, to charge into the building almost trampling over him with their steel boots. Terrified members crowding round the windows could see that outside, what a few moments ago had been a dimly lit area of tranquillity, was now a brightly floodlit area of the breakwater full of police officers putting up crime-scene tapes – some carrying guns – and all around the flashing lights of police cars and other attendant fire engines and ambulances.

What was going on?

A large uniformed policeman in a hat adorned with great encrustateons of silver, strode into the main room and shouted,

"Quiet please. Give me your attention. Please settle down and allow my men to go about their business. Would the President or Chairman or whatever you have here, please make himself known to me?"

Everyone in the room turned their eyes on Francey, still dusting himself down after his initial brush with the law, which, without anyone saying a word, identified him. The senior police officer turned to face Francey and continued,

"Please come with me, sir," and as he said it, two of his largest, body-armoured, gun-toting police constables took up station on either side of Francey, firmly grasped his elbows and escorted him out of the room.

The senior police officer turned back to the others,

"The rest of you just stay here and remain calm." With that, he turned to follow Francey and his escorts out of the building.

Once outside Francey saw that the whole neighbourhood was heaving with police activity and the bright beam of a searchlight was shining out into the middle of the harbour. Looking out, he could just discern what looked like a human form floating, face down on its oily waters.

"What can you tell us about *that*, sir?" the senior police officer demanded, pointing.

In a blue funk, his eyes wide open, his mouth even wider and speechless, Francey could only gaze at the spectacle. A police frogman in a boat was on the point of recovering the floating shape.

Leaning over the gunwales, he grabbed the floating mass, pulled an inert figure on board and then immediately headed back to where the silver-encrusted police officer and Francey were standing.

"Super!" he shouted, revealing the rank of the officer in charge, "Can I have a word?" The 'Super' went forward to meet the little boat as it touched the breakwater. After a whispered conversation, he came back to Francey and with a look of exasperation on his face hissed,

"What's going on here then? Is this some kind of a joke?"

Francey, still trying to work out what was happening, could only stutter,

"Wwwhy? Wwwhat? Hhhow?"

"Why, what, how, is that the best you can do? I'll ask the questions thank you."

The 'body' was brought ashore and dumped at the Superintendent's feet. Francey recognised the victim at once and with a sharp intake of breath, said,

"It's Charlie, our dummy; we use him for life saving and rescue practice." All the while thinking, *how did he get there? He should be locked up in the hall cupboard.*

Insistently the Superintendent's voice rang in his ears.

"Yes, it's a bloody dummy! I've been called out to rescue a bloody dummy!'

This statement brought no comfort to Francey, but did give him a moment or two to allow his addled brain to recover from its terror-induced inertia and he managed to utter

"Please come inside, Superintendent?"

"You can bet your sweet life I'm coming inside."

The Superintendent accompanied by a posse of bulky, heavily armed police accompanied the white-faced Francey inside.

"You lot," the grim faced superintendent said waving his arms to embrace everyone in the room, and with his voice shaking in anger demanded, "are going to tell me what you know about this stupid prank. In addition, why, on a freezing cold Christmas eve, you have had me bring out half the Lothian and Borders Armed Police Unit, as well as the Fire and Ambulance Services.

What I do know is that half an hour ago we received a 'phone call telling us that there was a body floating in the harbour and that the person who put it there was still in the area. Can any of you give me any information at all, that would help me in this matter?"

The uncomprehending audience looked blankly at the Superintendent. No one said a word.

After a brief pause he went on,

"So that's the way of it, is it? I can see this is going to be a long night. Will everyone please go back to their seats and wait to be interviewed."

Until well after midnight Francey, all of the members and their guests were held in the club, making statements to the police. It was only then that – the bedraggled, bleary-eyed bunch of ex revellers – thankfully no longer the subject of a police enquiry – were allowed to leave. They got into their cars, headed for home thinking, *the ignominy of it all and in **our** club!*

Next morning, when the secretary opened up the club-rooms, he found four white envelopes lying on the bar. In them were letters of resignation from each of the Emeraldeers, stating that they no longer wished to be associated with a club whose members were the subject of a police inquiry.

The Emeraldeers were now well and truly finished with the Club and had already disposed of the key to Charlie's room.

They may have severed their last link with the sea, but, what a way to go!

76

That's That   Edinburgh

The main chapel at Warriston Crematorium was packed. Sitting in the last row of pews, just inside the door, were three elderly men. They were there to say their final farewell to a former sailing colleague.

Four sombre, black-coated undertakers brought in the highly polished, brass-handled wooden coffin and with well-practiced ceremony, laid it on the altar at the front of the chapel, then reverently placing the many floral tributes on the floor between the coffin and the congregation, bowed, turned and walked slowly away.

Coupled with the sombre atmosphere of the chapel, Gilbert, Grunt and Murdo, three of the Emeraldeers, emotionally affected by the sad occasion, were not saying much. Although the religious element of the service was brief, the lengthy eulogy contained references that touched each one of them personally.

At the end of the service, the trio made a shuffling beeline for the exit, anxious to be first out of the Chapel of Rest before getting involved in the exchange of sympathetic words and handshakes with the family. For once, they succeeded and as the doors opened, they slipped out. Emerging into the daylight of the early spring afternoon. Directly in front of them, a watery sun setting in the West, was shining weakly through the trees. .

"Hello!" The call came from a silhouette edged with gold, coming out of the sun towards them. As the silhouetted figure made a valiant, if unsuccessful, attempt to run, a familiar voice gasped,

"Sorry I was late, boys. I missed the bus and when I got here, they wouldn't let me in. How did Fancy Boy's funeral go?"

Grunt admonished Zander with a glare.

"You'd be late for your own funeral, let alone Francey's, but if you really want to know, it went well enough."

Zander blundered on, ignoring Grunt's disapproval.

"Are we going to the wake?'

At this point Murdo decided to put his oar in, so to speak, piped up,

"No, we're not, and anyway it would be embarrassing now to take you along. You didn't even have the decency to get here in time for the committal service."

Gilbert trying to act as mediator suggested "How about just going to the pub to drink our *own* toast to Fancy Boy?" Everyone agreed.

To make up for his having missed the service Zander felt obliged to say something good about Francey, so in a somewhat grudging tone of voice, he said,

"He wasn't really such a bad sailor, was he?"

He then spoiled his pathetic attempt at atonement by adding,

"But he made a real mess of our departure from Ganavan Bay when he pulled that bollard off the pontoon and, come to think of it, he never did get to Saint Kilda, did he?"

"Neither did we!" chorused his exasperated crew, turning away in the direction of the nearest public house.

"At least *we're* all walking away from the crematorium!" Zander replied, trying to re establish control.

On the way to the pub Murdo, the occasional philosopher, made an observation.

"I've been thinking."

The others pricked up their ears at this almost unprecedented admission.

"If it was me that was dying, and I knew I was dying, I'd rather have the wake before I died, so that all these folk that I haven't seen for ages would see me and I'd see them. It's a real shame that when you go to the funeral of someone you've not seen for years, you don't see them and they don't see you. You read in the papers that so and so is dead and you say to yourself, what a shame I would like to have seen them before they went, but it is too late. Maybe folks should change their ways."

Gilbert took some time to digest Murdo's profound if wordy, suggestion before pricking the bubble of the well-meaning proposal with,

"Normally you don't know when you're going to go, so there's nothing you can do about it."

Zander, who had also been taking in Murdo's lengthy statement, added,

"I like that idea Murdo, but in practice, it just won't work, will it?'

With that, they got to the pub, went in and ordered. When the drinks arrived, Grunt, with a knowing smile to the barmaid, pointed at Zander and said,

"Skipper, here's your chance, you can have your wake right now!

It's your round!"

The End

ACKNOWLEDGEMENTS

As is often paraphrased, _no man is an island_ and equally no writer can complete the road to publishing without the help of others. Therefore, I would like to acknowledge the assistance of some of those to whom I am extremely grateful.

My wife **Ann** is where she always will be, right up there in number one spot. While acting as sounding board, proof-reader and editor, she has not only encouraged me and provided me with inestimable assistance but showed saintly tolerance during my long periods of 'isolation'.

I am also grateful to both of our sons. Big brother **Paul** who by creating the mood-setting illustrations makes a an obvious contribution. **Steven** who encouraged me to rewrite and publish the e books, maintains my web site and keeps me up to speed on technical matters.

Thanks must also go to my daughter in law **Heather,** who has applied her photographic talents to create the artwork in my website, and, to keep things in the family, to **Amber Jane** who is my Granddaughter and dispatcher

Thank you also to **Heather Macpherson,** Raspberry Creative Design who provided me with typesetting and cover design services and was the voice of experience and expertise during the lead-in to publication.

Finally, a big thank you to **my friends,** whose escapades and eccentricities inspired me to write this series. If I have offended anyone by not naming him/her individually, I sincerely apologise.

OTHER PUBLICATIONS

Old Edinburgh, Views from Above 2002 – Stenlake
Publishing

THE ZANDER TRILOGY
1 A Storm in Any Port   October 2019
3 A Storm In A Tin Cup   Late 2020

P.S If you have enjoyed this book, look out for the third
in the Zander Trilogy, A Storm in a Tin Cup, when Zander
turns his attention to Golf.